Wulf D. Hund, Michael Pickering,
Anandi Ramamurthy (eds.)

Colonial Advertising
&
Commodity Racism

RACISM ANALYSIS

edited by Wulf D. Hund

Series B: Yearbook

Volume 4

Colonial Advertising & Commodity Racism

edited by

Wulf D. Hund,
Michael Pickering,
Anandi Ramamurthy

LIT

Cover: Wulf D. Hund and Stefanie Affeldt
using two advertisements of Pears' Soap from ›Puck‹ (1887)

Layout and image editing: Stefanie Affeldt

Gedruckt auf alterungsbeständigem Werkdruckpapier
entsprechend ANSI Z3948   DIN ISO 9706

Bibliographic information published by the Deutsche Nationalbibliothek
The Deutsche Nationalbibliothek lists this publication in the Deutsche
Nationalbibliografie; detailed bibliographic data are available on the Internet at
http://dnb.d-nb.de.

ISBN 978-3-643-90416-4

A catalogue record for this book is available from the British Library

©LIT VERLAG GmbH & Co.
KG Wien,
Zweigniederlassung
Zürich 2013
Klosbachstr. 107
CH-8032 Zürich
Tel. +41 (0) 44-251 75 05
Fax +41 (0) 44-251 75 06
e-Mail: zuerich@lit-verlag.ch
http://www.lit-verlag.ch

LIT VERLAG
Dr. W. Hopf Berlin
2013
Fresnostr. 2
D-48159 Münster
Tel. +49 (0) 2 51-62 03 20
Fax +49 (0) 2 51-23 19 72
E-Mail: lit@lit-verlag.de
http://www.lit-verlag.de

Distribution:
In Germany: LIT Verlag Fresnostr. 2, D-48159 Münster
Tel. +49 (0) 2 51-620 32 22, Fax +49 (0) 2 51-922 60 99, e-mail: vertrieb@lit-verlag.de

In Austria: Medienlogistik Pichler-ÖBZ, e-mail: mlo@medien-logistik.at
In Switzerland: B + M Buch- und Medienvertrieb, e-mail: order@buch-medien.ch
In the UK: Global Book Marketing, e-mail: mo@centralbooks.com
In North America: International Specialized Book Services, e-mail: orders@isbs.com

Contents

Editorial   7

Exposés

Advertising White Supremacy   21
Capitalism, Colonialism and Commodity Racism
Wulf D. Hund

›Come and Join the Freedom-Lovers‹   69
Racism, Appropriation and Resistance in Advertising
Anandi Ramamurthy, Kalpana Wilson

Studies

Buffalo Bill's ›Wild West‹   97
The Racialisation of the Cosmopolitan Imagination
Robert W. Rydell

›Fun Without Vulgarity‹?   119
Commodity Racism and the Promotion of Blackface Fantasies
Michael Pickering

From Œcumene to Trademark   145
The Symbolism of the ›Moor‹ in the Occident
Malte Hinrichsen

Bittersweet Temptations   171
Race and the Advertising of Cocoa
Emma Robertson

›The German Alternative‹   197
Nationalism and Racism in ›Afri-Cola‹
Katharina Eggers, Robert Fechner

Editorial

In 1881 the Reverend Alexander Mackie from Lilydale, a township some 30 kilometres east of Melbourne, summarised his conception for a solution to the so-called half-caste problem in Australia in one, single sentence: »You can make them white here without soap«. To this end two measures were necessary. First of all, children had to be separated from their parents early on in their lives, and to be committed to the care of ›white‹ families. After an appropriate education, they then had to get married to a ›white‹ partner.[1]

This conviction united the cultural and the biological dimensions of racism. Already at the time of the developing of modern racism by the Enlightenment, Thomas Jefferson drew a distinction between indigenous American Indians who could be assimilated and African slaves with whom any intermixture should be avoided. The racial identification of the Aborigines in late-nineteenth-century Australia was characterised by their categorisation as ›black Caucasians‹. This classification allowed for racially improving existing ›half-castes‹ by the further admixture of ›white‹ blood, and in this manner facilitated breeding out their formerly ›black‹ colour as a symbol of their Aboriginality, once and for all.[2]

Mackie's racist association was alleviated at the time by its ironic reference to contemporary soap advertising. Even though, against the backdrop of the development of capitalism and of modified concepts of hygiene, cleanliness and fragrancy, soap evolved into a branded mass product only after the middle of the 19th century, the advertising connected with it rapidly became ubiquitous. It produced a wide range of promises, which, besides female beauty and hygienic homes, also encompassed the cleansing of the lower classes at home and of the savages overseas.[3]

---

1 Cf. Marguerita Stephens: White Without Soap. Philanthropy, Caste and Exclusion in Colonial Victoria 1835-1888. A Political Economy of Race. Melbourne: Melbourne University Custom Book Centre 2010, pp. 241 f.; for the quotation see p. 242.
2 Cf. Russell McGregor: Imagined Destinies. Aboriginal Australians and the Doomed Race Theory, 1880-1939. Carlton South: Melbourne University Press 1997, pp. 157 ff.; Warwick Anderson: The Cultivation of Whiteness. Science, Health, and Racial Destiny in Australia. Durham: Duke University Press 2006, pp. 195 ff.
3 Cf. Geoffrey Jones: Beauty Imagined. A History of the Global Beauty Industry. Oxford [et al.]: Oxford University Press 2010, pp. 71 ff.; Brian Lewis: So Clean. Lord Lever-

The political options associated with this, found, inter alia, iconographic expression in soap advertisements tied to Australia and its allegedly primitive natives. In 1889, Pears illustrated the theory of vanishing races with an advertisement in ›Puck‹ and other publications, which depicted an Aborigine passing away (see cover, left image). One of the lines below the picture assumed that »Ev'n the black Australian dying hopes he shall return, a white«.[4] As the readers of the magazine knew, this was a thoroughly serious statement. For only a few issues earlier, Pears had placed another advertisement, showing a black attendant being playfully washed by a naked pink-white little girl in an orientalised interior (see cover, right).[5] In this case, the advertisers could informally draw on the racist iconographic reservoir of European cultural history and borrow a scene from the tableau ›Die Mohrenwäsche‹ (›Washing a Moor‹) by the German genre painter Carl Joseph Begas.[6]

The short story in two pictures told an abridged version of modern racism's white supremacist worldview. In the beginning it was still combined with religious patterns of discrimination which kept ready an eternal ray of hope while justifying the racist purging of others. Already at the end of the 17th century, the ›Athenian Mercury‹ asked in which colour the ›Negroes‹ would rise at the ›last day‹. »Taking then this blackness of the Negro to be an accidental imperfection«, the gazette answered that he would »not arise with that complexion, but leave it behind him in the darkness of the grave, exchanging it for a brighter and better at his return again into the world«.[7]

hulme, Soap and Civilisation. Manchester [et al.]: Manchester University Press 2008, pp. 93 ff., 154 ff.

4   The image is from ›Puck‹, 21, 1887, 543, p. 377 and has the caption: »The Above Drawing illustrates the well known line in Lord Tennyson's Locksley Hall | ›Ev'n the black Australian dying hopes he shall return, a white.‹ | I have found Pear's soap matchless for the hands and complexion – Adelina Piatti«. The reference to the poem actually relates to Alfred Tennyson's ›Locksley Hall Sixty Years After‹ from 1886. Another version of the advertisement is addressed in Kay Heath: Aging by the Book. The Emergence of Midlife in Victorian Britain. Albany: State University of New York Press 2009, pp. 177 ff., image p. 172.

5   The image is from ›Puck‹, 21, 1887, 533, p. 217. Above the picture the message »The Best Soap in the World« is to be found, beneath is written: »Endorsed by the best judges. | Established in London 100 Years. | Sale Universal«.

6   Cf. Eberhard Ruhmer: Begas, Karl Joseph der Ältere. In: Neue Deutsche Biographie, ed. by Historische Kommission bei der Bayerischen Akademie der Wissenschaften, vol. 1, Berlin: Duncker & Humblot 1953, pp. 744 f.; there are a number of copies (partially by the painters own hand) from the 1841 painting – see http://www.kreismuseum-heinsberg.de/deutsch/gemaeldesammlung/carl-joseph-begas-der-aeltere/die-mohrenwaesche.html; cf. Nana Badenberg: Die Bildkarriere eines kulturellen Stereotyps. Mohrenwäsche im Leipziger Zoo. In: Mit Deutschland um die Welt. Eine Kulturgeschichte des Fremden in der Kolonialzeit, ed. by Alexander Honold, Klaus R. Schärpe. Stuttgart [et al.]: Metzler 2004, pp. 173-182.

7   Quoted from Colin Kidd: The Forging of Races. Race and Scripture in the Protestant Atlantic World, 1600 - 2000. Cambridge [et al.]: Cambridge University Press 2006, p. 68.

Ever since the Enlightenment this opportunity had been eradicated. ›Salvation‹ had made way for ›historical progress‹ and continual self-perfection had taken the place of immortal beatitude. God was remodelled as a metaphysical veneer behind which men were busy creating themselves. Under these premises even big philosophy felt certain that the future of humankind would be ›white‹, and Immanuel Kant wrote down that »[a]ll races will become exterminated [...], except for the whites«.[8] The change of paradigm in race sciences operated by evolutionary theory implied no substantial change for the so-called primitive races. Admittedly, they were exempted from their former incapability for development. But simultaneously the so called advanced ›white race‹ had become a merciless competitor in the ›struggle for existence‹. Herbert Spencer consequently counted the »effect of continually extirpating races« as a component of natural and social development which could only be successfully achieved by the »large-brained European«.[9]

The advertisers of Pears and other companies, geared toward the newly developing mass markets of consumerism, had no need to attend formally to social Darwinism or any other forms of evolutionist theory, for they could casually have recourse to comprehensive archives of a complex ›white‹ racist knowledge. In doing so they universalised and popularised racist concepts, stereotypes, and attitudes and made them available to a broad cross-class spectrum of actual and potential consumers. The advertisements show that Pears inadvertently exposed the facetious images of ›washing the Ethiopian white‹ and disclosed the barely hidden truth of all self-proclaimed civilising missions which never intended to concede an eventual equality. Such advertising in fact suggested that even steady toil would not suffice to blanchify people labelled as ›black‹. This ideologeme enabled even those recipients of the advertisements who could not afford the purchase of an expensive soap, and could not get rid of their underclass patina, to claim for themselves a place of belonging within the so-called

---

[8] Immanuel Kant: Entwürfe zu dem Colleg über Anthropologie. In: Kant's gesammelte Schriften, ed. by Königlich Preußische Akademie der Wissenschaften, Akademie der Wissenschaften der DDR, Akademie der Wissenschaften zu Göttingen, Berlin Brandenburgische Akademie der Wissenschaften. Berlin: Reimer and Berlin: de Gruyter 1900 ff., vol. 15, pp. 655-899, p. 878; cf. Wulf D. Hund: ›It must come from Europe‹. The Racisms of Immanuel Kant. In: Racisms Made in Germany, ed. by id., Christian Koller, Moshe Zimmermann [Racism Analysis | Yearbook 2]. Berlin [etc.]: Lit 2011, pp. 69-98.

[9] Herbert Spencer: The Study of Sociology. New York [et al.]: Appleton 1899, p. 175 (›extirpating‹), id.: The Principles of Biology. 2 vol. New York: Appleton 1883, vol. 2, p. 503 (›large-brained‹); cf. Patrick Brantlinger: Dark Vanishings. Discourse on the Extinction of Primitive Races, 1800-1930. Ithaca [et al.]: Cornell University Press 2003 and Thomas Gonderman: Evolution und Rasse. Theoretischer und institutioneller Wandel in der viktorianischen Anthropologie. Bielefeld: transcript 2007.

white race. As the little white girl attested, they were ›white‹ by nature and belonged to an imagined racial community which overrode age, gender and social class.

Soap advertising took account of that with a variety of stereotypical oppositions. These were built around a sense of racial identity that associated whiteness with cleanliness, healthiness, regeneration, purity, improvement in standards, civilisational advancement and imperial progress. Blackness was constructed in stark contrast to these putative qualities and attributes. The whole point of a white child washing a black person – adult or child – with a certain brand of soap was then to impart magical properties to it. Making black white not only connected soap to quite miraculous powers as a commodity, but also as a commodity extended these powers into the realm of empire, so reinforcing the ideology of the imperial civilising mission, the main intent of which was to wash the ›black savage‹ out of a state of primitiveness. Of course, the cleansing trick could never really be complete. It could never really counter what were regarded as innate racial attributes, a point graphically illustrated by the famous Pears' soap ad in which a white boy washes a black boy in his bathtub, turning his body white in the process. The result of this imperious experiment is that he is left as a peculiar hybrid, with a whitened body but a head that is still black. The message is clear: progression towards a state of racial equality can only ever be partial. Allowing black to become partially white nevertheless served to endorse – by being complicit with – the colonialist and imperialist exploitation of Africa, and as one of us has previously suggested, »we can view the washing of the black boy's body, but not his head, as a reference to the form of influence established by Britain in West Africa – the protectorate«.[10] With the head remaining black, the African would always be inferior in intelligence and rationality to the white, while the whitening of the body offered legitimation of the exploitation of African material resources, and of tropical trade routes and arrangements coming under British or European control.

The ideological affirmations and endorsements of soap advertising in the period of the late nineteenth and early twentieth century were underwritten by the binary oppositions upon which the racist stereotyping of black people depends. Stereotyping of this kind polarises being and identity around widely circulating racial markers which serve to ›other‹ those targeted by the stereotyping, so making them seem utterly distinct from

---

10 Anandi Ramamurthy: Imperial Persuaders. Images of Africa and Asia in British Advertising. Manchester [et al.]: Manchester University Press 2003, p. 30.

those who construct and reproduce the stereotypes.¹¹ Notions of Otherness operate through the fixing of reductive and restrictive characteristics of racial difference, which are then regarded as the opposite to those associated with the sameness of ›us‹ in ›our‹ national and racial identities, with this putative sameness subsuming differences of gender, generation and social class, as we noted above. Through what is always a two-way, but one-sided relationship, racist stereotypes implicitly affirm those who stereotype in their own sense of superiority, and because race-thinking involves mobilising ideas of large-scale collectivities, they extend beyond this in validating particular social orders and culturally sanctioned hierarchies. The forms of representation such stereotypes traffic in provide support for existing structures of power, relations of domination and oppression, and inequalities of resource and opportunity. Stereotyping implicitly ratifies these inequalities by explicitly invalidating its targets in some manner.

Soap advertising played upon this process by setting off white against black. The black child, itself an allegory of the notion of blacks as childlike, could not wash off its blackness, and hence could never escape a state of racial backwardness and inferiority, whereas the white middle-class or lower middle-class consumer, concerned to maintain or aspire to social respectability, could readily buy into this via the simple purchase of a bar of soap. It was then at the intersection of notions of social respectability and racial superiority that soap triumphed in its stereotypical opposition of blackness and whiteness. Soap became at once an icon of domestic hygiene and racial stock. It established a hearth-and-home familiarity and acceptability for imperialism, colonialism and racist conceptions of evolutionism, making the ideas and values associated with them commonplace in ways that relatively elitist theories of ›scientific‹ racism had never been able to achieve. Through such ads as those displayed on our front cover, soap became synonymous with both imperial progress and the civilising mission. As a Pears' ad of 1899 explained: »The first step towards lightening The White Man's Burden is through teaching the virtues of cleanliness. Pears Soap is a potent factor in brightening the dark corners of the earth«.¹² The conviction of the ›explorer‹ Henry Morton Stanley that »he had a mission to civilise Africans by teaching them the value of commodities« was directly in step with this.¹³

---

11   Cf. Michael Pickering: Stereotyping. The Politics of Representation. Basingstoke [et al.]: Palgrave 2001, pp. 47-78.
12   See the reproduction in Richard M. Ohmann: Selling Culture. Magazines, Markets, and Class at the Turn of the Century. London [et al.]: Verso 1996, p. 203.
13   Thomas Richards: The Commodity Culture of Victorian England. London [et al.]: Verso 1990, p. 123.

While it is important to acknowledge the construction and perpetuation of racist stereotypes in the way we have, to confine our attention to them would result in an abbreviated analysis. The sheer volume of black and other non-white figures populating the world of commodity racism indicates the nexus of advertising and profitable economic interests as well as imperialist political interests. The advertisements imply that the propagation of soap was not only targeted at the distribution of promises of use value but also served as legitimisation of the acquisition and protection of colonial raw material. From the middle of the 19th century, palm kernel oil was exported from West Africa, and being affordable even for the lower classes, »was ideal for the mass market for soap«.[14]

The mass marketing of soap was directly connected to the shift in the export trade in West Africa from slaves during the transatlantic slave trade, to a trade in raw materials that was described by British merchants and colonisers as ›legitimate‹ commerce. The kingdom of Dahomey for instance switched directly from slave trading with Europeans to one in palm oil and palm kernel oil, both essential in the production of vegetable oil-based soaps – a market that grew exponentially during the second half of the nineteenth century.[15] The shift to palm oil production in West Africa and the desire to develop new outlets for European manufactured goods led to the financing of three expeditions by the British Government along the Niger in the mid-nineteenth century. This aimed to open up the interior of the African continent to European trade. William Baikie who led the final expedition in 1854 noted the importance of the region as »an outlet for home manufactures as the unclad millions of central Africa must absorb thousands of cargoes of soft goods, eagerly bartering their raw cottons, their vegetable oils and their ivory for our calicoes and cloths«.[16] The principle of the civilising mission to clothe Africans, as well as encourage capitalist trading relations, fitted economic imperatives. When the depression of the 1880s led European merchants to seek cheaper raw materials, and the price of palm oil in Europe was halved from £37 - £45 a ton in 1860 to about £20 - £25 in 1890,[17] African traders resisted demands for price

14   Cf. Martin Lynn: Commerce and Economic Change in West Africa. The Palm Oil Trade in the Nineteenth Century. Cambridge [et al.]: Cambridge University Press 1997; for the quotation see ibid., pp. 117 f.; cf. also Kristin Mann: Slavery and the Birth of an African City. Lagos, 1760-1900. Bloomington: Indiana University Press 2007, pp. 118 ff.
15   Cf. Elisee Soumonni: The Compatibility of the Slave and Palm Oil Trades in Dahomey, 1818-1858. In: From Slave Trade to ›Legitimate‹ Commerce. The Commercial Transition in Nineteenth Century West Africa, ed. by Robin Law. Cambridge [et al.]: Cambridge University Press 1995, pp. 78-92.
16   Nancy Clark: Africa and the West. From the Slave Trade to Conquest, 1441-1905. Oxford [et al.]: Oxford University Press 2010, p. 170.
17   Anthony G. Hopkins: An Economic History of West Africa. London: Longman 1973, pp. 132 f.

reduction. As the profit margins of European traders became reduced, this encouraged European merchants to favour imperialist annexation in West Africa.[18]

Support for colonial intervention by soap manufacturers was made explicit in Pears' first advertisement to feature a black child that was published in December 1884 following the start of the Berlin Conference during which European nations carved up the continent amongst themselves, in a process where imperialist intervention was presented as ›a moral duty‹ – the white man's burden.[19]

The economic imperatives behind racialised discourses can be seen explicitly in Lord Lever's frustrated attempts to establish a plantation-based economy in West Africa, where palm oil production became increasingly supplied through small-scale producers. As Anne Phillips has pointed out: in the 1890s West Africa still offered contrasting possibilities for development. While the centralised power of elites, established during the transatlantic slave trade, were still in existence and large estates dependent on indigenous slave labour were an important part of palm oil production, the increase of small-scale subsistence producers of palm oil contained the basis for a future peasantry. However, »[t]he vision of British West Africa as a world of small peasants became possible in the twentieth century, but was not yet determined in the years of colonial conflict«.[20]

While Lord Lever sent an investigator to West Africa to explore supplies of palm oil and palm kernel oil in 1902, which were defined as ›inexhaustible‹, and was keen to maintain full control over all processes of production, attempting to buy and run plantations in West Africa, he was frustrated by the increasing development of a policy of native land tenure that would eventually support small-scale peasant farming and indirect rule in West Africa. Lever's support for direct rule can be seen in his written accounts: »a native cannot organise. He cannot even run a wooding post on the river satisfactorily. You have only to compare one run by a native with one run by a European to prove that«.[21]

The diminution of Africa to a child in many soap advertisements links directly to the attitudes of Lord Lever who argued that »West Africans have to be treated very much as one would treat children« and that they »will be happier, produce the best [...] when his labour is directed and organised by his white brother«. In pushing for plantation models of pro-

18 Robin Law: Introduction. In: From Slave Trade to ›Legitimate‹ Commerce, p. 11.
19 Anandi Ramamurthy: Imperial Persuaders, pp. 27-30.
20 Anne Phillips: The Enigma of Colonialism. British Policy in West Africa. London: James Currey 1989, p. 22.
21 William Hulme Leverhulme: Viscount Leverhulme, by his Son. London: Allen and Unwin 1927, p. 312; for the following quote see ibid., p. 315.

duction, which favoured smaller and powerful elites that would rely on domestic slavery, Lever also tacitly accepted domestic slavery in West Africa as a form of labour organisation and such attitudes even manifested themselves in Pears' advertisements, such as the one on the cover that was reproduced in ›The Graphic‹ on 26 January 1907 with the phrase ›Look how the black slave smiles‹.[22] Such racialised representations in advertising do not simply reflect generalised cultural stereotypes but often assert ideological positions that are consolidated through specific economic and political interests.

Against this backdrop the following essays discuss the relations of advertising and commodity racism. As »commodity racism [...] converted the narrative of imperial progress into mass-produced consumer spectacles«[23] it was (besides blackface minstrelsy, human zoos, world exhibitions and other gadgets of popularisation) a pivotal module of the last stage in the development of modern racism, when the race concept »became paradigmatic in anthropology«, »spread in the sciences and humanities«, and, at the same time, was socially generalised to such an extent that »the lower classes were granted membership in the ›master race‹« and in this way were definitively integrated in the realms of whiteness.[24] This was no unique event but a social process which passed through several stages of alteration – not least because the challenge of anti-colonial struggles and anti-racist movements induced »the reformulation, not the elimination of commodity racism«.[25] Focusing on the various crossover points between racism and commodity marketing, the contributions to this volume illuminate a variety of facets of modern advertising whose racist interspersions are traced and analysed from their earliest manifestations up to the present day. It becomes evident, that along with more obvious changes advertising is characterised by both a striking adaptability and a tenacious persistence of racist discrimination.

In the opening chapter, *Wulf D. Hund* (Universität Hamburg) analyses the connections between capitalism, imperialism, mass production, advertising, and racism. He shows that racism has been so closely related to the development of modern advertising that it constituted a pivotal component of commodity aesthetics and led to a doubling of the advertisements'

22 See the reproduction in Anandi Ramamurthy: Imperial Persuaders, p. 58.
23 Anne McClintock: Imperial Leather. Race, Gender and Sexuality in the Colonial Context. New York [et al.]: Routledge 1995, p. 33 (emphasis omitted).
24 Wulf D. Hund: Negative Societalisation. Racism and the Constitution of Race. In: Wages of Whiteness & Racist Symbolic Capital, ed. id., Jeremy Krikler, David Roediger [Racism Analysis | Yearbook 1]. Berlin [et al.]: Lit 2010, pp. 57-96, p. 59.
25 C. Richard King: Commodity Racism Now. In: Studies in Symbolic Interaction, vol. 33, ed. Norman K. Denzin. Bingley: Emerald 2009 pp. 97-108, p. 104.

promises of use value. They not only praised the advantages of certain (branded) commodities but also provided racist symbolic capital even for all those viewers of their propaganda who could not afford the lauded commodities. Hereby commodity racism contributed to the social stabilisation of a capitalist society, which was substantially in trouble after the formation of the working class. Some products of colonial expropriation (like sugar and tea) became available to the lower classes, of course, but the routine consumption of many commonly advertised commodities was refused to them. It was not by chance that commodity racism advertised not only goods, but also, as a surrogate, whiteness as promise of belonging (and antidote against social discontent).

Anandi Ramamurthy (University of Central Lancashire) and *Kalpana Wilson* (London School of Economics) explore the changes in racialised representations in contemporary advertising from the 1960s until the present, highlighting the ways in which these changes have been shaped by transformations in patterns of global capital accumulation – particularly the rise of neoliberal globalisation – as well as new forms of resistance to racism and imperialism. The chapter examines advertising's engagement with notions of social justice in three contexts and argues that in each case, these forms of advertising seek to represent consumerism as a force for progressive social change, while reproducing and reinforcing racialised global hierarchies that have their roots in racialised discourses established during the transatlantic slave trade and colonial era. Further, these engagements can be understood as attempts to appropriate, redeploy and simultaneously undermine the discourses which resistance to racism and imperialism produces.

Robert W. Rydell (Montana State University) examines the familiar example of late Victorian/Edwardian popular entertainment, Buffalo Bill's Wild West show, by looking at it in a novel way. He argues that rather than simply offering a fond look back to the old days of the American frontier, this show hitched a modern cosmopolitan outlook to existing racial categories and in that way promoted the interests of western imperialism. This combination transmitted the reassuring message that, as the world became increasingly modernised and globalised, those assigned to particular racialised identities would conform to them and continue to enact them. Both through the Wild West performances and its representations in poster art, the show advanced a form of commodity racism and imperialism that could readily pose as cosmopolitan spectacle. This was especially the case after it amalgamated with Pawnee Bill's Great Far East show.

Michael Pickering (Loughborough University) turns to another example of popular entertainment that took off from the mid-nineteenth century and was at its peak of commercial success during the late-nineteenth century period of ›high‹ imperialism. Blackface minstrelsy in Britain was always a commercial form of entertainment, both in its shows and in its associated products, such as sheet music and song albums, but it became increasingly commodified as the Victorian era advanced, particularly in its grand-scale urban manifestations. As a type of commodity racism, British minstrelsy contributed enormously to the production and reproduction of Africanist ideology and the racist stereotyping of black people. Attending primarily to the sheet music covers, programmes, posters and promotional images associated with British minstrelsy, the chapter shows that it was highly successful in this regard because of the way its deployment of racist depictions, attitudes and values resonated deeply within the popular aesthetics of its theatrical form.

Malte Hinrichsen (Universität Hamburg) examines the history of European advertising ›moors‹ and reveals their origin in medieval representations of œcumene and tolerance. During the rise of transatlantic slave trade and influenced by the emergence of scientific racism, the initial image of the ›moor‹ became increasingly objectified and racialised. The example of a prominent German coat of arms ›moor‹, the Tucher-Mohr, illustrates how the figure was gradually redefined and, eventually, commodified since the 19th century, selling ideas of white supremacy to Western consumers. Up to the present day, derogatory images of the ›moor‹ are part of European commodity culture and belie the history of its noble and sacred iconographic precursors.

Emma Robertson (La Trobe University) analyses the ways in which cocoa was marketed and promoted as a popular drink from the late-nineteenth to the late-twentieth century. Cocoa advertising in Britain became a significant vehicle of racialised meanings and attitudes. It did so through advancing particular notions of blackness and whiteness, though with considerable variation in different countries of western Europe, as for example in respect to the salience accorded to relations of production and consumption, and the type of characters used to help sell cocoa to white consumers. As well as making clear what was specific to British cocoa advertising, this chapter shows how the decline of British imperialism found expression in the ads of the later twentieth century.

Katharina Eggers (Martin-Luther-Universität Halle-Wittenberg) and *Robert Fechner* (Goethe-Universität Frankfurt) tell a story of racist flexibility and perseverance. They survey the different stages of advertising

›Afri-Cola‹, which from its commercial launch was passed off as the ›German alternative‹ to ›Coca-Cola‹. From the beginning, ›Afri-Cola‹ promotion made use of racist items like antisemitism, colonial revisionism, white suprematism, exotism and chauvinism. Neither the defeat of German fascism nor the success of the antiauthoritarian movement could prevent the advertisers from promoting their product, affiliated by its name (›Afri‹) and its logo (›palm tree‹) with the times of colonialism, through the vehicle of racist motifs.

(Wulf D. Hund, Michael Pickering, Anandi Ramamurthy)

Exposés

Advertising White Supremacy
Capitalism, Colonialism and Commodity Racism
Wulf D. Hund

Abstract: Commodity racism was always more than the mere usage of racist images and insinuations in advertising. From the beginning, it set up a social system of promoting mores as well as goods, hereby not only mediating between producers and consumers but also between classes. Racist advertisements distribute exotic or insolent promises of use value and additionally offer an extra ideological use value available even for non-buyers of the praised commodities. The socially uncoded and widely distributed information purportedly free of charge established the condition of possibility for the acquisition of racist symbolic capital by the general public. Historically, the basis for this was the transformation of capitalist profit interest and colonial violence into auspicious temptations. Racism was a pivotal component of this mélange. Looked at in that light, commodity racism implied not only the announcement of brands but also an enduring advertising of white supremacy.

Some time ago in Germany, a large-scale advertising billboard promoted rum of the brand ›Captain Morgan‹. One of the posters showed a scene from a football game: five players set up a defensive wall prepared to parry a free kick. With fearful expression, four of them tried to protect what apparently they were more scared for than their heads. The fifth by contrast provokingly takes up an imperious attitude. It corresponds with the slogan ›Got a little captain in you?‹ and with the label of a prominently depicted bottle of rum which, above the trade name, features the figure of a buccaneer who nonchalantly leans his hand on a sabre and possessively sets foot on a barrel.

This is no innocent tableau. When in 1944 the ›Captain Morgan Rum Company‹ was founded in Jamaica, the island had been a British colony for almost three hundred years. The pirate Henry Morgan took such an active part in the promotion of this pearl of the Antilles that eventually he was knighted and rewarded with the rank of Lieutenant Governor.[1] Having witnessed the misery of slavery as an indentured servant in his younger days, did not hinder him afterwards, as a wealthy man, from investing in plantations and slaves. After he »transferred his plunder into a Jamaican plantation«,[2] Morgan was directly involved in the exploitation of slave labour. This did not only produce sugar for the incidental side-product, molasses, was inter alia distilled to rum which, in turn, in the form of the rum ration of the navy, developed into a power source of colonialism and, as a high-proof equivalent, evolved into a considerable means of barter in the transatlantic slave trade.[3]

Metamorphosed into an advertising icon, ›Captain Morgan‹ sets foot on an inverted Pandora's box. It contains distilled black workforce. Although the labourers themselves, as well as their activity, are completely eliminated from the scene, the barrel containing the product of their labour refers to the history of colonialism and the appropriation of enslaved Africans whose acquisition was calculated with a high mortality rate on the slave ships and whose exploitation had no regard for the survival of the human merchandise. For that reason alone, the rum advertisement is as thoughtless as distasteful. Overall, it indicates a cultural ambience in which, until today, it obviously seems to be unproblematic for producers, advertisers, and consumers to communicate a picture charged with colonial violence and racist oppression as an animating sales message (see fig. 1).

Its discriminating implications are additionally intensified by the representation of the players, divided between a weak-spirited group and a triumphant, fearless individual. The players in the group are genderised and racialised. In order to become aware of the sexist dimension of their depiction it is sufficient to visualise them with the handbags with which a photomontage circulating on the internet outfitted a similar group of (Argentine) players. The recipients were familiar with the macho contrast because of an interview with the most famous German goalkeeper at that time. After a defeat of his team, he had simply claimed: »Wir brauchen Eier« (literally: we need eggs – meaning: balls).[4]

---

1   Concerning Henry Morgan cf. Terry Breverton: Admiral Sir Henry Morgan, pp. 82 (knighting), 84 (Lieutenant-Governor), 88 (sugar plantations); John F. Richards: The Unending Frontier, pp. 444 f. (plantations and slaves). The fore-mentioned advertising campaign was implemented in 2008.
2   Michael Cranton: Empire, Enslavement and Freedom in the Caribbean, p. 52.
3   Cf. A. James Pack: Nelson's blood; Richard B. Sheridan: Sugar and Slavery, pp. 339 ff.; Eric Williams: Capitalism and Slavery, pp. 78 ff.
4   Cf. http://www.guy-sports.com/fun_pictures/football_handbags_argentine.jpg and Süddeutsche Zeitung, 5.11.2003 (›Rumeiern geht nicht‹).

The pictorial design of the sales message is not composed much differently. The feminised players in the group secure with their hands exactly what, in the opinion of the sexist advertisers, they are lacking: cojones. In contrast to them, the footballing doubleganger of Captain Morgan presents himself as hotshot. His posture is modelled on the Caribbean slaveholder and racistly supplemented by his position contiguous to the flinching black teammate. The multi-culturally customised surface of the advertisement does not suffice to mask the tradition of European racism. The gesture of superiority is based on a history of oppression, at once veiled and warranted by the iconography. On the one hand, the historic slave plantations

Fig. 1: ... the slaveholder as advertiser ...

are situated beyond the picture. The contemporary black footballer, on the other hand, has voluntarily joined the team and by his juxtaposed timidity authenticates the supremacy of his white teammate.

The clandestine yet sinister linkage, implied in the triumphant gesture, has obtained its most prevalent legitimisation and representation in the allegedly voluntary subordination of Friday to Robinson. Propagating colonialism and calling for imperialism, Daniel Defoe's Robinson trilogy has been underestimated even by master thinkers. Jean-Jacques Rousseau considers that the novel would be ideal if confined to the island episode. Karl Marx did not lag behind him as he characterised the political economy of the robinsonade without even mentioning Man Friday.[5]

---

5   Cf. Jean-Jacques Rousseau: Émile, p. 455 and Karl Marx: Das Kapital, pp. 90 f.

Actually, the self-sufficient island living is only a spectacle presented by Defoe on the front stage of his novel whereas on the backstage the profane exploitation of the colonial plantation economy took place. The stage metaphors shaped by Erving Goffman[6] are well suited to characterise the ideological curtain in front of which Robinson tirelessly pretends to toil whilst behind it the slaves of his Brazilian plantation are invisibly exploited. When Defoe finally considered that his protagonist had performed enough ideological work he saved him, and Robinson turned out to be a wealthy man. He was »Master [...] of above 5000. l. Sterling in Money, and had an Estate [...] in the Brasils, of above a thousand Pounds a Year«. The labour of the slaves on the back stage of his sugar plantation enabled him to acquire a country estate in England and establish himself as a gentleman and member of the gentry.

In view of the legitimation of property by one's own labour, Defoe was a docile disciple of John Locke. With regard to the vindication of slavery he surpassed him by far. Just as Robinson sedulously pottered around on his island in order to emphasise his ownership, so he symbolically gained a slave who willingly bowed to him and in doing so likewise veiled the slavery on Robinson's Brazilian plantations. The latter neither had to capture nor to buy Man Friday, for instead he saved him from a certain death threatened by his cannibalistic tribesmen. Friday submitted himself to his saviour out of inner conviction and deep gratitude. The description of this scene is an epigram for slaveholders: »he came nearer and nearer, kneeling down every Ten or Twelve steps in token of acknowledgement for my saving his Life [...]; at length he came close to me, and then he kneel'd down again, kiss'd the Ground, and laid his Head upon the Ground, and taking me by the Foot, set my Foot upon his Head; this it seems was in token of swearing to be my Slave for ever«.[7]

This episode has been illustrated too often and circulated too widely to fall into oblivion (see fig. 2).[8] Ideologically as well as iconographically, it bears a straight relation to Captain Morgan's foot imperially set on the barrel of rum, which contained a high-proof concentrate of looted slave labour. The question as to why the continuation of slavery as advertising after its abolition as policy has been possible until today cannot simply be answered with reference to the short memory of the advertisers or the long half-life of stereotypes. Racist advertising is not designed unwittingly or

---

6   Cf. Erving Goffman: The presentation of self in everyday life.
7   Daniel Defoe: Robinson Crusoe, pp. 205 (›estate in Brasil‹), 147 (›set may foot upon his head‹).
8   The version reproduced in fig. 2 is from Voyages et Aventures Surprenantes de Robinson Crusoé. Dessinées et Gravées par F. A. L. Dumoulin. Vevey: Lœrtscher et Fils (n.d.); (see http://www.gutenberg.org/files/24915/24915-h/24915-h.htm).

accidentally. It is consistently connected to ideological patterns of degradation in other social areas as well as embedded in cultural traditions of racist arrogance and social structures of racist oppression. Commodity racism is informed by »[e]pistemic violence« and represents »structures of power«.⁹

This is made drastically evident by responses to the promotion of ›Banania‹. The breakfast food initially used the image of a dark-skinned belle from the Antilles emptying her colonial cornucopia over the people

Fig. 2: ... slavery as self-submission ...

of France. But after the beginning of the First World War, the advertising featured the character of ›Bonhomme Banania‹, a tirailleur sénégalais who, sitting beside a crate with the label ›Banania‹, had put aside his rifle and, spooning the cereal out of a bowl, smilingly professed: »Banania y'a bon«. His smile was created to undermine his soldierly manliness and the words put into his mouth served to emphasise his cultural inferiority: »The Bonhomme's smile became an iconic synecdoche for the black other as

---

9 Anne Donadey: ›Y'a bon Banania‹, p. 11 (›epistemic violence‹); Michael Pickering: Stereotyping, p. 3 (›structures of power‹).

a grand enfant« and »[t]he language [...] was used to place him along a civilizing index«.[10]

Frantz Fanon has described how his »body schema [...] collapsed« under the weight of such impertinences and was »giving way to an epidermal racial schema«: »I cast an objective gaze over myself, discovered my blackness, my ethnic features; deafened by cannibalism, backwardness, fetishism, racial stigmas, slave traders, and above all, yes, above all, the grinning Y a bon Banania«. Only slightly earlier, Léopold Sédar Senghor had sworn that he »will tear off the Banania grins from all the walls of France«.[11] Only three years after Senghor came to France for study, in 1931 the Exposition coloniale was taking place. It was staged in grand style as an exhibition of humans and, like its predecessors, was intended to demonstrate the amenities of colonialism as well as the simpleness and harmlessness of the colonial subjects to the metropolitan populace.[12]

Human zoos and commodity racism emerged simultaneously and represent two sides of the coin with which capitalist societies attempted to appease the rigours of exploitation and convince the lower classes of the advantages of imperialism. At the opening of the first great world exposition in London's Crystal Palace in 1851, this connection was comparatively rudimentary, but the reopening in 1854 showcased exotic panoramas populated with plaster casts of ›savage‹ people. For the centenary of the French Revolution and the quadricentennial of the ›discovery‹ of ›America‹ the World Fairs in Paris (1889) and Chicago (1893) celebrated the success of white supremacy with spacious native villages. Especially in Chicago, these could even be examined by visitors having personally experienced persecution, oppression, and slavery.[13] They came face to face with the racist achievements of anthropology and the promotion of commodities like cigarettes or pancake mixtures advertised by the racist stereotypes of noble ›red savages‹ or caring ›black mammies‹ or ›uncles‹.

The fundamental basis of racist advertising and commodity racism is the dialectic of *advertised temptation and imperialist violence*. It is discussed in the first chapter which shows that the nexus of the political development of imperialism and the emergence of modern advertising is not coincidental. Against this background the second chapter investigates the

10 Brett A. Berliner: Ambivalent Desire, p. 15 (›smile‹); Peter J. Bloom: French Colonial Documentary, p. 41 (›language‹); see also Malte Hinrichsen: Racist Trademarks, pp. 63 ff.
11 Frantz Fanon: Black Skin, White Masks, p. 92; Léopold Sédar Sengor: Poème liminaire, p. 55 (»je déchirerai les rires banania sur tous les murs de France«).
12 Cf. Herman Lebovics: Les zoos de l'Exposition coloniale internationale de Paris en 1931.
13 Cf. Christopher Robert Reed: ›All the World is Here!‹

relations of *racist discrimination and commodity aesthetics*, thereby explaining how racist advertising does not only represent a special promise of use value but also a specific use value: the promotion of an imagined racial community. The third chapter addresses *a pentagon of phantasmagorias* resulting from the intertwining of commodity racism with anthropological science and entertainment and the intersectionality of racist, classist and sexist discrimination. The relationship of *commodity racism and racist symbolic capital* is the topic of the concluding fourth chapter which deals with the significance of racism for classist societalisation and the social function of racist advertising in this context.

Advertised Temptation and Imperialist Violence

In the vortex of discourse, information occasionally gets lost. Sometimes it also falls victim to hasty interpretation. This is suggested by the way two prominent analyses of commodity culture deal with two of its significant pictorial examples. The one, George Cruikshank's frontispiece for Henry Mayhew's novel of the ›Great Exhibition‹, is bisected in Thomas Richards' depiction of consumerism. The other, an advertisement for Pears' soap captioned ›The formula of British conquest‹, is curtailed in Anne McClintock's characterisation of commodity racism.[14]

When in 1851 ›Crystal Palace‹ opened its doors in London's Hyde Park the first »monument to consumption« was inaugurated, whose »[e]xhibition fashioned a phenomenology and a psychology for a new kind of being, the consumer, and a new strain of ideology, consumerism«. In respect to this thesis, Thomas Richards takes the period of time into account, after which a development that started as a soliloquy of the bourgeoisie reached the majority of the working people. Nonetheless, consumerism was a cross-class phenomenon and Crystal Palace the point of no return. This was demonstrated by the Shilling day which allowed ordinary people access to commodities they could contemplate but not afford. That was, at least symbolically, an »imprimatur of social consensus«. It transformed wide sections of the population into supporters of imperialism and allowed commodity holders and exhibition organisers »to sell imperialism to the domestic public«.[15]

---

14 Cf. Thomas Richards: The Commodity Culture of Victorian England, p. 18; Anne McClintock: Imperial Leather, p. 57.
15 Thomas Richards: The Commodity Culture of Victorian England, pp. 3 (›monument‹), 5 (›new‹), 70 (›impremature‹), 71 (›imperialism‹); for a detailed discussion of the integration of the labouring classes into early consumerism see Peter Gurney: An Appropriated Space.

This correlation included a vision of a civilising mission for a modernity without any alternative, whose success would be ensured by the attractiveness of its message. This, too, was one of the subtexts of an etching by George Cruikshank, illuminating the attractive power of Crystal Palace as gravitational attraction and proclaiming ›All the World Going to See the Great Exhibition of 1851‹ (see fig. 3).[16] The scene plays on a globe obviously divided between north and south. The majority of the people are located in, or heading to, the northern hemisphere. They appear to be attracted by the Crystal Palace that is palatially topping this part of the world. This procession, predominantly walking, is flanked by modern means of transport, railways and steamships, on the horizon.

Richards takes this as a proof of the Great Exhibition as an »outburst of the phantasmagoria of commodity culture« and »the still centre of the turning earth, the focal point of all gazing and the endpoint of all pilgrimages«.[17] To uphold this view, however, he has to present a bisected version of the etching. It is cut off just below the equator. As a result, the palace appears not only as a magic sign of desire en masse but also as the crowning peak of an architectural triangle, whose basis is composed of palm huts (left) as signs of persistent primitivity and pyramids (right) as witnesses of a bygone culture. The southern hemisphere with its pagodas and temples completely disappears from view.

By this move the Union Jack, which also flutters over this southern part of the earth, is blocked out of the picture and the analysis. It was not set up over a crystalline construction of glass and iron, as in the north, but waves over a crude fortification. Viewers nevertheless could be sure that behind its palisades there is a technology of repression and domination that has no need to shy away from comparison with the achievements displayed in the wondrous palace.[18] The duality of commodities and cannons is the ultima ratio of imperialism. Who refuses the allegedly peaceful pervasion with the capitalist range of goods has to reckon with penalties. The East Asian expedition to Crystal Palace can tell a thing or two about it. Recently, China has lost the Opium War and has been forced by the Treaty of Nanking to open ports and markets to British trade and to surrender Hong Kong as a

16 Cf. Henry Mayhew, George Cruikshank: 1851, frontispiece; recently, the edging was used as the cover picture of Jeffrey A. Auerbach, Peter H. Hoffenberg (eds.): Britain, the Empire, and the World at the Great Exhibition of 1851.
17 Thomas Richards: The Commodity Culture of Victorian England, p. 18.
18 Anne McClintock: Imperial Leather, p. 57, despite reproducing the complete etching, comes to the same conclusion as Richards: »In an exemplary image the Great Exhibition literally drew the world's people toward the monumental display of the commodity« (ibid., p. 58). In Tanya Agathocleous: Urban Realism and the Cosmopolitan Imagination in the Nineteenth Century, p. 39 the entire picture is to be seen as well, but the author also disregards the military antipole of Crystal Palace.

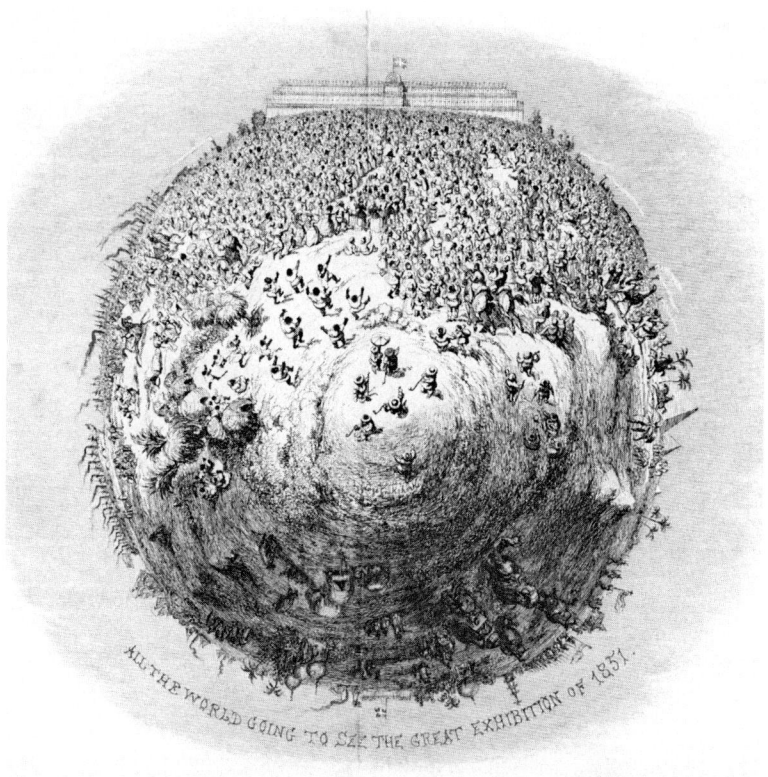

Fig. 3: ... consumerism and imperialism ...

crown colony – a procedure which should be repeated after the Arrow War on an enlarged scale in that the empires of Britain, France, Russia and the United States expected distinctly more extensive concessions of China.[19]

If Crystal Palace radiates the light of an incipient consumer culture, then this was not least because it was a cultural imperialism made manifest. It combined the enticements of a developing commodity production with the violence of a colonialism mutated into Empire. Military outposts were crucially conductive to its glitter. They enforced and secured unequal terms of trade as well as the formation and preservation of political and ideological zones of influence. Racist advertising must be understood against this background. Its seductive appeal cannot be sustained without the element of power.

19 Cf. Peter Ward Fey: The Opium War; John Y. Wong: Deadly Dreams.

Fig. 4: ... the formula of British conquest ...

A frequently discussed implementation of such an amalgam of temptation and violence was offered by Pears. It was designed in 1887 and printed in several gazettes. In ›The Illustrated London News‹ it was arranged as a double advertisement. On the left it showed several text passages and on the right it displayed a scene with the headline ›The formula of British conquest‹ and the legend ›Pears' soap in the Soudan‹ (see fig. 4). Thomas Richards reproduces only the right side of this complex message, Anne McClintock acts in the same way and furthermore even removes the text lines below the picture.[20]

20 Cf. Thomas Richards: The Commodity Culture of Victorian England, pp. 121 ff. and Anne McClintock: Imperial Leather, pp. 225 f.; for the advertisement see ›The Illustrated London News‹, 27.8.1887, p. 249 – on the same day a similar double advertisement with the same left part but a different right part was published: cf. ›The Graphic‹, 27.8.1887, p. 239. Comparable to Richards precede Janice Boddy: Civilizing Women, p. 39, David Ciarlo: Advertising Empire, p. 111, Enda Duffy: Molly's Throat, figure 2, Eric J. Hobsbawm: The Age of Empire, illustration 21, Anandi Ramamurthy: Imperial Persuaders, p. 38; for a complete reproduction see Julia V. Emberley: Defamiliarizing the Aboriginal, p. 125.

Advertising White Supremacy

Fig. 5: ... advertising as system promotion ...

This decontextualisation leads to an analytical curtailment and a constriction of argument. The halving of the advertisement obscures its clandestine reference to the instant advantage of racist promises of use value and the omission of text withholds evidence of the association of imperial military power and capitalist economic expansion. In the case of the Pears' advertisement this attitude generated a self-fulfilling prophecy that did not need any further historical evidence. But as it happens, the advertisement was a mixture of »pictorial realism« and »play of imagination«.[21] In August 1885 ›The Illustrated London News‹ published a picture with the caption ›Private enterprise in the Soudan‹, depicting a tableau of a rock formation, and several people with camels resting at the foothills (see fig. 5). In the foreground, a railway track is to be seen. On one of the rocks is written the slogan ›Pear's [sic] soap is the best‹. The comment refers to the ›Berber railway‹, which would have opened the land »for commercial enterprise«. The writing on the rock would be the oeuvre of »some clever agent of a well-known branch of retail trade«. However, »an Arabic trans-

---

21 Andrzej Piotrowski: Architecture of Thought, p. 176.

lation« for the »Soudanese natives« would be missing. Hence the instruction »how the best of soaps will serve to wash a blackamoor white« would remain hidden to them.[22]

This derivation of the writing on the wall is rather doubtful. As it happens, with white letters on a rock, British soldiers had labelled the spot ›Otao Junction‹ and, misspelling the brand name, might have painted the advertising phrase as well. Similar slogans like ›Drink Eno's Fruit Salts‹ could be deciphered even decades later on the neighbouring hills.[23] At the same time the troops' camp must have been flagged with the Union Jack. George Cruikshank's allegory was realised at the final stop of a military railway, built by workers from India called ›coolies‹ and guarded by imperial formations including contingents from Canada and New South Wales. A desert hollow, where rocks served as billboards and commodities were represented by their mere brand name, substituted the crystal emporium of consumerism. The crowds in this amphitheatre of imperial culture were no equals in front of a commodity display, but racistly divided into conscripted labourers and violent conquerors. The slogans on the rocks were as Janus-faced as the beholders – promise to some, menace for the rest. The benedictions of consumerism in the imperial centre came along with underdevelopment at the colonial periphery.

In the pictorial representation of this scenario violence is sublimated to technical and advertising signs. The completion of the railway line signals the capability to bring in troops and to carry away raw materials. The soap slogan reveals the intimate alliance of imperialist expansionism and capitalist profit interests. Evidently, it is not addressed to the small group of locals integrated into the picture. They camp at the foot of the rock formation with their camels and turn their backs on the inscription. Yet a German recipient of the image captions its reprint in his ›Book of Advertising‹ with the phrase »Ankündigung von Pears' Seife an einem Felsen im Sudan« – »Announcement of Pears' soap on a rock in the Sudan«.[24]

›Announcement‹ is a comprehensive term. In this context it certainly included ›advertisement‹. However, the author omitted to ask who has advertised in which manner for what? The writing actually dated back to the campaign of a company, but it was not installed by its order. Its designers were no commissioners of a single capital but agents of an imperial capital. Its message had multiple connotations. By its painters it was consid-

---

22 Illustrated London News, 22.8.1885, pp. 193 (picture), 194 (›enterprise‹, etc.); see also Anandi Ramamurthy: Imperial Persuaders, p. 40.
23 Cf. Janice Boddy: Purity and Conquest in the Anglo-Egyptian Sudan, p. 181.
24 Cf. Rudolf Cronau: Buch der Reklame, p. 1, 27; see also David Ciarlo: Advertising Empire, p. 109.

ered as a landmark of a proposed occupation, the insolvent ›natives‹ could at best see it as a symbol of colonial usurpation in the guise of a civilizing mission, to its spectators at home it was a sign of national grandeur and destiny. If the ›announcement of Pears' soap on a rock in the Sudan‹ was advertising, then in the first instance it was not for a product for which there was no outlet far and wide. It was rather a form of system promotion, merging the spatial dimensions of colonialism with the political dimensions of imperialism, the economical dimensions of capitalism, and the ideological dimensions of racism.

The advertisers of Pears' Soap were quite acquainted with this complexity. For some time after the British forces had to leave Otao, they made use of the report on the rock painting for a promotion. At that time the siege of Khartoum and the death of Gordon Pascha were altogether known to the public. Already symbolically born as the son of a ship owner's daughter and a military officer, Charles George Gordon was practically an incarnation of imperial power politics, had fought in the Crimean War against Russians and in the Opium War against Chinese, had controlled the construction of fortifications for the river Thames and searched for the actual location of Golgotha in Palestine, was the Secretary of the Viceroy of India, Commander in Mauritius and Commander-in-chief in South Africa, when he, who had already earlier been the Governor of the Turkish-Egyptian-ruled Sudan and had been appointed Pasha, was sent by the British government, under pressure of a jingoist press, to Khartoum, where, officially, he was supposed to care only for the security of the civilian population but instead autocratically decided in favour of resistance against the Mahdi insurgence and defended the city for ten months, until he was killed during its seizure shortly before the compensatory expedition which had been staged with tremendous public attention and support reached the city. It was regarded as authentic that he fell victim to a multitude armed with archaic weapons. Concerning the circumstances of his death the suggestion prevailed that he was speared. This was epitomised in George William Joy's painting ›General Gordon's Last Stand‹ (and afterwards re-enacted in Madame Tussaud's Wax Museum).[25]

Quite recently having given a painful defeat to the empire and having been the death of one of its most heroic sons, the spears soon attained literary honours. Rudyard Kipling would pass a poisoned compliment to the Mahdist soldier and praise the ›Fuzzy-Wuzzy‹ who »'s 'oppin' in an' out

---

25 Cf. C. Brad Faught: Gordon (Gordon's life); Stephanie D. Laffer: Gordon's Ghost, p. 33 (›speared‹); Edward Berenson: Heroes of Empire, p. 118 (painting, wax museum).

among the bush | [w]ith 'is coffin-headed shield an' shovel-spear«.[26] In the advertisement for Pears' soap the spears played a likewise prominent role: they indicated a process of capitulation which would have done Man Friday credit and, from left to right, are rapidly lowered until they are laying on the ground and the fighters are disarmed. The reason for this surrender seems to be the writing on the wall whose blazing apparition even forces one of the men to his knees.

In interpreting this image various scholars content themselves with Foucauldian or Marxist deliberations on the fetishisms of signs or commodities. Apparently, a glance into the bible seems to be far too profane, even though the contemporaries at that time were well acquainted with the scripture and therefore also knew the story of Belshazzar. As the prophet Daniel explained the writing on the wall to the king of Babylon in the language of commerce (counting, weighting, dividing), similarly the Pears company declared to the Mahdist rulers their imminent end in the language of modern capitalism (advertising). But, to be sure, the reign of Belshazzar was not ended by merchants but by the Persians. Just as in his days Cyrus, as ancient ›King of the four corners of the World‹ really no bad example for a modern empire, had captured Babylon, likewise Britain would conquer the realm of the Mahdi. For this purpose, Queen Victoria did not even have to put herself on the line. She sent Horatio Herbert Kitchener, who, before dying during the First World War, had been Consul-General in Egypt, Commander-in-Chief in India and responsible for concentration camps in South Africa. He had celebrated his first military triumph as the victor of the battle of Omdurman, which ended the realm of the Mahdi and placed Sudan under English rule, whereupon the Queen ennobled him at first as a baron and ultimately as Earl Kitchener of Khartoum.[27]

It so happened that not only Kitchener himself knew about the close affiliation of imperialism and capitalism as he had similarly well-informed soldiers in his troops. Hence, Lever Brothers, which a good ten years later would acquire Pears Ltd., could place a noteworthy advertisement (see fig. 6).[28] Under the slogan ›The march of civilisation: Sunlight soap at Khartoum‹ it depicted two British soldiers who have just painted the logo of the soap on the local city walls – watched by dark-skinned local inhabitants (who have completely lost their weapons). The text beneath the picture refers to a »message« cabled to England by Kitchener: »I trust that the opening up of these extensive countries will benefit the City of London and British trade and commerce in general«. After that there is a notice that

26 Rudyard Kipling: Fuzzy-Wuzzy, p. 223.
27 Cf. Daniel, 5, 25-27; concerning Kitchener see Philip Magnus: Kitchener.
28 Cf. ›The Illustrated London News‹, 8.10.1898, p. 525.

the company claims to have received from a soldier in Khartoum. After the capture he was commandeered »to bore holes to erect the flag-staffs on top of the Palace« and has taken the opportunity to place a ›Sunlight‹ advertisement »on a wall [...] within one hundred yards of Gordon's Palace«.

He described the triumph of a transcended Crystal Palace under the flag of the Royal army. George Cruikshank's version of the global collaboration of imperial power and capitalist economy condensed as brand name at the walls near the very palace, in which Gordon Pascha lost his life and on which eventually the Union Jack flew. An epiphany of imperialism, this message, as well as Pears' previous writing on the wall, was not intended for the Sudanese who witnessed the manifestations of capitalist advertising. Both were in fact addressed to the readers of the illustrated

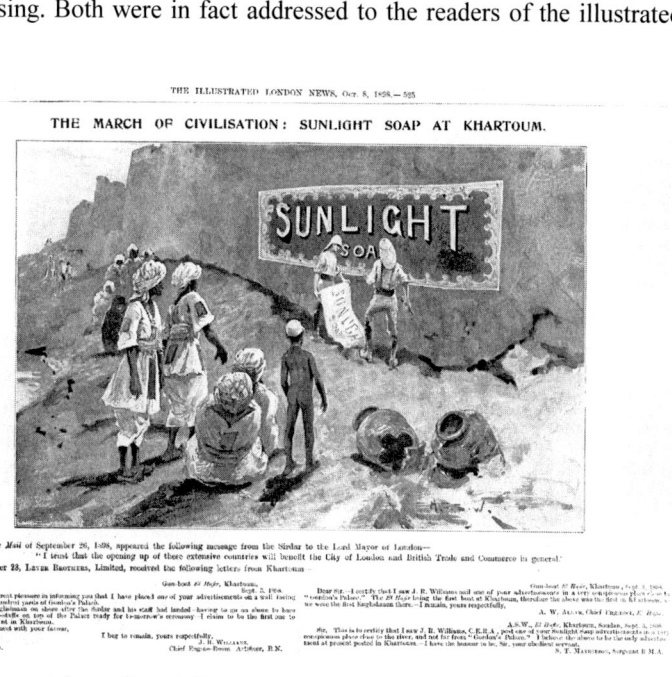

Fig. 6: ... an epiphany of imperialism ...

press and the consumers of soap.[29] They were well-prepared to decipher such a subtext. The press had intensely reported the conflict from the beginning and encouraged the jingoist atmosphere already in existence. The war correspondents made use of the ›language of empire‹ which could be

---

29 Cf. Julia V. Emberley: Defamiliarizing the Aboriginal, pp. 124 ff.

acquired from an early age by the reading of numerous juvenile books.[30] Moreover, ideological accessory was produced on all cultural fields. The Grand National Amphitheatre, for example, staged ›Khartoum‹ as a play. The audience not only could delight in heroic actions of British soldiers but also gaze at ›Sudanese Natives‹.[31]

Racist Discrimination and Commodity Aesthetics

When the advertisers of ›Pears' Soap‹ designed their Sudanese dervishes, they could not have read either Karl Marx or Walter Benjamin, Jean Baudrillard or Pierre Bourdieu. They had no notion of commodity fetishism and no understanding of phantasmagorias, and were not acquainted with sign values and ignorant of symbolic capital.[32] But they still chose an exceptional form of configuration. It almost seemed as if two advertisements were placed side by side (see fig. 4). This, at least, must have been the view of those analysers who relinquished the examination of the left part of the advertisement.

As a result they missed a far-reaching aspiration of the division: the doubling of the advertisement disclosed the fact that it not only conveyed a promise of use value but also had an instant ideological use value. On the one side it declares that »[n]othing adds so much to personal attractions as a bright, clear complexion« and it alleges that such an appearance could be gained by using Pears' soap. This is supported by two statements of a ›professor‹, ›Sir‹, and ›eminent authority on the skin‹ and of an acclaimed contemporary prima donna. However, to enjoy this promise, the soap has to be purchased. This is the plain economic purpose of the advertisement.

Its other part is composed of a headline, a picture, and a text placed below quoting a sentence of the ›War Correspondent (in the Soudan) of the Daily Telegraph‹.[33] By this means, the advertisement assimilates to its editorial context. All media commodities containing advertisements circulate on two markets. They produce news and entertainment as commodities for

30 Cf. Roger T. Stearn: War Correspondents and Colonial War; Robert H. MacDonald: The Language of Empire.
31 Cf. Edward Ziter: The Orient on the Victorian Stage, p. 180.
32 As overviews see i.a. Anne M. Cronin: Advertising Myths; Robert G. Dunn: Identifying Consumption; Martyn J. Lee: Consumer Culture Reborn; Robert Miklitsch: From Hegel to Madonna.
33 The caption of the text is »»Pears' soap in the Soudan« and it reads: »»Even if our invasion of the Soudan has done nothing else it has at any rate left the Arab something to puzzle his fuzzy had over, for the legend Pears' Soap is the best, described in huge white characters on the rock which marks the farthest point of our advance toward Berber, will tax all the wits of the Dervishes of the Desert to translate.‹ – Phil Robinson, War Correspondent (in the Soudan) of the Daily Telegraph in London, 1884««.

readers and lookers and they produce space for advertisements as commodities for advertisers. The use value of the media commodity consists in the communication of information and amusement on the one hand and in the generation of a setting for advertising on the other. Admittedly, advertisements also pretend to provide information – just as Pears on the left side of its double notice with the hint to the significance of soap for skin care and the importance of fine soap for the success of washing – but this information commonly serves the promise of use value: those who use Pears' become not only clean but also attractive.

In this respect the enticements of different soaps are alternative. Their promises are bound to the brand name that signals singularity and suggests the realisation of ordinary soapy use values with wondrous vigour. Concerning the atmosphere of soap advertising, by contrast, the manufacturers can act in concert, embellish it with colonial clichés and colourise it in a racist manner. Beyond the specific promise of use value their advertisements present a joint message. It is available for those viewers as well, who do not turn into consumers. They can read racist promises of value as information about white supremacy, and therein lies the ideological significance of advertising.

Historically, the overlapping of both dimensions shaped commodity aesthetics. It inevitably went, as Wolfgang Fritz Haug has emphasised, hand in hand with the production of commodities in order to bridge the contradiction between the producers (profit) and the consumers (use): »a beauty developed in the service of the realisation of exchange value«.[34] Groundwork of this consideration is the analysis of the commodity and the form of value by Karl Marx. To produce value, commodities have to be produced with »use value for others, social use value«. This is definitively not easy, because commodities are values but have no use values for their producers and sellers, and use values but with no values for their buyers and consumers. To realise the value for the producer and the use value for the consumer, commodities must change hands. That is quite a hazardous procedure, so that Marx called it the »salto mortale of the commodity«. Despite the commodities making amorous eyes at the money of the buyers with their prices, the feat can only go well if the commodities do not fail to »*show* that they are use-values before they can be realised as values«.[35]

This is the birth of what Haug calls the promise of use value and what after the shift to monopoly capitalism evolves into modern advertising

---

34 Wolfgang Fritz Haug: Kritik der Warenästhetik, p. 23; for the following see ibid, pp. 29 f. (›promise of use value‹), 226 (›communicated commodity aesthetics‹).
35 Karl Marx: Das Kapital, pp. 55 (›social use value‹), 100 (›values‹ and ›use values‹), 120 (›salto mortale‹), 124 (›amorous eyes‹), 110 (›show‹ etc. – my emphasis).

which is nothing more than »communicated commodity aesthetics«. With its help all those who were exploited during the production of commodities are eventually hoodwinked by the promise of use value and, after having reproduced capital as a social relation, reproduce the phantasmagorias of consumerism as well – so much that they themselves actually serve as agents of the sellers. Haug has illustrated this correlation with a photograph showing pigeons on the Piazza San Marco in Venice. The birds have been stimulated by the arrangement of feed to form, while eating, the logo ›Coca-Cola‹ with their bodies (see fig. 7).[36]

However, the symbolism of this arrangement does not only refer to the »manipulation of people (as of pigeons)« by »advertising and the mass media«.[37] The advertised beverage initially was a syrup served in soda bars. Hence its consumption was subjected to racial segregation and made it into a ›white‹ drink of the middle class. This tradition was extended when, from 1900 on, the liquid was bottled. Even the vending did not go without racist discrimination and as late as 1953 ›The Crisis‹ chronicled ›Jim Crow Coca Cola Machines‹. At the same time a comprehensive promotion entirely relied on ›white‹ role models like the legendary Coca-Cola girls – indeed, »there was a day when even Ebony still had the white faces advertising the Coke«.[38]

Fig. 7: ... pigeons on duty ...

The president of the company opposed the civil rights movement and entertained »a traditional master-slave relationship« with his black attendants into the middle of the twentieth century. But finally in North Carolina four black students sat down at a segregated lunch counter in Greensboro.

36 Cf. Wolfgang Fritz Haug: Critique of Commodity Aesthetics, p. 118: »In Venice a picture postcard is on sale which advertises both the city and an American company. It shows St Mark's Square, empty of people, but with its famous flock of pigeons. The pigeons are sitting in an organized shape: in huge letters they form the name Coca-Cola. The letters are those of the ›copyright protected‹ trademark design. The lay-out for the advertising photo was achieved by the advertising manager hiring casual labourers to spread birdseed on the square in the shape of the trademark. The pigeons did not gather with the intention of forming the trademark but to satisfy their hunger. But equally the seed was not scattered to feed the pigeons but to employ them on its tracks as extras. The arrangement is totally alien and external to pigeons. While they are consuming their feed, capital is subsuming, and consuming, them. This picture, a triumph of capitalist advertising technique, symbolizes a fundamental aspect of capitalism«; Joseph G. Links: Venice, p. 65, already referred to the advertising experiment with the pigeons.
37 Arthur Asa Berger: Media Analysis Techniques, p. 59.
38 Cf. Wendy A. Woloson: Refined Tastes, p. 89 (»Soda fountains became key meeting and socializing places for the urban elite [... and] continued to reinforce the cultural hierarchies among consumers«); The Crisis, 60, 1953, 6, p. 350 (›Jim Crow‹); Chris H. Beyer: Coca-Cola Girls; Dick Gregory: [Interview from 1961], p. 84 (›Ebony‹).

Advertising White Supremacy

In doing so they were even confronted twice with references to that soft drink whose consumption was refused to them here, while almost at the same time the pigeons of Venice formed its logo (see fig. 8).

Back then, the ›girls‹ advertising the product were still mainly ›white‹. But even after the company had to change its advertising strategy during

Fig. 8: ... unmasked consumer culture ...

the course of the sixties, the attached white supremacy did not vanish. In the early seventies an advertisement united »a field of young, good-looking representatives of various ›racial types‹« in enjoying Coca-Cola. But it was the prerogative of the white woman to proclaim the »multicultural but universalist« message: »people can live ›in perfect harmony‹, when brought together within white, American commodity culture«.[39]

Viewed in this light, the pigeons of Venice indeed showcased »the devouring nature of the advertising sign, which could shape anything to its own consuming logic«.[40] But at the same time they symbolised the efforts

---

39 Mark Pendergrast: For God, Country and Coca-Cola, p. 267 (›master-slave‹); William H. Chafe: Civilities and Civil Rights, pp. 71 ff.(›Greensboro‹; the picture of the ›Greensboro Four‹ has been frequently published, i.a. ibid., p. 84); Alastair Bonnett: Anti-Racism, p. 79 (›perfect harmony‹).
40 Nigel Wheale (ed.): The Postmodern Arts, p. 3.

of the consumers to identify with the label and the prestige of an object of preference. This included the appropriation and reproduction of its ›white‹ connotation. Modern commodity aesthetics emerged against the background of a development associating new conditions of the valorisation of capital with imperialism and racism. For that reason modern advertising from the beginning not only proclaimed the indispensability of particular commodities but also propagated the blessings of European-American imperialism and its aspiration of white supremacy as well. Commodity aesthetics and commodity racism developed at the same time in a reciprocal relationship.

In this way ›whiteness‹ became so taken for granted that it was disregarded or blocked out even in critical researches. In particular, Walter Benjamin's ›Arcades Project‹ shows this obviously. Theoretically central to his critique of modernity are its phantasmagorias – of time and space, of urbanity and interiors, of culture and world exhibitions. The latter are considered as »places of pilgrimage to the commodity fetish« – they »glorify the exchange value of the commodity« and »propagate the universe of commodities«.[41] But despite the fact that Paris, Benjamin's capital of the nineteenth century, was the metropolis of a colonial empire, from where Caribbean slavery was restored, Algeria was occupied, an intervention to Mexico emanated, French Indochina was annexed and the participation in the Scramble for Africa was organised, one of the most significant perversions of the nineteenth century is absent in Benjamin's deliberations: the phantasmagoria of human races and of their supposed racial inequality.

And yet the world fairs, emphasised by Benjamin alongside the fetishised commodities, exposed ›natives‹ specifically brought along for that purpose to public viewing.[42] Moreover, French philosophers and scientists made a tremendous contribution to the development of scientific racism; a Frenchman championed the idea that all history is race history; and polygenetic opinions regarding the origin(s) of mankind were held with particular intensity in France. Eventually modern advertising, which used stylised ›têtes noires‹ to promote all kinds of commodities, was generated on the basis of such an ideology.[43]

41 Walter Benjamin: The Arcades Project, pp. 34 (›signage‹), 7 f. (›places of pilgrimage‹, ›exchange value‹, ›universe‹); for the following see ibid., 12 f. (›revolution‹).
42 Cf. the information in Gilles Boëtsch, Yann Ardagna: Zoos humains: le ›sauvage‹ et l'anthropologie; Pascal Blanchard, Nicolas Bancel, Sandrine Lemaire: Les zoos humaines: le passage d'un ›racisme scientifique‹ vers un ›racisme populaire et colonial‹ en Occident; William H. Schneider: Les expositions ethnographiques du Jardin zoologique d'acclimatation.
43 Concerning scientific racism see Tzvetan Todorov: Nous et les autres; Martin S. Staum: Labeling People; for the popularisation of racism cf. William H. Schneider: An Empire for the Masses; Anne McClintock: Imperial Leather, pp. 31 ff. refers to »commodity

Benjamin so rigorously ignores this correlation that he censors his own cognition when describing an advertisement. In the context of the idea that, »[w]ith the dramatic signage of the magasins de nouveautés, art enters the service of the businessman«, he considers a »poster that, if things had their due in this world, would have found its admirers, historians, exegetes, and copyists just as surely as any great poem or painting«.[44] Concerning this poster he suggests that he had experienced it as such a »shock«, that its subject burst through his consciousness »and for years lay irrecoverable somewhere in the darkness«.

He only wants to have memorised the name of the advertised product: »Bullrich Salt«. And despite repeatedly passing the store where it was sold, he neglected to go in and to enquire about the poster. Not until a later accidental encounter with the brand name, did he purportedly remember the illustration pictured on the poster: »In the foreground, a horse-drawn wagon was advancing across the desert. It was loaded with sacks bearing the words ›Bullrich Salt‹. One of these sacks had a hole, from which salt had already trickled a good distance on the ground [...] and formed [...] the word ›Bullrich Salt‹«.[45]

Evidence suggests that this poster never existed.[46] But in any case the shop of the company in question had a display window that showed the scene described by Benjamin in a quite different configuration (see fig. 9b). It strongly contradicted the ironic compliment with which Benjamin appreciated the salt which was writing its own name by explaining: »Was not the pre-established harmony of a Leibniz mere child's play compared to this tightly orchestrated predestination in the desert? And didn't that poster furnish an image for things that no one in his mortal life has yet experienced? An image of the everyday in Utopia?«

Actually, the ›pre-established harmony‹ was nothing other than a promotional version of the manifest destiny of capitalism, the ›everyday in

racism«; concerning the mentioned advertisements see Dana S. Hale: Races on Display, pp. 25 ff.
44 Walter Benjamin: The Arcades Project, pp. 34 (›signage‹), 173 (›poster‹). Already in the late 19th century Georg Simmel (using the example of a Berlin industrial exhibition) has described the »peculiar attraction« of »world fairs«. It included an enhanced »shop-window-quality of things«, the necessity to give commodities »a tempting appearance« and to provide them with »aesthetic significance« (cf. Georg Simmel: Berliner Gewerbeausstellung, pp. 65, 67). Simmel indeed felt positive about this and did not stand alone. Even decades later a witness seemed to agree with him when Sergei Tretyakov wrote (on Berlin shopwindows): »Who wants to see where the arts of the bourgeoisie are still alive, militant, and innovative, doesn't have to go to the theatre or an art exhibition. He has to look at the shopwindows of the department stores« (Sergej Tretjakow: Schaufensterreklame, p. 542).
45 Walter Benjamin: The Arcades Project, p. 174; for the following quote (›Leibniz‹) see ibid.
46 Cf. in detail Wulf D. Hund: Prädestination in der Wüste.

Fig. 9 a & b: ... the ›shock‹ of racist advertisements ...

Utopia‹ was the vulgar daily routine of colonial exploitation, and the ›predestination in the desert‹ was just another writing on the billboard of commodity racism. On the poster (fig. 9a) the salt de facto did not trickle out of a sack but, wholly in the spirit of the promotion strategy, from its specially designed package. And this did not lie on a horse cart but was carried by an African on his back. This strictly conformed to the company's advertising campaign relying on »the aesthetics of the colonial era«.[47]

47   Matthias Gerschwitz: Bullrich-Salz, p. 71 (I wish to thank the author for the permis-

The »shock« which Benjamin claims to have felt upon first sight of the poster, arose from the action of a profane advertising agency. On one side, it ensured that materiality (body) and essence (soul) of the commodity did not fall apart. The sodium bicarbonate has incorporated its brand name in its chemical structure to such an extent, that particles getting lost from the identity-establishing packaging automatically arrange themselves and form the tradename. This brand, on the other side, was inextricably linked to the labour of black colonial others. The African carrier obviously was not conceptualised as consumer but rather as deliverer of the salt. That, to be sure, was not least a combination of exoticism and exclusivity meant to elevate the self-assurance of the white customers by imagined black servants. But such imagined figures were based on the reality of colonial expropriation. As Anandi Ramamurthy has shown, the mendacious pictures of jolly natives harvesting palm seed, cocoa, coffee or tea frequently functioned as ideological screen as well, at the rear of which the respective capitals and companies pursued their interests in alliance with the politics of their imperialist states.[48]

Benjamin's salt showed this connection, too. The designers of the advertisement consciously located the scenario in front of a prominent mountain range. It shows Africa at the foot of the snow covered slopes of ›Germany's highest mountain‹.[49] Ahead of its peak in fact, in the lowlands of the Great Rift Valley, a unique lake is located in an area formerly being a part of German East Africa. Already in 1911 a reichstag deputy enthused about »the large treasures of the Lake Natron«, where »100 million tons of natron« would represent an asset of four billion reichsmark«. And even after German colonies were lost, the German Colonial Encyclopedia referenced to the sodium carbonate in the Lake Natron and speculated about the »chance of its practical exploitation«.[50] The writing in the desert was nothing more than the imagined unification of imperialism, capitalism and consumerism operated by colonial exploitation and racist discrimination. The hand of the writer was not guided by the deity of pre-established harmony but by the gods of advantage, prejudice and whitewash who already

---

sion to reproduce the figures 9 a & b; the copyright is held by the Bullrich salt archive Matthias Gerschwitz, Berlin).

48 Cf. Anandi Ramamurthy: Imperial Persuaders.

49 Cf. Joachim Zeller: Bilderschule der Herrenmenschen, p. 158: »A question often raised in the German Kaiserreich, during geography lessons, was: ›What is the name of the highest German mountain?‹ In the years after 1885 the answer had to be: ›Mount Kilimanjaro in the colony German East Africa‹««; see also Alexander Honold: Kaiser-Wilhelm-Spitze.

50 Verhandlungen des Reichstags, pp. 5791 f. (session 155, 23.3.1911 – ›large treasures‹); Deutsches Kolonial-Lexikon, vol. 2, p. 474 (›Lake Natron‹), vol. 1, p. 164 (›exploitation‹).

had instructed the calligraphers of Pears' writing on a Sudanese Rock and Sunlight's manifestation on the walls of Khartoum.

A Pentagon of Phantasmagorias

In revenge for Khartoum, Kitchener ordered the destruction of the Mahdi's tomb and his bones to be thrown into the Nile. But the skull was desecrated further and retained as a trophy. Apparently for a while Kitchener was thinking about using it as an inkstand or a drinking cup. It was only after the queen had expressed her consternation that he wrote to her explaining that »the Mahdi's skull [...] was brought to me, and [...] I had thought of sending it to the College of Surgeons where, I believe, such things are kept«. Finally, however, he allowed the reburial of the skull.[51]

The latter was not predictable everywhere in the Commonwealth. So ›The West Australian‹ chronicled as a matter of course that »[t]he skull of the Mahdi [...] has been forwarded to London to the Royal College of Surgeons«.[52] For the members of the settler society down under, such a handling of the mortal remains of so-called savages was absolutely not indecent. The conjunction of scientific expertise and public entertainment frequently practised in this regard is a distinctive feature of that climate of racist system advertising that also let flourish a consumer racism provided by corresponding advertising campaigns for all kinds of commodities. The handling of the bodies of the conquered, oppressed, exhibited, assassinated, and defiled people of the colonial periphery was a substantial element of this setting. With skin and hair, ritual body painting and insufficient clothing they had to guarantee the state of being backward in the development of mankind. They were fixed by the instruments of anthropology and apportioned so-called primitive features. And they were marked out for the living proof of the theory of progress which demonstrated that history in the guise of white civilisation justifiably brushed them aside.[53]

In 1879 a letter to ›The Argus‹ stated that »the aborigines of Australia [...] are doubtless at the lowest range of humanity and form a race that is apparently irretrievably doomed to disappear before the more vigorous Caucasian«. Hence, the writer demanded that they be put on display as

---

51   Cf. Martin W. Daly: Empire on the Nile, p. 6; Simon Harrison: Dark Trophies, p. 76; Kitchener to the Queen, 7.3.1899, quoted in Max Hastings (ed.): The Oxford Book of Military Anecdotes, p. 310.
52   ›The West Australian‹, 28.9.1898 (›The Mahdi's Skull Sent to London‹).
53   Cf. i.a. Cressida Fforde, Jane Huber, Paul Turnbull: The Dead and their Possessions; Wulf D. Hund: Die Körper der Bilder der Rassen.

long as this would still be possible.⁵⁴ At that time Truganini had already been dead for three years. She was referred to as the ›last‹ Tasmanian not least to let the English emerge as the legitimate heirs of an ›extinct race‹. Born only a few years after the occupation of Tasmania, Truganini had witnessed the violent (›Black War‹) and the cultural (›Friendly Mission‹) attacks on the indigenous population, of which before long she was de-

Fig. 10: ... the ›savages‹ outside ...

clared to be the sole survivor. Already before her death she knew that her corpse would be desecrated in the name of science. Eventually, in 1888 her skull was put on display during the Victorian International Exhibition in Melbourne (and her entire skeleton was shown from 1904 to 1947 at the Tasmanian Museum in Hobart).⁵⁵

54 ›The Argus‹, 27.6.1879 (›Aborigines at the Exhibition‹).
55 Cf. ›The Mercury‹ (Hobart), 2.8.1888 (›The Tasmanian Court‹); see Cressida Fforde: Collecting the Dead, p. 98 and Antje Kühnast: ›In the interest of science and the colony‹.

An Aborigine from North Queensland called Billy was spared this fate. But when in 1889 a larger-than-life image of ›Billy the Australian‹ (see fig. 10, right), together with the one of ›Esther the Hottentot‹ (see fig. 10, left), decorated the entrance of the anthropological section of the Universal Exposition in Paris, he presumably was no longer alive. He had toured large parts of the world with a group of Australians and had been presented as ›cannibal‹ and ›boomerang thrower‹. In the USA, where they had an engagement at Barnum's ›Greatest Show on Earth‹, one member of the group died. His corpse, sold by the impresario to an operator of a dime museum, was mummified and put on display. In Europe the Aborigines performed in the Crystal Palace, too. During their tour through Germany, France, Ireland, Scotland, Scandinavia, Russia, Turkey, Italy and Austria another four of them died. Lastly, their traces were lost in England, whereas the impressario returned to Australia and recruited a new troop.[56]

During their stay in Paris, the Australians had been photographed by Prince Roland Bonaparte and scientifically examined by Paul Topinard, the deputy director of the Laboratoire d'anthropologie de l'École pratique des hautes études who had published studies like ›Études sur les Tasmaniens‹ and ›Études sur les races indigènes de l'Australie‹.[57] In 1888, three years after the inspection of the aboriginal Australians, Topinard had the opportunity of examining a group of South Africans guesting as ›Hottentots‹ in the Jardin d'acclimatation. Their ›chief‹ Jacob had a wife called Esther. She pertained to Topinard's objects of study and was referred to as »venus of the Kalahari desert« by him.[58]

This label could be easily deciphered as reference to Sarah Baartman. She had acted as ›Hottentot Venus‹ in England and France and after her death in Paris had been dissected by George Cuvier in a brutal procedure of racist-sexist science. He had thereby provided the basis for the anthropological typing of the ›Hottentot Venus‹. In 1876, when Topinard published his ›Anthropology‹, he could qualify Sarah Baartman as »an excellent sample of this race« and use this characterisation to denote the »bushman type« as the most »inferior of the human family«.[59] Specified according to this pattern, Esther quickly turned into the eponym of the

---

56 Cf. Roslyn Poignant: Professional Savages, pp. 106 f., 145, 154, 160, 164.
57 Cf. Stephanie Anderson: ›Three Living Australians‹ and the Société d'Anthropologie de Paris.
58 Paul Topinard: La stéatopyge des Hottentotes du Jardin d'acclimatation, pp. 194 f.; already previously a profile image of the topless Esther by Prince Bonaparte was published in Joseph Deniker: Les Hottentots aux Jardin d'acclimatation, p. 3.
59 Paul Topinard: L'Anthropologie, pp. 522 f.; concerning Sarah Baartman see at length Sabine Ritter: Facetten der Sarah Baartman, regarding the context addressed here esp. pp. 118 f., and Clifton Crais, Pamela Scully: Sara Baartman and the Hottentot Venus, pp. 131 ff.

female entrance figure at the anthropological section of the 1889 World's fair in Paris and, together with Billy, made the visitors feel they were taking a look at their own success story through the lens of two primitive representatives of mankind.

Anthropology did not only have a section in the palais des arts libéraux but was literally celebrated as »une science essentiellement française«. It moulded the character of the whole exhibition. Along with images of and information on the different human races, it provided the public with a show about the development of mankind since the Stone Age and with ethnographic exhibits from Africa, America, and Asia which should demonstrate that these continents had not come very far since the beginnings of humanity. A representative synopsis of the World Fair on two opposite pages thus depicted obviously ›white‹ ›métallurgistes‹ from the Bronze Age and ›forgerons nègres‹ of the present. The readers could thereby assure themselves, once again, that the ancient Europeans were technologically further developed than the Africans of today.[60] As in this vein a hierarchy of time had been constructed, the colonial and native villages represented a hierarchy of space. The visitors of the exhibition could roam the distance between the prestigious constructions of the European-North American show, the exotic buildings of the Asian colonies, and the simple dwellings of ›natives‹ labelled as ›savages‹.[61]

All this was overshadowed by the ›Tour Eiffel‹ which simultaneously was considered as a symbol of human ingenuity, epitomizing the harmony of the art of engineering, the daring of entrepreneurship and the diligence of labour. In this respect it was much more enthusiastically frequented by the masses than by the elites so that Guy de Maupassant disdainfully professed that the tower was a »triomphe complet de la démocratie«.[62] And in fact the organisers of the exhibition deemed it urgently proper to give their attention to the social question. As a result, the Exposition universelle did not only have native villages and colonial pavilions but also a »cité sociale«.[63] The latter stood entirely in the tradition of the conservative social reform of a Frédéric Le Play who, by the revolutions of 1830 and 1848, felt compelled to pursue extensive studies on the condition of the working classes in France and Europe and who was commissioner general of the Paris World Fairs of 1855 and 1867. In 1889, the commission responsible

---

60 La société, l'école et le laboratoire d'anthropologie de Paris a l'exposition universelle de 1889, p. 1 (›science française‹); Émile Monod: L'exposition Universelle de 1889, pp. 296 (›métallurgistes‹), 297 (›forgerons‹).
61 Cf. Lynn E. Palermo: Identity under Construction, pp. 294 f.
62 Quoted in Hubertus Kohle: Der Eiffelturm als Revolutionsdenkmal, p. 126.
63 Laure Godineau: L'économie sociale à l'Exposition universelle de 1889, p. 78; cf. Marieke Bloembergen: Colonial Spectacles, p. 115.

for the social question was composed of his followers. They advocated a social peace organised by social economy as a palliative against state intervention and socialism.

The exhibition of anthropological images, living indigenous people and means for a social peace had its nexus in the increasing delegitimation of imperial governance outward as well as inward. The World Fair of 1889 was pointedly conceived as centenary of the French Revolution which already had relentlessly unveiled the dialectics of Enlightenment and reacted to the association of the workers with a ban on organising, to the confident behaviour of women with the interdiction of their revolutionary clubs, and to the self-liberation of slaves with war and the reintroduction of slavery. But in France as elsewhere the emancipation movements could not be permanently suppressed. In 1865, after a remorselessly conducted civil war, the Thirteenth Amendment to the United States Constitution abolished slavery. In 1871, the Paris Commune proclaimed women's suffrage (which, after its defeat, admittedly was abolished again and, in France, was not re-established before the end of the Second World War). In 1890 the Social-Democratic Party emerged from the repression under the Anti-Socialist Laws as the party with the most voters in Germany.

Modern advertising developed in this climate and was shaped by it from the beginning. This found expression in a pentagon of phantasmagorias, held together by the gravity of commodity fetishism. The reification of social relations as commodities generated the phantasmagorias of advertising as a penetrating polyphony of promises of use values. The colonial ambience of this development was clad in the legend of peripheral servility to metropolitan superiority that evaporated the phantasmagorias of exoticism. Thus, capitalism appeared as the destination of a worldwide development and could be displayed as a civilising mission, so much so that the private pursuit of profit was hidden by the phantasmagorias of progress. The violence of this process was converted into a natural development by means of the phantasmagorias of race. Eventually, this mélange facilitated the development of an imagined racial community manifesting itself in the phantasmagorias of whiteness.

In 1872 John Gast assembled these phantasmagorias in his painting ›American Progress‹ (see fig. 11). It was a commissioned work designed to be an advertising message itself: George Crofutt, who commissioned it and specified the scene, used a chromolithography of the motif as a free gift to subscribers of his monthly ›Western World‹, and as a steel engraving for the frontispiece of his tourist guide through the West which was widely spread in numerous editions. The scenery combines the expan-

Advertising White Supremacy 49

Fig. 11: ... the march of civilisation ...

sion of civilisation from the seaport towns of the Atlantic to the coasts of the Pacific with an apotheosis of technology, depicts the Brooklyn Bridge already years before the completion, and installs telegraph and railway into the vastnesses of the West (where they had actually surmounted the Rockies already between 1861 and 1867).⁶⁴ The (male) pioneers of civilisation, across all social boundaries, are doubly accounted as ›white‹ – by the female allegory of progress under whose protection they move forward and by the humans backing away from them together with the animals, whereby, as well as by their partial nakedness, they are labelled as ›savages‹. Augmented by images of industrial technology, this scenario illustrates nothing less than the Enlightenment's racist philosophy of history, which the aged Thomas Jefferson expressed when, using the example of the United States, he described the »march of civilization advancing from the sea coast« and »passing over us like a cloud of light«.⁶⁵

64 Cf. Crofutt's Trans-Continental Tourist, frontispiece; see Pamela Walker Laird: Advertising Progress, p. 129 (lithograph‹, ›engraving›); J. Valerie Fifer: American progress, p. 202 (Brooklyn Bridge); Richard R. John: Network Nation, p. 110 (Rockies).
65 Cf. Mark Rawlinson: American Visual Culture, p. 34 (gender, class, race); Thomas Jefferson: Letter to William Ludlow, pp. 1496 f. (›march of civilization‹; the reasoning goes as follows: »Let a philosophic observer commence a journey from the savages of the Rocky Mountains, eastwardly towards our sea-coast. These he would observe in the earliest stage of association living under no law but that of nature, subscribing and

Fig. 12: ... commodity aestheticisation ...

Not by chance, Gast has set the first group of his pioneers in the same perspective with which Cruikshank had recorded ›Crystal Palace‹ twenty years earlier. The man in front carries a rifle, the last of the group smokes a pipe. Colonial violence and consumption affiliated to it are familiarly combined. The pipe could well have been stuffed with ›Westward Ho‹ tobacco which shared the same name by which Gast's painting occasionally was termed. An old advertising label shows three frontiersmen leading an endless procession of settlers (see fig. 12, left). Displaced by them, the native Americans finally become subject to the »commodity aestheticisation of the North American natives« (see fig. 12, right) and are subsumed to the type of the ›Tobacco Indian‹ to be seen on numerous tobacco advertisements and standing until today in front of the ›Westward Ho‹ shop

covering themselves with the flesh and skins of wild beasts. He would next find those on our frontiers in the pastoral state, raising domestic animals to supply the defects of hunting. Then succeed our own semi-barbarous citizens, the pioneers of the advance of civilization, and so in his progress he would meet the gradual shades of improving man until he would reach his, as yet, most improved state in our seaport towns. This, in fact, is equivalent to a survey, in time, of the progress of man from the infancy of creation to the present day«); cf. Wulf D. Hund: Der inszenierte Indianer, pp. 48 ff.

in Disney's ›Frontierland‹.⁶⁶ The racist proclivity of the tobacco industry obviously exceeded the infamous dictum of General Philip Sheridan. For them, the best Indian was a dead Indian advertising.

Tobacco, of course, was likewise counted among the commodities displayed in the Crystal Palace by the United States. By pointing out that »[i]t

Fig. 13: ... blaming the victim ...

is exported to England in [... an] enormous annual sum«, it was classed as a »valuable article of commerce«. At the same time the exhibition left no doubt regarding the destiny of the North Americans who once welcomed the Europeans with a pipe filled with tobacco. The entry to the USA section was flanked by two sculptures, one of them being Peter Stephenson's ›The Wounded American Indian‹ (see fig. 13). It embodied a noble savage whose »collapsing form was commonly taken as symbolizing the Indian in terminal decline«.⁶⁷ His death, caused by an arrow and thus by one

66 Cf. Angela Miller: American Expansionism and Universal Allegory, p. 464 (Gast's ›Westward Ho‹); David Holloway, John Beck: Introduction to Part 1, p. 13 (tobacco ad from 1868); Hans-Peter Rodenberg: Der imaginierte Indianer, p. 76 (›commodity aestheticisation‹); the ›Tobacco Indian‹ stands in the Disneyland Resort of Anaheim, Los Angeles (http://www.flickr.com/photos/peterpanfan1953/7769631552/); concerning the ongoing use of constructed Indianness in advertising see the Chapter »Commodified Racism: Brand Images of Native Americans« in Debra L. Merskin: Media, Minorities, and Meaning, pp. 174-190.
67 Official Descriptive and Illustrated Catalogue of the Great Exhibition of the Works of Industry of all Nations, p. 1453 (›article of commerce‹); Kate Flint: Exhibiting America, p. 171 (›terminal decline‹) – for a picture of the sculpture see http://www.chrysler. org/images/collections/stephenson-wounded-indian.jpg. The battle at the Little Bighorn River and the Massacre of Wounded Knee at that time were yet to come. But even

of his kind, unequivocally refers to the ideology of dying races: they do not perish of the consequences of colonialism and imperialism, but due to their own savageness.

Commodity Racism and Racist Symbolic Capital

After the Great Exhibition in London had closed its doors, the Crystal Palace was transferred from Hyde Park to Sydenham. The reopening was frenetically celebrated as »raising a palace for the people«, being »the possession of the British people« and »the production of their own unaided and independent enterprise«. In 1854, when the thus lauded public was let in again, it could additionally judge its ingenious ability with the assistance of the popularised statements of the race sciences. The new palace was equipped with an ›ethnological collection‹, informing visitors about the history and variety of the »›two-handed‹ mammals who constructed the Crystal Palace«. Following Johann Friedrich Blumenbach, they were classified into five races, whose enumeration began not by chance with the »Caucasian, or white race« and subsequently listed the »Mongolian, or yellow race«, the »Æthiopian, or black race of Africa«, the »American, or red race« and the »Malay, or brown race, inhabiting the Asiatic Islands, Australia, and New Zealand«. That this was meant to be a hierarchic numeration came to light at the latest in the description of the Australians: »The pure Austral negro holds about the lowest position in civilization, that of the naked, houseless, cannibal«.[68]

The entire exhibition was actually designed in a mode that »could be read as a model of Progressive order«, »displaying the progress that had led to modern civilisation«.[69] This conception found its caricatured expression in the sketch ›Crystal Palace – Some Varieties of the Human Race‹.[70] Two fair-skinned young ladies sit at a coffee table in front of a panorama with tropical plants and swarthy naked men. One of these ›savages‹ with a nasal piercing is in the process of throwing a spear and in the background two men with outsized underlips combat each other (see fig. 14).

they would be marketed. The Anheuser Busch Brewing Association used a lithograph of ›Custer's Last Fight‹ to promote Budweiser beer – Cf. Lucy A. Ganje: Marketing the Sacred, pp. 94 f.
68   Routledge's Guide to the Crystal Palace and Park at Sydenham, pp. 16 (›palace for‹ and ›possession of‹ the ›people‹), 171 (›mammals‹), 172 (›races‹), 174 (›Australian‹).
69   James A. Secord: Monsters at the Crystal Palace, p. 140.
70   See Punch, 28, 1855, p. XIII – the impression of a gendered racial difference was furthermore enhanced by a second caricature on the same page showing a father explaining to his scared son the figures of primeval dinosaurs displayed in Sydenham.

Advertising White Supremacy 53

Fig. 14: ... savouring whiteness ...

The scene was as realistic as constructed. The savages were the life-size plaster casts of the natural history department of the exhibition, including »a party of Botocudos, two of whom are engaged in a fierce fight with sticks«, who not only are »excessively savage« but also »give themselves a still wilder appearance by the introduction of blocks of hard wood in the under-lip«. Tables were placed straight aside in the refreshment court and also »among the surrounding inhabitants of Africa and America«.[71] For the visitors, the exhibition of the savages should have been already sufficient to forget all Rousseauist illusions. A stroll from there to the cultural achievements of modernity would do the rest to elucidate the gulf between the races.[72] Looked at that way, even those who, for mere cost reasons,

71 Cf. Samuel Phillips: Guide to the Crystal Palace and Park, p. 107 (›Botocudos‹); Jan R. Piggott: Palace of the People, p. 59 (›tables‹); for the following reference to the third-class refreshment room see ibid., p. 60.
72 The Crystal Palace, pp. 35 (»[t]he lip of the Botocudo [...] will dispel many illusions as to the simplicity and happiness of nature's children«), 39 (»[f]rom the Ethnological Groups, exhibiting man in his lowest conditions, to the Industrial Courts, exhibiting the domestic arts in the highest state of culture, the transition is great«).

Fig. 15: ... an achievement of civilisation ...

could not take a seat alongside the ladies but, at best, could sit down in the third-class refreshment room, were able to identify with the young women. The stereotyping and stigmatisation of the ›savages‹ created a distance which made the differences of the spectators dwindle to a negligible factor. Sauntering past the panoramas of ›dark-skinned primitives‹, the flaneurs could veneer the social gap between them and collectively imagine themselves as ›civilised whites‹ – because, to extrapolate from a phrasing by Michael Pickering, »it is easier to imagine a shared belonging to a (unified) [race] than to a (divided) society«[73] (see fig. 15).

Commodity racism transfers this configuration to the field of advertising and everyday consumption. To participate in the racist prestige offered thereby, it was not even necessary to buy the praised commodities. Racist advertising is characterised by a doubling of use value and promise of use value and additionally provides an extra ideological use value. It signals a social surplus related to the consumption of the commodity and in the

---

73 Michael Pickering: Stereotyping, p. 90 (instead of ›[race]‹ the author refers to ›nation‹ here; for a contemporaneous example of the overlapping and fluidity of the categories ›race‹ and ›nation‹ see the discussion of Benjamin Disraeli in Simone Beate Borgstede: ›All is Race‹). For models of a group of Zulus at the Crystal Palace (fig. 15) see Sadiah Qureshi: Peoples on Parade, p. 196: »The *white* plaster casts were painted in tones simulating *[black]* skin« (my emphasis and addition) – the ›construction‹ of ›race‹ had been taken literally (for the image see ibid., p. 197).

inclusion in an imagined racist community. This equally applies to those who cannot afford the purchase of commodities advertised in such a way.[74]

Trade cards represented a special form of this added value. They were considered as effective advertising material and already in 1885 a US journal alleged that »[t]he ultimate destination of all cards is to swell some collection or to adorn some home, and they may be found in even the remotest parts of the land«. The cards often were available only by an act of purchase but not uncommonly were handed over for free as a bait or frequently cadged by youngsters. The London socialist Walter Southgate, as with many of his friends during their childhood around 1900, collected cigarette cards and remembered in his ›working class autobiography‹ that »[w]e pestered the life out of passers-by for them«. Trading cards indeed aimed »to create a desire for the advertised commodity«. But after the act of purchase they parted with the close connection to the commodity and became »part of a public discourse« and »of the informal mass instruction of the new language of modernism«. In a range of versions and series they propagated colonial and racist images and in this way established, as Joachim Zeller has called it, a true »picture school of the master race«.[75]

With their trade cards, capitals from different economic branches branded time and space and inscribed their marks into colonial landscapes, subjected lifestyles, and historical eras. The advertising writing on the wall could not only be read on a rock in the Sudan or at the foot of the Kilimanjaro but also overwrote non-European cultures and traditions bathed in the fallacious light of white supremacy. Thus the Liebig Company, a multinational enterprise with »German leadership«, »British capital« and »Uruguayan production site providing the land, cattle and labour« for the fabrication of Liebig's extract of meat, manufactured for an international market and its trading cards reached up to three million copies per card. Significant motifs of the cards were colonial and racial topics. The compa-

74 On that ground alone, Baudrillard's ›sign value‹ is not helpful here – to acquire a certain sign and to accumulate prestige, the commodity to which the sign is bound must be bought. (cf. Jean Baudrillard: For a Critique of the Political Economy of the Sign, pp. 112 ff.). Besides, Baudrillard's definition of racism is impractical. He considers the »hallucination of difference known as racism« and the »temptation to fetishize difference« affiliated to it as a component of the universal ›melodrama of difference‹ and essentially links racism to the otherness of the others: »Racism does not exist so long as the other remains Other, so long as the stranger remains foreign. It comes into existence when the other becomes merely different – that is to say, dangerous similar. This is the moment when the inclination to keep the other at a distance comes into being« (Jean Baudrillard: The Melodrama of Difference, p. 129).
75 Joachim Zeller: Bilderschule der Herrenmenschen – for the preceding citations see Robert Jay: The Trade Card in Nineteenth Century America, p. 3 (quoting a U.S. journal); Ginger S. Frost: Victorian Childhoods, p. 76 (quoting Southgate); Kyla Wazana Tomkins: Racial Indigestion, p. 155 (›desire‹, ›discourse‹); Lenore Metrick-Chen: Collecting Objects / Excluding People, p. 170 (›mass instruction‹).

ny associated its extract tin with the entire history of colonialism including legitimising contracts (see fig. 16a), ›civilising‹ labour (see fig. 16b), ridiculing minstrelisation (see fig. 16c) or reactions to resistance (see. fig. 16d) – in this manner disclosing the concomitant effects of consumerism for the affected others: defraudation, exploitation, degradation, and violence.[76]

In view of such advertising it is hardly surprising that the mere product itself was soaked with colonial violence. As often, the product was just as contaminated as the advertisements. Its whitewashed story ran: »Liebig always kept an eye open for commercial opportunities. So hearing that in [...] Uruguay there was a superfluity of cattle, which were slaughtered for their hides, while most of the meat was thrown away, he devised a process for rendering the beef into a concentrated broth«. Actually, European meat was a scarce and expensive commodity and Justus Liebig was even criticised for wasting it for the production of his meat extract. Hence, he bargained with Australian ›cattle barons‹ (who had expropriated land of the Aborigines and destroyed their natural resources) before he engaged in a company which affordably produced in Uruguay.[77]

This was only possible because the indigenous Charrúas had been struck by a genocidal massacre. At first, »the ecosystem of the pampa had been traumatized by the whites and their animals«. Afterwards the Amerindians seized escaped European horses, became brilliant equestrians and lived on cattle. Therefore the cattle barons finally drew up »an extermination plan that would erase the Charrúa from the face of the earth«.[78] While most of the survivors were sold as slaves, the leader Vaimaca Perú and a small group were brought to France and exhibited as the ›last of the Charrúas‹. Vaimaca Perú starved himself to death in protest. Subsequently, his corpse was scientifically examined, preserved, committed to the Musée de l'Homme (and not repatriated until 2002).[79]

The depopulated pampas yielded the ›natural‹ resource of which Liebig suggested that for one pound of his meat extract 30 pounds of meat have

76 David Ciarlo: Advertising Empire, pp. 183 (›leadership‹ etc.), 185 (›copies per card‹); for the trade cards see Joachim Zeller: Bilderschule der Herrenmenschen, pp. 36 (a colonial contract in Pennsylvania), 114 (preparing the soil for cotton), 97 (battleships in Kiautschou), 202 (minstrel clowns).
77 Walter Gratzer: Eureka and Euphorias, p. 227 (Liebig's ›open eyes‹); Mark R. Finlay: Early Marketing of the Theory of Nutrition, p. 57 (criticism); William H. Brock: Justus von Liebig, pp. 223 ff. (Australia, Uruguay); in the beginning of the 20th century the company also produced in German South-West Africa (see Adolf Heilborn: Die deutschen Kolonien, p. 76) and thereby benefited from the suppression of the Herero, Nama, and other peoples.
78 Alfred W. Crosby: Ecological Imperialism, pp. 160 f. (›ecosystem‹); Gustavo Verdesio: The Original Sin Behind the Creation of a New Europe, pp. 151 f. (›extermination plan‹).
79 Cf. Jean-Paul Duviols: Le miroir du Nouveau Monde, pp. 320 ff.; Annie Houot: Un cacique Charrúa en Paris; Wulf D. Hund: Die Körper der Bilder der Rassen, pp. 49 f.

to be used and that he was proud of having introduced such a fabrication to an area where »meat has no trading price«.[80] Advertising properly contributed to the success of such a product. In the course of this it closed the

Fig. 16 a – d: ... a picture school of the master race ...

circle of colonial violence in a mendacious advertisement. To that end it drew on a story of Henry Morton Stanley who organised his expedition for the relief of Emin Pascha as a ›commodity procession‹ through ›darkest Africa‹. That perfectly corresponded with the international attention – Emin, a German physician and adventurer, whose name actually was Eduard Schnitzler, had, after all, been appointed by no one less than Gordon Pascha as governor of Equatoria and now was threatened, as was Gordon before, by the Mahdists. Even prior to starting his expedition, Stanley lauded his supply of Liebig extract. On the move, sick carriers frequently had to be pepped up with Liebig soups and some of them sometimes misappropriated a »tin of Liebig«. Finally, the day approached, when an enfeebled carrier was saved with »a pint of hot broth made from the Liebig Company's extract of meat«.[81] The company did not miss this scene and

80 Justus von Liebig: [Brief an Theodor Reuning, 7.5.1865], pp. 168 f.
81 Henry Morton Stanley: In Darkest Africa, pp. 1/39 (extract), 1/89 (soup), 1/200 (›tin‹), 2/58 (›broth‹); the phrase ›commodity procession‹ originates from Thomas Richards: The Commodity Culture of Victorian England, p. 138; the advertisement was printed in ›Lady's Pictorial‹, 1891 – cf. Lori Anne Loeb: Consuming Angels, p. 80-83.

Fig. 17: ... saints of imperialism ...

developed it as a tableau of a colonial pietà, who surrounded by apostles of imperialism, claimed to revive a suffering African by the muddy broth composed of European ingenuity and transatlantic capitalism (see fig. 17).

In practice, the famous meat extract was not for everybody. A popular German cookbook writer who contributed to Liebig's success with a recipe booklet, requested to him »that the extract's price be lowered ›in the interest of the working classes, as well as in the interest of society as a whole‹‹‹.[82] But even though the lower classes had to be content with the promise of use value because they could not afford the product, they could partake of the ideological use value of the racist promotion. The advertisements and trading cards were available for them, too, and submitted to the offer to classify themselves, if not as consumers of meat extract, so at least as members of their race.

Those who were not equipped with economic capital and whose cultural capital was limited by their social status, thus could leastwise accumulate racist symbolic capital (as Anja Weiß has put it in extension of Pierre Bourdieu).[83] In this way they could, by (racistly) discriminating others, feel a sense of belonging to those by whom they were (socially) discriminated themselves. Racist symbolic capital on the one side constitutes a precluded liability company with deposits at the expense of outsiders. On the other side it most notably is a resource of those who have no economic capital and no or only meagre cultural capital because it allows an imagined community ideologically bridging the economic, cultural, and social barriers between different classes.

Advertising substantially contributed to this racist community building. Its socio-economic base of operations was the phantasm of egality originating in the circulation sphere. It fostered the illusion that the promises of use value emitted by the advertising agencies were indistinctively addressed to a shopping public, whose access to the promoted commodity depended only on the willingness to pay the retail price. Hence advertisements even appealed to all potential buyers. In addition commodity racism not only exuded promises of use value charged with diverse exoticisms, but also supplied the spectators of its messages with the chance to ascribe themselves to the ›white race‹, which thereby was not only reproduced by the conformations of science, the expositions of museums, the displays of world fairs, and the spectacles of human zoos, but also by compliance or purchase reconstructed in everyday action and behaviour. Commodity racism transformed consumption into one of the factories of the social construction of race, and intertwined the commendation of capitalism and the laudation of colonialism within a permanent advertisement that promoted the blessings of white supremacy.[84]

---

82 Henriette Davidis, quoted in Mark R. Finlay: Early Marketing of the Theory of Nutrition, p. 62.
83 Cf. Anja Weiß: Racist Symbolic Capital; cf. also Wulf D. Hund: Negative Societalisation. For a drastic example of commodity racism reflective to politics and economy to such an extent that it influenced the process of nation building and fiscal and customs policy see Stefanie Affeldt: Consuming Whiteness; id.: A Paroxysm of Whiteness.
84 I wish to thank Tina Antenucci, Bärbel Kirchhoff-Hund and Michael Pickering for their precise reading of the text and Stefanie Affeldt for her splendid finishing of the images.

References

Affeldt, Stefanie: A Paroxysm of Whiteness. ›White‹ Labour, ›White‹ Nation and ›White‹ Sugar in Australia. In: Wages of Whiteness & Racist Symbolic Capital, ed. by Wulf D. Hund, Jeremy Krikler, David Roediger (Racism Analysis | Yearbook 1). Berlin [et al.]: Lit 2010, pp. 99-131.

—: Consuming Whiteness. Australian Racism and the ›White Sugar‹ Campaign. (Racism Analysis | Studies 4). Berlin [et al.]: Lit 2014 [in preparation].

Agathocleous, Tanya: Urban Realism and the Cosmopolitan Imagination in the Nineteenth Century. Visible City, Invisible World. Cambridge [et al.]: Cambridge University Press 2011.

Anderson, Stephanie: ›Three Living Australians‹ and the Société d'Anthropologie de Paris, 1885. In: Foreign Bodies. Oceania and the Science of Race 1750-1940, ed. by Bronwen Douglas, Chris Ballard. Canberra: ANU E Press 2008, pp. 229-255.

Auerbach, Jeffrey A., Peter H. Hoffenberg (eds.): Britain, the Empire, and the World at the Great Exhibition of 1851. Aldershot [et al.]: Ashgate 2008.

Baudrillard, Jean: For a Critique of the Political Economy of the Sign. St. Louis: Telos Press 1981.

—: The Melodrama of Difference. In: id., The Transparency of Evil. Essays on Extreme Phenomena. London [et al.]: Verso 1993, pp. 124-138.

Berenson, Edward: Heroes of Empire. Five Charismatic Men and the Conquest of Africa. Berkeley [et al.]: University of California Press 2011.

Berger, Arthur Asa: Media Analysis Techniques. 4th ed. Thousand Oaks [et al.]: Sage 2012.

Berliner, Brett A.: Ambivalent Desire. The Exotic Black Other in Jazz Age France. Amherst: University of Massachusetts Press 2002.

Beyer, Chris H.: Coca-Cola Girls. An Advertising Art History. Portland: Collectors Press 2000.

Blanchard, Pascal, Nicolas Bancel, Sandrine Lemaire: Les zoos humaines: le passage d'un ›racisme scientifique‹ vers un ›racisme populaire et colonial‹ en Occident In: Zoos humains. Au temps des exhibitions humaines, with a new preface ed. by Nicolas Bancel, Pascal Blanchard, Gilles Boëtsch, Éric Deroo, Sandrine Lemaire. Paris: La Découverte 2004, pp. 63-71.

Bloembergen, Marieke: Colonial Spectacles. The Netherlands and the Dutch East Indies at the World Exhibitions, 1880 - 1931. Singapore: Singapore University Press 2006.

Bloom, Peter J.: French Colonial Documentary. Mythologies of Humanitarianism. Minneapolis: University of Minnesota Press 2008.

Boddy, Janice: Purity and Conquest in the Anglo-Egyptian Sudan. In: Dirt, Undress, and Difference. Critical Perspectives on the Body's Surface, ed. by Adeline Masquelier. Bloomington: Indiana University Press 2005, pp. 168-189.

Boëtsch, Gilles, Yann Ardagna: Zoos humains: le ›sauvage‹ et l'anthropologie. In: Zoos humains. Au temps des exhibitions humaines, with a new preface ed. by Nicolas Bancel, Pascal Blanchard, Gilles Boëtsch, Éric Deroo, Sandrine Lemaire. Paris: La Découverte 2004, pp. 55-62.

Bonnett, Alastair: Anti-Racism. Key Ideas. London [et al.]: Routledge 2000.

Borgstede, Simone Beate: ›All is Race‹. Benjamin Disraeli on Race, Nation and Empire. (Racism Analysis | Studies 2). Berlin [et al.]: Lit 2011.
Breverton, Terry: Admiral Sir Henry Morgan. King of the Buccaneers. Gretna: Pelican 2005.
Brock, William H.: Justus von Liebig. The Chemical Gatekeeper. Cambridge [et al.]: Cambridge University Press 1997.
Chafe, William H.: Civilities and Civil Rights. Greensboro, North Carolina, and the Black Struggle for Freedom. Oxford [et al.]: Oxford University Press 1980.
Chun, Elaine W.: Ideologies of Legitimate Mockery. Margaret Cho's Revoicings of Mock Asian. In: Pragmatics, 14, 2004, 2/3, pp. 263-289.
Ciarlo, David: Advertising Empire. Race and Visual Culture in Imperial Germany. Cambridge, Mass. [et al.]: Harvard University Press 2011.
Crais, Clifton, Pamela Scully: Sara Baartman and the Hottentot Venus. A Ghost Story and a Biography. Princeton [et al.]: Princeton University Press 2009.
Cranton, Michael: Empire, Enslavement and Freedom in the Caribbean. Oxford: James Currey 1997.
Crofutt's Trans-Continental Tourist, [...] From the Atlantic to the Pacific Coast. New York: Carleton 1875.
Cronau, Rudolf: Buch der Reklame. Geschichte, Wesen und Praxis der Reklame. 5 vol. Ulm: Wohler 1887.
Cronin, Anne M.: Advertising Myths. The Strange Half-Lives of Images and Commodities. London [et al.]: Routledge 2004.
Crosby, Alfred W.: Ecological Imperialism. The Biological Expansion of Europe, 900-1900. Cambridge [et al.]: Cambridge University Press 1986.
Daly, Martin W.: Empire on the Nile. The Anglo-Egyptian Sudan, 1898-1934. Cambridge [et al.]: Cambridge University Press 1986.
Daniel: Das Buch Daniel. In: Neue Jerusalemer Bibel. Einheitsübersetzung. 8th ed. Freiburg [et al.]: Herder 1985, pp. 1259-1285.
Defoe, Daniel: Robinson Crusoe. An Authoritative Text, Contexts, Criticism, ed. by Michael Shinagel. 2nd ed. New York [et al.]: Norton 1994.
Deniker, Joseph: Les Hottentots au Jardin d'Acclimatation. In: Revue d'Anthropologie, 4, 1889, 1, pp. 1-27.
Deutsches Kolonial-Lexikon, ed. by Heinrich Schnee. 3 vol. Leipzig: Quelle & Meyer 1920.
Donadey, Anne: ›Y'a bon Banania‹. Ethics and Cultural Criticism in the Colonial Context. In: French Cultural Studies, 11, 2000, 31, pp. 9-29.
Duffy, Enda: Molly's Throat. In: Joyce: Feminism / Post / Colonialism. European Joyce Studies 8, ed. by Ellen Carol Jones. Amsterdam [et al.]: Rodopi 1998, pp. 231-244.
Dunn, Robert G.: Identifying Consumption. Subjects and Objects in Consumer Society. Philadelphia: Temple University Press 2008.
Duviols, Jean-Paul: Le miroir du Nouveau Monde. Images primitives de l'Amérique. Paris: Presses de l'Université Paris-Sorbonne 2006.
Emberley, Julia V.: Defamiliarizing the Aboriginal. Cultural Practices and Decolonization in Canada. Toronto [et al.]: University of Toronto Press 2007.
Fanon, Frantz: Black Skin, White Masks. New ed., transl. by Richard Philcox, Foreword by Kwame Anthony Appiah. New York: Grove Press 2008.
Faught, C. Brad: Gordon. Victorian Hero. Washington: Potomac 2008.

Fay, Peter Ward: The Opium War, 1840-1842. Barbarians in the Celestial Empire in the Early Part of the Nineteenth Century and the War by which they Forced Her Gates Ajar. Chapel Hill: The University of North Carolina Press 1975.

Flint, Kate: Exhibiting America. The Native American and the Crystal Palace. In: Victorian Prism. Refractions of the Crystal Palace, ed. by James Buzard, Joseph W. Childers, Eileen Gillooly. Charlottesville [et al.]: University of Virginia Press 2007, pp. 171-185.

Fforde, Cressida: Collecting the Dead. Archaeology and the Reburial Issue. London: Duckworth 2004.

—, Jane Huber, Paul Turnbull: The Dead and their Possessions. Repatriation in Principle, Policy and Practice. New York [et al.]: Routledge 2002.

Fifer, J. Valerie: American Progress. The Growth of the Transport, Tourist, and Information Industries in the Nineteenth-Century West, Seen Through the Life and Times of George A. Crofutt, Pioneer and Publicist of the Transcontinental Age. Chester: Globe Pequot Press 1988.

Finlay, Mark R.: Early Marketing of the Theory of Nutrition. The Science and Culture of Liebig's Extract of Meat. In: The Science and Culture of Nutrition, 1840 - 1940, ed. by Harmke Kamminga, Andrew Cummingham. Amsterdam: Rodopi 1995, pp. 48-74.

Frost, Ginger S.: Victorian Childhoods. Westport: Praeger 2009.

Ganje, Lucy A.: Marketing the Sacred. Commodifying Native-American Cultural Images. In: Images that Injure. Pictorial Stereotypes in the Media, ed. by Susan Dente Ross, Paul Martin Lester. 3rd ed. Santa Barbara: Praeger 2011, pp. 91-106.

Gerschwitz, Matthias: Bullrich-Salz. Marke, Mythos, Magensäure. Auf den Spuren eines der ältesten deutschen Markenartikel. Norderstedt: Books on Demand 2007.

Gleason's Pictorial, 1, 1851, 12.

Godineau, Laure: L'économie sociale à l'Exposition universelle de 1889. In: Le Mouvement social, 149, 1989, pp. 71-87.

Goffman, Erving: The presentation of self in everyday life. Garden City: Doubleday 1959.

Gratzer, Walter: Eureka and Euphorias. The Oxford Book of Scientific Anecdotes. Oxford [et al.]: Oxford University Press 2002.

Gregory, Dick: [Interview from 1961]. In: Paul Krassner's Impolite Interviews. New York: Seven Stories Press 1999, pp. 75-86.

Gurney, Peter: An Appropriated Space. The Great Exhibition, the Crystal Palace and the Working Class. In: The Great Exhibition of 1851. New Interdisciplinary Essays, ed. by Louise Purbrick. Manchester [et al.]: Manchester University Press 2001, pp. 114-145.

Hale, Dana S.: Races on Display. French Representations of Colonized Peoples 1886 - 1940. Bloomington: Indiana University Press 2008.

Harrison, Simon: Dark Trophies. Hunting the Enemy Body in Modern War. New York: Berghahn 2012.

Hastings, Max (ed.): The Oxford Book of Military Anecdotes. Oxford [et al.]: Oxford University Press 1985.

Haug, Wolfgang Fritz: Critique of Commodity Aesthetics. Appearance, Sexuality, and Advertising in Capitalist Society. Minneapolis: University of Minnesota Press 1986.
—: Kritik der Warenästhetik. Rev. new ed., followed by: Warenästhetik im High-Tech-Kapitalismus. Frankfurt: Suhrkamp 2009.
Heilborn, Adolf: Die deutschen Kolonien (Land und Leute). Zehn Vorlesungen. 2. exp. Ed. Leipzig: Teubner 1908.
Hinrichsen, Malte: Racist Trademarks. Slavery, Orient, Colonialism & Commodity Culture. (Racism Analysis | Studies 3). Berlin [et al.]: Lit 2012.
Hobsbawm, Eric J.: The Age of Empire, 1875-1914. New York: Vintage 1989.
Holloway, David, John Beck: Introduction to Part 1. In: American Visual Cultures, ed. by id. New York [et al.]: Continuum 2005, pp. 13-20.
Honold, Alexander: Kaiser-Wilhelm-Spitze. 6. Oktober 1889: Hans Meyer erobert den Kilimandscharo. In: Mit Deutschland um die Welt. Eine Kulturgeschichte des Fremden in der Kolonialzeit, hg. v. id., Klaus R. Scherpe. Stuttgart [etc.]: Metzler 2004, pp. 136-144.
Houot, Annie: Un cacique Charrúa en Paris. Montevideo: Costa Atlántica 2002.
Hund, Wulf D.: Der inszenierte Indianer. In: id., Rassismus. Die soziale Konstruktion natürlicher Ungleichheit. Münster: Westfälisches Dampfboot 1999, pp. 39-53.
—: Die Körper der Bilder der Rassen. Wissenschaftliche Leichenschändung und rassistische Entfremdung. In: Entfremdete Körper. Rassismus als Leichenschändung, ed. by id. Bielefeld: transcript 2009, pp. 13-79.
—: Negative Societalisation. Racism and the Constitution of Race. In: Wages of Whiteness & Racist Symbolic Capital, ed. by id., Jeremy Krikler, David Roediger (Racism Analysis | Yearbook 1). Berlin [et al.]: Lit 2010, pp. 57-96.
—: Prädestination in der Wüste? Marginalie zu einer Fata Morgana von Walter Benjamin. In: Das Argument, 300 (54, 2012, 6), pp. 833-844.
Jay, Robert: The Trade Card in Nineteenth Century America. Columbia: University of Missouri Press 1987.
Jefferson, Thomas: Letter to William Ludlow, September 6, 1824. In: id., Writings. New York: The Library of America 1984, pp. 1496 f.
John, Richard R.: Network Nation. Inventing American Telecommunications. Cambridge: Belknap Press of Harvard University Press 2010.
Kipling, Rudyard: Fuzzy-Wuzzy. In: Stories and Poems from Kipling, ed. Mary E. Burt. New York: Burt [1909], pp. 222-224.
Kohle, Hubertus: Der Eiffelturm als Revolutionsdenkmal. In: Frankreich 1871-1914, ed. by Gudrun Gersmann, Hubertus Kohle. Stuttgart: Steiner 2002, pp. 119-132.
Kühnast, Antje: ›In the interest of science and the colony‹. Truganini und die Legende von den aussterbenden Rassen. In: Entfremdete Körper. Rassismus als Leichenschändung, ed. by Wulf D. Hund. Bielefeld: transcript 2009, pp. 205-250.
Laffer, Stephanie D.: Gordon's Ghost. British Major-General Charles George Gordon and His Legacies, 1885-1960. PhD dissertation. [Tallahassee]: Florida State University 2010.
Laird, Pamela Walker: Advertising Progress. American Business and the Rise of Consumer Marketing. Baltimore [et al.]: Johns Hopkins University Press 1998.

La société, l'école et le laboratoire d'anthropologie de Paris a l'exposition universelle de 1889. Instruction publique. Paris: Imprimeries réunis 1889.

Lebovics, Herman: Les zoos de l'Exposition coloniale internationale de Paris en 1931. In: Zoos humains. Au temps des exhibitions humaines, with a new preface ed. by Nicolas Bancel, Pascal Blanchard, Gilles Boëtsch, Éric Deroo, Sandrine Lemaire. Paris: La Découverte 2004, pp. 367-373.

Lee, Martyn J.: Consumer Culture Reborn. The Cultural Politics of Consumption. London [et al.]: Routledge 1993.

von Liebig, Justus: [Brief an Theodor Reuning, 7.5.1865]. In: Briefwechsel zwischen Justus v. Liebig und Theodor Reuning über landwirtschaftliche Fragen aus den Jahren 1854 bis 1873. Dresden: Schönfeld's Verlagsbuchhandlung 1884, pp. 168-170.

Links, Joseph G.: Venice. London: Lutterworth 1967.

Loeb, Lori Anne: Consuming Angels. Advertising and Victorian Women. Oxford [et al.]: Oxford University Press 1994.

MacDonald, Robert H.: The Language of Empire. Myths and Metaphors of Popular Imperialism, 1880-1918. Manchester [et al.]: Manchester University Press 1994.

Magnus, Philip: Kitchener. Portrait of an Imperialist. London: Murray 1958.

Marx, Karl: Das Kapital. Kritik der politischen Ökonomie. Vol. 1. In: id., Friedrich Engels: Werke (MEW), vol. 23, Berlin: Dietz 1988.

Mayhew, Henry, George Cruikshank: 1851: Or, The Adventures of Mr. and Mrs. Sandboys and Family, Who Came Up to London to ›Enjoy Themselves‹, and to See the Great Exhibition. London: David Bogue 1851.

McClintock, Anne: Imperial Leather. Race, Gender and Sexuality in the Colonial Contest. New York [et al.]: Routledge 1995.

Merskin, Debra L.: Media, Minorities, and Meaning. A Critical Introduction. New York: Peter Lang 2011.

Metrick-Chen, Lenore: Collecting Objects / Excluding People. Chinese Subjects and American Visual Culture, 1830-1900. Albany: State University of New York Press 2012.

Miklitsch, Robert: From Hegel to Madonna. Towards a General Theory of ›Commodity Fetishism‹. Albany: State University of New York Press 1998.

Miller, Angela: American Expansionism and Universal Allegory. William Allen Wall's Nativity of Truth. In: The New England Quarterly, 63, 1990, 3, pp. 446-467.

Miller, Randall M.: Daily Life through American History in Primary Documents. The Colonial Period to the American Revolution. Santa Barbara: ABC-CLIO 2012.

Monod, Émile: L'Exposition Universelle de 1889. Grand ouvrage illustré. Vol. 1. Paris: Dentu 1890.

Official Descriptive and Illustrated Catalogue of the Great Exhibition of the Works of Industry of all Nations. Part V. London: Spicer Brothers 1851.

Pack, A. James: Nelson's Blood. The Story of Naval Rum. Havant: Mason 1982.

Palermo, Lynn E.: Identity under Construction. Representing the Colonies at the Paris Exposition Universelle of 1889. In: The Colour of Liberty. Histories of Race in France, ed. by Sue Peabody, Tyler Stovall. Durham [et al.]: Duke University Press 2003, pp. 285-301.

Pendergrast, Mark: For God, Country and Coca-Cola. The Definitive History of the Great American Soft Drink and the Company That Makes It. 2nd rev. and exp. ed. New York: Basic Books 2000.
Phillips, Samuel: Guide to the Crystal Palace and Park. Illustrated by P. H. Delamotte. London: Crystal Palace Library, Bradbury and Evans 1854.
Pickering, Michael: Stereotyping. The Politics of Representation. Basingstoke [et al.]: Palgrave 2001.
Piggott, Jan R.: Palace of the People. The Crystal Palace at Sydenham, 1854-1936. London: Hurst 2004.
Piotrowski, Andrzej: Architecture of Thought. Minneapolis: University of Minnesota Press 2011.
Poignant, Roslyn: Professional Savages. Captive Lives and Western Spectacle. New Haven [et al.]: Yale University Press 2004.
Pollard, Tanya: The Pleasures and Perils of Smoking in Early Modern England. In: Smoke. A Global History of Smoking, ed. by Sander L. Gilman, Zhou Xun. London: Reaktion Books 2004, pp. 38-45.
Qureshi, Sadiah: Peoples on Parade. Exhibitions, Empire, and Anthropology in Nineteenth-Century Britain. Chicago [et al.]: University of Chicago Press 2011.
Ramamurthy, Anandi: Imperial Persuaders. Images of Africa and Asia in British Advertising. Manchester [et al.]: Manchester University Press 2003.
Rawlinson, Mark: American Visual Culture. Oxford [et al.]: Berg 2009.
Reed, Christopher Robert: ›All the World is Here!‹ The Black Presence at the White City. Bloomington [et al.]: Indiana University Press 2000.
Rex, Cathy: Indians and Images. The Massachusetts Bay Colony Seal, James Printer, and the Anxiety of Colonial Identity. In: American Quarterly, 63, 2011, 1, pp. 61-93.
Richards, John F.: The Unending Frontier. An Environmental History of the Early Modern World. Berkeley etc.: University of California Press 2003.
Richards, Thomas: The Commodity Culture of Victorian England. Advertising and Spectacle, 1851-1914. Stanford: Stanford University Press 1990.
Ritter, Sabine: Facetten der Sarah Baartman. Repräsentationen und Rekonstruktionen der ›Hottentottenvenus‹. (Racism Analysis | Studies 1). Berlin [etc.]: Lit 2010.
Rodenberg, Hans-Peter: Der imaginierte Indianer. Zur Dynamik von Kulturkonflikt und Vergesellschaftung des Fremden. Frankfurt: Suhrkamp 1994.
Rousseau, Jean-Jacques: Émile ou de l'éducation. In: id.: Œuvres complètes, vol. 4. Paris: Gallimard 1969.
Routledge's Guide to the Crystal Palace and Park at Sydenham. London [et al.]: George Routledge 1854.
Schneider, William H.: An Empire for the Masses. The French Popular Image of Africa, 1870 - 1900. Westport, Conn.: Greenwood Press 1982.
—: Les expositions ethnographiques du Jardin zoologique d'acclimatation. In: Zoos humains. Au temps des exhibitions humaines, with a new preface ed. by Nicolas Bancel, Pascal Blanchard, Gilles Boëtsch, Éric Deroo, Sandrine Lemaire. Paris: La Découverte 2004, pp. 72-80.

Secord, James A.: Monsters at the Crystal Palace. In: Models. The Third Dimension of Science, ed. by Soraya de Chadarevian, Nick Hopwood. Stanford: Stanford University Press 2004, pp. 138-169.
Senghor, Léopold Sédar: Poème liminaire. In: id., Œuvre poétique. Paris: Seuil 1964, 55 f.
Sheridan, Richard B.: Sugar and Slavery. An Economic History of the British West Indies, 1623-1775. Baltimore: Johns Hopkins University Press 1973.
Simmel, Georg: Berliner Gewerbeausstellung. In: Georg Simmel in Wien. Texte und Kontexte aus dem Wien der Jahrhundertwende, ed. by David Frisby. Wien: WUV Universitätsverlag 2000, pp. 64-68.
Stanley, Henry Morton: In Darkest Africa, or the Quest, Rescue, and Retreat of Emin Governor of Equatoria. 2 vol. in 1. New York: Charles Scribner's Sons 1913.
Staum, Martin S.: Labelling People. French Scholars on Society, Race, and Empire, 1815-1848. Montreal [etc.]: McGill-Queen's University Press 2003.
Stearn, Roger T.: War Correspondents and Colonial War, c. 1870-1900. In: Popular Imperialism and the Military, 1850-1950, ed. by John M. MacKenzie. Manchester [et al.]: Manchester University Press 1992, pp. 139-161.
Sweet, John Wood: Bodies Politic. Negotiating Race in the American North, 1730-1830. Philadelphia: University of Pennsylvania Press 2003.
The Crystal Palace. An Essay, Descriptive and Critical. 2nd ed. London [et al.]: Walton and Maberly 1855.
Todorov, Tzvetan: Nous et les autres. La réflexion française sur la diversité humaine. Paris: Seuil 1989.
Tomkins, Kyla Wazana: Racial Indigestion. Eating Bodies in the 19th Century. New York [et al.]: New York University Press 2012.
Topinard, Paul: L'Antropologie. Paris: Reinwald 1876.
—: La stéatopyge des Hottentotes du Jardin d'acclimatation. In: Revue d'Anthropologie, 4, 1889, 2, pp. 194-199.
Tretjakow, Sergej: Schaufensterreklame. In: Russen in Berlin. Literatur, Malerei, Theater, Film 1918-1933, ed. by Fritz Mierau. 2nd ed. Leipzig: Reclam 1990, pp. 540-544.
Verdesio, Gustavo: The Original Sin Behind the Creation of a New Europe. Economic and Ecological Imperialism in the River Plate, In: Mapping Colonial Spanish America. Places and Commonplaces of Identity, Culture, and Experience, ed. by Santa Arias, Mariselle Meléndez. London [et al.]: Associated University Presses 2002, pp. 137-158.
Verhandlungen des Reichstags. 12. Legislaturperiode. Stenographische Berichte, Bd. 265. Berlin: Norddeutsche Buchdruckerei und Verlags-Anstalt 1911.
Weiß, Anja: Racist Symbolic Capital. A Bourdieuian Approach to the Analysis of Racism. In: Wages of Whiteness & Racist Symbolic Capital, ed. by Wulf D. Hund, Jeremy Krikler, David Roediger. (Racism Analysis | Yearbook 1). Berlin [et al.]: Lit 2010, pp. 37-56.
Wheale, Nigel (ed.): The Postmodern Arts. An Introductory Reader. London [et al.]: Routledge 1995.
Williams, Eric: Capitalism and Slavery. With a new introduction by Colin A. Palmer. Chapel Hill: University of North Carolina Press 1994.

Winter, Joseph C.: Traditional Uses of Tobacco by Native Americans. In: Tobacco Use by Native North Americans. Sacred Smoke and Silent Killer, ed. by id. Norman: University of Oklahoma Press 2000, pp. 9-58.

Woloson, Wendy A.: Refined Tastes. Sugar, Confectionery, and Consumers in Nineteenth-Century America. Baltimore: Johns Hopkins University Press 2002.

Wong, John Y.: Deadly Dreams. Opium and the Arrow War (1856-1860) in China. Cambridge [et al.]: Cambridge University Press 1998.

Zeller, Joachim: Bilderschule der Herrenmenschen. Koloniale Reklamesammelbilder. Berlin: Christoph Links 2008.

Ziter, Edward: The Orient on the Victorian Stage. Cambridge [et al.]: Cambridge University Press 2003.

›Come and Join the Freedom-Lovers‹
Racism, Appropriation and Resistance in Advertising
Anandi Ramamurthy, Kalpana Wilson

Abstract: This chapter explores changes in racialised representations in contemporary advertising from the 1960s until the present, highlighting the ways in which these changes have been shaped by transformations in patterns of global capital accumulation – particularly the rise of neoliberal globalisation – as well as new forms of resistance to racism and imperialism. In this context it examines advertising's engagement with notions of social justice in three contexts – mainstream commercial advertising, fair trade advertising, and the publicity materials of international development organisations, and argues that in each case, these forms of advertising seek to represent consumerism as a force for progressive social change, while reproducing and reinforcing racialised global hierarchies. Further, these engagements can be understood as attempts to appropriate, redeploy and simultaneously undermine the discourses which resistance to racism and imperialism produces.

Advertising as a form of cultural expression has played a powerful role in the consolidation of racist ideologies. Research on racism in advertising has focused primarily on the production and reproduction of stereotypes, social hierarchies and the reinscribing of otherness in contemporary commercial culture.[1] It has also asserted the value for advertisers of addressing diverse markets and gaining cultural understanding.[2] In developing its languages of representation advertising has been forced to respond to changing global politics in the late twentieth century where civil rights, anti-colonial and national liberation movements intervened to challenge white supremacy. In the majority of narratives the response by advertisers to this process has been discussed in terms of the way in which advertisers attempted to ›tone down‹ stereotypical images to make them more acceptable or address the Black consumer.

---

1 Cf. William M. O'Barr: Culture and the Ad; Jan Nederveen Pieterse: White on Black; Stuart Hall: The Spectacle of the Other.
2 Cf. Guilherme D. Pires, P. John Stanton: Ethnic Marketing; Russell Luyt: Representation of Masculinities and Race in South African Television Advertising; Timothy de-Waal Malefyt, Brian Moeran (eds.): Advertising Cultures.

Such narratives continue to be dominated by the notion of ›positive images‹ that have been incorporated into advertising in contrast to the negative racist stereotypes that continue to litter commercial messages, although there has been a recognition of the bifurcation of representations into those of ›good blacks‹ (middle class and respectable) and ›bad blacks‹ (ghetto types) in the 1970s and 1980s.[3] Psychological approaches that have preferenced the impact of advertising images on the formation of identities and the self-esteem of those subject to racism have also been explored.[4] Such narratives have suggested that certain images (such as that of a black Santa cited by Nederveen Pieterse) are ›set breaking‹ because they do not refer to stereotypes associated with colonialism and slavery of black people as servants, entertainers or sportsmen.[5] This approach fails to examine the implications of these images in a context where deep structural inequalities between the global North and South persist and continue to be legitimised by race, materially constraining the participation of the majority of people in the global South in a world of consumption which is dependent on their labour. As this implies, political economy is crucial in understanding how ›race‹ is constituted and reproduced, and is all the more indispensible in the context of a field where cultural production is so clearly tied to economic interests.

This chapter will argue for the importance of exploring advertising's relationship with political economy in order to understand the way in which discourses surrounding ›race‹ operate within the context of contemporary imperialism and neo-liberal globalisation. How is advertising today reshaped by neo-liberal discourses which are involved in maintaining global and racial inequalities? We will explore the discourse and structures of race and imperialism from which promotional images derive, tracing the impacts of post-independence modernisation theories of development (first observable in commercial imagery in the 1950s) which projected the South as ›catching up‹, advancing through and into a US style consumer society, and of contemporary neoliberalism in which notions of difference and multiple subjectivities are selectively appropriated and commoditised. With these models encountering day-to-day resistance as well as organised anti-colonial, anti-imperialist and anti-racist struggles, advertising has also sought to appropriate and transform representations of resistance, ironically seeking to incorporate these representations within discourses

---

3   Cf. Jan Nederveen Pieterse: White on Black, p. 203.
4   Cf. Adrienne Ward: What Role Do Ads Play in Racial Tension?; Julia M. Bristor, Renée Gravois Lee, Michelle R. Hunt: Race and Ideology.
5   Cf. Jan Nederveen Pieterse: White on Black, pp. 3 f.; Carol Nathanson-Moog: The Psychological Power of Ethnic Images in Advertising, pp. 19-22.

of consumption. Going beyond a simplistic notion of stereotypes, we argue that a wider array of imagery works towards mobilising ideas about not just the benign nature of contemporary capitalism but its potential as a force for the advancement for global equality. We explore the ways in which advertising in an era of globalisation and neo-liberalism continues to reproduce and naturalise racialised inequalities even when it appears to promote the very opposite – ›progress‹ and social change.

We will examine the patterns of – and relationships between – charity, development publicity and commercial imagery through this chapter in order to understand the ways in which representations of black people in commodity culture operate in contemporary society to uphold social inequalities at the very moment when they appear to be breaking them down. We will explore three categories of imagery that engage with ideas of social justice to consider how they have been employed to encourage ideologies of consumerism and globalisation as a benign and progressive force for social equality and how such narratives often operate to reinforce racial hierarchies. We look first at representations of resistance in commercial advertising; second, at how these have been developed in fair trade advertising; and third, at how they have been used in publicity produced by international development organisations, which attempts to mimic and appropriate the language and practices of movements for social justice.

Race, Capital, Commodification and Resistance

The intimate historical and contemporary relationship between race and capital can be understood as beginning with racialised slavery within which human beings themselves were transformed into commodities. The very development of capitalism in Europe was made possible by transatlantic slavery and early colonialism, and the huge transfer of resources to the global North involved in these processes. Conversely, the enslavement and transportation of millions of people, the direct appropriation of resources, the extraction of surpluses through taxation, exploitation and unequal trade, the shift of resources away from productive activities and enforced deindustrialisation, and the forcible integration into global markets on unequal terms which accompanied European incursions were instrumental in producing the structures and conditions associated with the countries in the global South.

The consolidation of constructions of race was central to these processes from the outset. With the restructuring of Western societies associated with the transition to metropolitan industrial capitalism, liberal Enlightenment ideas about freedom, the rights of the individual and universal humanism became increasingly important. Enlightenment ideas were clearly inconsistent with the dynamics of colonialism – and in particular with the system of transatlantic slavery – on which continuing capital accumulation depended, as they were with the continuation – or consolidation – of patriarchal gender relations within capitalism. Not surprisingly then, Enlightenment ›universalism‹ was from the outset based on multiple exclusions with only the white, property-owning man ultimately defined as capable of ›rational‹ thought and action and therefore fully human and entitled to rights.[6] As Paul Gilroy writes of plantation slavery, there is a »need to indict those forms of rationality which have been rendered implausible by their racially exclusive character and further too explore their complicity with terror systematically and rationally practiced as a form of political and economic administration«.[7] Racialised slavery must therefore be understood not as an anomaly of capitalism but its epitome, in which race makes possible the full commodification and therefore non-integrity of the body which is »fully opened to capital«.[8]

In this context, discourses of ›race‹ came to be structured around a set of binary oppositions (such as civilisation/savagery; reason/emotion and culture/nature) which characterised Enlightenment definitions of the human. Influential liberal philosophers such as Locke and Hume were explicitly racist in their writings, defining black people as lacking the capacity for rationality and therefore agency.[9] These claims were not however simply philosophical speculations but direct interventions into contemporary political debates[10] and crucially, responses to the multiple forms of continuous and sustained resistance by the enslaved people themselves. They sought to provide a justification for plantation slavery as a form of surplus accumulation and its institutionalisation in forms such as France's ›Code Noir‹, which applied to black slaves in its colonies,[11] and »legalized not only slavery, the treatment of human beings as moveable property, but the branding, torture, physical mutilation, and killing of slaves for attempting to defy their inhuman status«.[12] As this implies, the invention of ›race‹ was itself from the outset conditioned by the resistance of those it sought to exclude from humanity.

6   Cf. Allison Jaggar: Feminist Politics and Human Nature; David T. Goldberg: Racist Culture; Emmanuel C. Eze: Race and the Enlightenment.
7   Paul Gilroy: The Black Atlantic, p. 220.
8   Eva Cherniavsky: Incorporations, p. xvii.
9   Cf. David T. Goldberg: Racist Culture; Emmanuel C. Eze: Race and the Enlightenment.
10 Cf. id.: Hume, Race and Human Nature.
11 Cf. Cyril Lionel Robert James: The Black Jacobins.
12 Susan Buck Morss: Hegel and Haiti, p. 380.

Our discussion of the contemporary ›commodification of social justice‹ in this chapter is underpinned by the understanding that changing dominant notions of ›race‹ have been shaped by, and in turn have made possible, changing patterns of global capital accumulation, and equally significantly that ideas about racial hierarchy have been deployed in response to multiple forms of resistance, and have been themselves altered and reconfigured by this resistance. Within this context, we understand commodity racism to refer to the global structural inequalities inherent in the production, circulation and consumption of commodities that continue to be both legitimised and reinforced by racism.

Imperialism and the Commodification of Resistance

In the period since the end of formal colonialism, particularly at moments of crisis, advertisers have sought to absorb or represent conflict which could not be ignored. We can see advertising's ability to transform itself in the wake of dissent and to absorb all forms of representation, including symbols and narratives of dissent in a whirl of signs that become increasingly difficult to disentangle – as an attempt to shore up hegemony and to sustain imperialism through successive phases of Cold War decolonisation and neoliberal globalisation. Lenin argued that parasitism was a feature of imperialism: he noted how, with the rise of finance capital, the bourgeoisie of Europe were increasingly concerned with acting as rentiers rather than engaging in production. Imperialism based on the export of capital to the colonies reinforced this process, and in Lenin's words »set the seal of parasitism on the whole country that lives by exploiting the labour of several overseas countries and colonies«.[13]

Anti-colonial and anti-racist struggles in the post-war period meant that in order to sustain this parasitic imperialism under new conditions, capital was compelled to implement a shift in representations (albeit an incomplete one) from the previous dehumanising stereotypes of formerly colonised and enslaved peoples as child-like, savage or as born to labour. Advertisers first responded to the changing political climate by banishing images of black people from consumer advertising. However, during the Cold War period, Melamed has argued that the development of a liberal race paradigm which »recognised racial inequality as a problem [...] secure[d] a liberal symbolic framework for race reform centred in abstract equality, market individualism and inclusive civic nationalism«, in a

13 Vladimir Ilich Lenin: Imperialism, the Highest Stage of Capitalism, p. 120.

framework in which race equality thus defined became a nationally recognised social value in the US.¹⁴ Racial liberalism became increasingly employed as part of the Cold War arsenal to represent the West as the upholder of human rights and freedom. Such an ideology is perceivable as early as the 1950s where images of a transforming and industrialising Africa were associated with Western firms such as English Electric whose advertisements of an industrialising Africa present the firm as benevolent, encouraging and driving ›development‹ in Africa and the global South. In these corporate images, the black man was no longer the worker serving the interests of Europe, but rather framed as a worker reaping the benefit of Western science and development or as a simple, leisured individual dependent on Western productivity for his/her needs. In all the advertisements the corporate firm retained the image of benefactor aiding processes of social change. Such images did not employ explicitly degrading stereotypes of black people but maintained the colonial ideology of the white man's burden in developing an underdeveloped world. In one 1958 advertisement the Cold War conflict is made explicit with a text that asserts: »Rival ideologies are competing for the future of the world, the one that wins will be that which offers more people a better life« juxtaposed with the image of an African man looking contemplatively at an English Electric engine powering the Johannesburg Mail, projecting the improved conditions of life as belonging to corporate development.¹⁵

In the struggle to be represented as human and not rendered invisible, civil rights discourses often treated the question of media representations as separate from those of political and economic rights. As the Congress for Racial Equality argued: »What Negro consumers want now is recognition of their humanity and an industry wide respect for the Negro image«.¹⁶ The civil rights movement's campaign for a wider range of imagery was to establish a black presence within the plethora of idealised images produced by advertisers, so as to humanise black Americans, represent them as objects of desire and permit a black presence within the American dream. The racialised political economy of the production remained unchallenged however within this framework. As Kim and Chung have argued, the US economy has relied increasingly on unequal relations between the US and the global South to sustain profits by incorporating the devalued labour of outsourced workers and migrants, many of whom are women, within new economic structures. In this context the diversification

---

14 Jodi Melamed: The Spirit of Neo-liberalism, p. 2.
15 Anandi Ramamurthy: Imperial Persuaders, pp. 173-213; id: Images of Industrialisation in Empire and Commonwealth During the Shift to Neo-Colonialism, pp. 43-69.
16 Quoted in Jason Chambers: Madison Avenue and the Color Line, p. 120.

of images in advertising to include the visual consumption of the bodies of women of colour in particular has enabled corporations to expand their market share to a racially diversified population of consumers, as well as »to re-package and obscure the exploitative labour machinery that produces them«.[17]

In Britain, the Sunday Times magazine of 5 March 1969 heralded this shift for the British establishment media. The magazine featured a black woman on the front cover with the title »Black is Beautiful«. The powerful and radical black power message which directly confronted the dehumanisation of black people within racist discourses was here transformed into a simple fashionable accompaniment to the objectification of black women by the white gaze. In the same year, Bahama's tourist advertising, which had previously represented the attractions of the Bahamas as those of sandy beaches, swimming pools and palm trees with the people of the Bahamas rendered invisible, altered their advertising to add another attraction – the black Bahamian, whose body, culture and labour act as an exotic appendage to the tranquil sandy beaches of the previous advertisements. Much has been written about the racialised commodification inherent in tourism promotion, particularly in the Caribbean[18] and it is significant to note the precise moment at which images of black people themselves were incorporated into those of ›unspoilt‹ nature. ›Are you big enough for the Bahamas?‹ was the new slogan that projected images that focused on the bodies of local fishermen, market sellers or companions on the golf course, to present their material and affective labour as objects of consumption. Their bodies are inscribed with a complex array of meanings which allude to manual labour, exotic appeal, a racialised de-sexualisation as well as a racialised hyper-sexuality through a series of advertisements which focus on the pleasure of the white tourist. The commodification of the black body in Bahamas tourist advertising was further consolidated in 1989 when a 1967 advertisement for the Bahamas which has been critiqued for its presentation of a white woman as ripe for penetration – lying in a tranquil sea, staring up at the viewer with the slogan »lets assume I'm an island« was reproduced in 1989 to feature a black woman in the same context with the same slogan, confirming the limit of the ›black is beautiful‹ concept in advertising to contexts of sexual objectification.

The rising political conflicts of 1969 also produced images in which resistance itself was commodified such as the series of advertisements for Berlei underwear with the tag line ›Come and Join the Freedom Lovers‹.

17 Minjeong Kim, Angie Y. Chung: Consuming Orientalism, p. 72.
18 Cf. Kamala Kempadoo: Sexing the Caribbean; Jacqueline Sánchez Taylor: Female Sex Tourism.

The terms and insignia of protest were appropriated in a campaign to persuade women to purchase lycra rich lingerie. The ads featured white women dressed in their underwear standing in the desert, carrying flags for ›freedom‹ implicitly referencing – and trivialising – the Palestinian struggles that had intensified following the 1967 Arab-Israeli war. »Feel free« as one advertisement suggested, »follow the freedom lovers into the beautiful world of Berlei«.[19] The struggles for social transformation centred around race, gender, and imperialism referenced here were evacuated of political content in such images that implicitly equated freedom with participation in consumer culture and transformed the desire for revolutionary change into the desire for sexualised consumption, prefiguring neoliberal and postfeminist inspired discourses of ›girl power‹.

The appropriation of histories of dissent is particularly visible at moments in history where political change and conflict impacts on corporate capitalism most dramatically. The late 1980s which saw the collapse of the Soviet Union and the dismantling of apartheid marked another moment that saw an appropriation of images of struggle and social change by large corporations. In 1990 for example, the Anglo American Corporation of South Africa that had colluded for decades with the apartheid regime sought to ›clean up‹ its image as the apartheid system began to collapse. Two full page advertisements placed in the broadsheet newspapers sought to allay investors' fears over the corporation's future direction in the month that Nelson Mandela was released from prison. One ad featured an image of victorious black miners outside the mine owners headquarters after a strike with the tag line ›Do we sometimes wish we hadn't fought to have black trade unions recognised‹?[20] The history of black resistance to racism is here reduced to a single struggle which Anglo America shamelessly appropriates as theirs at a transitional moment in South Africa's history.

Multiculturalism and Neoliberalism

By the 1980s, anti-colonial struggles, the civil rights movement and the articulation of black power had consolidated a shift away from explicit racism in dominant discourses, with ›culture‹ increasingly being substituted for ›race‹ in these discourses. Racial discourse could no longer be employed as a rationale for the organisation of society. Yet at the same

---

19 For the ads see http://old-ads-and-mags.tumblr.com/post/29900661935/come-join-the-freedom-lovers (›Old Ads and Mags‹); http://www.calectasia.com/History/Brands/Berlei.php (›Famous Brands‹) – all URLs have been revised on 30.5.2013.
20 Cf. ›The Guardian‹, 2.4.1990.

time, neo-liberal globalisation had extended and entrenched inequalities between the North and the global south. The late 1980s was the exact moment when images of multiculturalism became a key element in commercial advertising.

Hale and Melamed have both argued that the adoption of multicultural policies in both the US and Latin America have been used effectively to neutralise political opposition to neo-liberal economic policies.[21] In advertising, the first widespread use of multiculturalism as a brand image was adopted by Coca Cola in 1971 with their advertisement ›I'd like to buy the world a coke‹.[22] The hilltop advertisement gathered individuals from a variety of nations who sing together ›in perfect harmony‹ eliding the values of sharing and love with the purchase of Coke, which the advertisement visualises as a levelling and equalising factor. For a brand that relied on a global market it was an ideal image and foreshadowed 1980s multicultural marketing practices.

As multiculturalism became more widespread in advertising imagery in the 1980s, culminating in Benetton's assertive embracing of it as a core brand identity, its suturing to neo-liberal production practices became more apparent and provides an important case study of a racialised discourse projected as the embracing of cultural diversity. Giroux has argued that Benetton's employment of multicultural imagery in the 1980s fitted their embracement of globalised post-Fordist manufacturing systems, in which flexibility in manufacturing was the key to its success, using new technologies to create small batch production and transferring risk to multiple small sub-contracted units (in the global South as well the North where vulnerable workers, often migrant women, were employed), which allowed workers to be denied rights.[23] Benetton's multiculturalism was initially presented by the company as an accident when their photographer Oliviero Toscani noticed that »it wasn't just the sweaters that came in different shades«[24] yet this shift in advertising imagery also coincided with the launch of the company as a global firm in the mid-1980s. Benetton's politics of difference can be seen as not simply a naïve expression of multiculturalism to promote an »apolitical egalitarianism veiled in an appeal to international harmony« but the cultural articulation of a post-Fordist »world without borders« where difference was embraced to exploit low la-

---

21 Cf. Charles Hale: Neoliberal Multiculturalism; Jodi Melamed: The Spirit of Neoliberalism.
22 Cf. Ted Ryan: The Making of ›I'd Like to Buy the World a Coke‹.
23 Cf. Henry Giroux: Consuming Social Change.
24 Quoted in ›The Face‹, November 1987, p. 83.

bour costs in the global south while at the same time denying its potential for resistance and social struggle.²⁵

These early Benetton images can be understood as a multiculturalism constructed within a »grammar of race«²⁶ where national cultures were reduced to caricatures and difference was deliberately marked by the choice of blond and blue-eyed European models in juxtaposition with dark-skinned African models. But Benetton's images of ›harmony‹ were also often ideologically loaded. An advertisement from 1987 which represented both the USSR as well as the USA wearing Benetton clothes structured the USSR as more rigid and aggressive in contrast to the softer and more playful image of the USA.²⁷ Similarly a Benetton's ›Colors‹ perfume from 1988, while superficially suggesting unity between black and white, was constructed to project the white male hand as giver and black female hand as receiver of perfumes. Along with the title ›Her first perfume‹ it was reminiscent of charity advertisements that draw attention to what the white male philanthropist can provide – her first book, her first shoes etc., and, like them, irresistibly evoked the civilising mission.²⁸

This bland multiculturalism that could be critiqued as ignoring social inequalities and conflict was transformed in 1989 when Benetton began to employ imagery representing social issues and conflicts that did not directly relate to the promotion of their products. This marked a shift in the company's brand strategy, which sought to not simply articulate ideas about social justice in a world of consumerism, but where the questions raised by social consciousness and activism appear to be addressed through consumption rather than changing oppressive relations of power. Benetton's campaigns were the beginning of a process that has increasingly seen consumer culture as a force that can create progressive change. This has created »a new form of violence against the public«, which offers an image of the social that is »stripped of all social and political antagonisms«.²⁹

War, racism, HIV/AIDS, birth, death and religion were some of the issues highlighted in Benetton advertisements from 1989 onwards. The shift in Benetton's advertising strategy from one of directly selling a product, to selling the idea of corporate social responsibility, included many advertisements that engaged with controversies over race and representation. The images employed were deliberately decontextualised and dehistoricised, which Luciano Benetton argued was a deliberate strategy because »the im-

---

25 Henry Giroux: Consuming Social Change, p. 18.
26 Les Back, Vibke Quaade: Dream Utopias Nightmare Realities, p. 65.
27 Cf. Anandi Ramamurthy: Spectacles and Illusions, pp. 253-256.
28 See. id.: Imperial Persuaders, pp. 219 f.
29 Henry Giroux: Consuming Social Change, p. 15.

age is understandable by itself«. Yet the images were carefully contrived ambiguous statements inviting interpretation. While Benetton played with the notion that readers create the meaning of any text, it is clear that certain interpretations are privileged in a society in which systematic racism exists. As Stuart Hall has argued, the reading of individual images depends on an accumulation of meanings: one image implicitly refers to a series of others, or has its meaning altered by being read in the context of others in a process which establishes ›regimes of representation‹.[30] Thus the image of a black and white hand handcuffed together is likely to be read by white viewers as a representation of black criminality even if this is nowhere made explicit. Similarly the image of a black woman with a white baby cannot easily be removed from the context of slavery and colonialism. Its banning in America made this clear. »Restaging race relations in these terms exploits the racially charged tensions that underlie current racial formations in the Western industrial countries while simultaneously reducing the historical legacy of white supremacy to a representation of mere equality or symmetry«.[31]

While the first ›social issue‹ images were constructed by Toscani, soon the company moved to reproduce hyperrealist documentary images on their billboard advertisements. This strategy collapsed the boundaries between the fantasy images of advertising and the social documentary images that we often consume to try to understand social realities. The advertisements included the image of David Kirby dying of AIDS, a car in flames, an anonymous African soldier carrying a human femur bone and the blood soaked clothes of a dead (and again unnamed) Bosnian soldier. The images carefully avoided any comment or perspective on the issues that they highlighted and could therefore provide no indication of the possibilities for social transformation. Most importantly, with both historical continuities and contemporary global connections erased from these contexts, they acted to reinforce racialised tropes such as those of Africans as irrational, brutal and dehumanised and of the war in Bosnia as the product of unchangeable ›ancient hatreds‹. In the packaging of political and social issues within a commercial context, the purchase of clothing became a triumph for justice. In one series of advertisements from 1993, the white and wealthy Luciano Benetton posed nude with the text ›I want my clothes back‹ to encourage the rich to give away their old clothes to charity, arguing that »business has to go on for everybody. Rich people should buy new stuff and be pleased that others can profit from (their old clothes)«.[32]

30 Cf. Stuart Hall: The Spectacle of the ›Other‹.
31 Henry Giroux: Benetton's ›World without Borders‹.
32 Sharon Waxman: Benetton Laid Bare.

What is unspoken is that this divide between ›rich people‹ and ›others‹ globally is also racialised as structural inequalities between the North and the global South leave the rich as largely white and the poor as predominantly non-white.

Contemporary advertising by charities and development organisations also extensively represents and reproduces the racialised inequalities of neoliberal globalisation. In a particularly explicit example, an advertisement by the Danish charity Humana in 2009, presents even the North's rubbish as more dynamic than African people, and as a catalyst for change in Africa. In the advertisement a truck travels through an (unidentified) ›African‹ landscape in which every African figure is passive and unproductive, staring at the camera or sitting on a wall. The truck moves dynamically before stopping in a city space to deposit what first appears to be unidentifiable rubbish on the ground. Soon camera close ups reveal this rubbish to be second hand clothes which literally ›come alive‹ to transform Africa. Disembodied trousers and shirts move through the streets watched passively by African children to eventually enter a classroom to teach children, play football, cradle a child and drag a water pump unaided by any other labour to a village where we see the disembodied shirt even pumping the water out of the ground for the villagers. Nowhere is the labour of Africans represented or acknowledged and the ad ends with the tag line »let your second hand clothing help the third world«.[33] The advertisement consolidates a world of consumption as a trigger for social transformation. The fact that Humana, which describes itself as a non-profit organization that supports sustainable development in Southern Africa, has since been exposed as being involved in a multinational trading company running fruit plantations in Belize, Brazil and Equador (as well as fraudulently running for-profit second hand clothes shops in some European countries and collecting donations that have disappeared into tax havens) only further highlights exploitative relationships between the North and the global South which are shored up by racism.[34]

Yet more established and ›respectable‹ NGOs like Oxfam are equally implicated in these relationships, and in racialised advertising and promotion campaigns. The recurring theme of the detritus of people in the global North representing ›hope‹ to those in the South was replayed once again in Oxfam's ›Big Bra Hunt‹ launched in April 2012 which urged women in Britain to donate their ›unwanted‹ bras to the charity.[35] These bras, they

---

33 Cf. http://www.youtube.com/watch?v=NxE4HQKQWWo (›Humana – let your 2-nd hand clothes help 3-rd world‹).
34 Cf. Anne L. Mösken: Second Hand Scam.
35 Cf. Oxfam: The Big Bra Hunt (http://www.oxfam.org.uk/donate/the-big-bra-hunt).

were informed, if not sold in Oxfam's UK shops, »could end up getting sorted and sold in Senegal at Frip Ethique, Oxfam's social enterprise« because »British bras are seriously sought after in Senegal – where few businesses have the complex technology needed to make good-quality bras«. Oxfam was heavily criticised for a campaign which, with its ubiquitous pink and surfeit of lace, represented (mainly white) women in the global North in postfeminist terms as sexualised consuming subjects deriving pleasure from their own objectification, and those in the global South, and ›Africa‹ in particular, as gratefully aspiring to ›civilisation‹ now defined in these terms. Racialised hierarchies of consumption in which that which is ›unwanted‹ in the North is assumed to be transformed into an object of desire – ›seriously sought after‹ – in the South, were not challenged but reaffirmed and reinforced in the absence of any recognition of structural relationships of inequality underpinning these processes. The colonial resonances of the ›bra‹ campaign were so unavoidable that even Duncan Green of Oxfam, responding to critics, referred uneasily to »overtones« of »colonial administrators wives advising ›native‹ women on decent dressing« before dismissing these concerns by invoking the spurious logic of the market – »the bras are being sold, not given away – women can choose whether or not to buy them«.[36] Equally striking was the way in which the campaign naturalised and racialised the unequal global value chains and distribution of resources inherent in global capitalism, which are reduced to ›businesses‹ in Africa apparently inevitably lacking the ›complex technology‹ to produce ›good quality‹ products, a problem for which Oxfam's solution appears to be the dumping of second-hand underwear from Europe.

But while the Oxfam ›bra‹ campaign attracted considerable criticism in NGO circles, other recent promotional campaigns by Oxfam and other NGOs as well as development institutions such as DfID and the World Bank which seek to promote ›positive, active‹ representations of ›poor women in the global South‹ have been welcomed as recognising the ›agency‹ of these women. However, these ›new‹ images, which were produced partly in response to the critiques of earlier representations of ›Third World women‹ as a homogenous category of ›passive victims‹,[37] contribute to and extend, rather than challenge, racialised regimes of representation. They are consistent with the current requirements of neoliberal capital in reproducing the notion of the ›poor woman in the global South‹ as a reliable, hyper-industrious entrepreneurial subject with a gendered and

36 Duncan Green: Should Oxfam be Collecting a Million Bras From the Public and Selling Them? (http://www.oxfamblogs.org/fp2p/?p=9725).
37 Cf. Chandra Talpade Mohanty: Under Western Eyes.

racialised propensity for hard work and altruism, whose labour can and should be further extended and intensified.[38] This is particularly marked in the increasing volume of advertising which blurs the boundaries between consumerism and philanthropy, epitomised by what is considered ethical consumerism, where consumers can effect positive change by exercising the ›choice‹ to buy fair-trade.

Ethical Consumerism and Fairtrade

Established in 1992, the Max Havelaar Foundation has spearheaded a niche in mainstream consumer markets which has been described as marrying the pleasure and shame of consumption for those in the privileged North, where the access to expanded choice of goods and services only available to them has enabled a ›choice‹ of ethical consumption which by its very existence reaffirms the structural inequalities that it is supposed to allay.[39] While it is claimed that »by requiring companies to pay sustainable prices, Fairtrade addresses the injustices of conventional trade«[40] it remains rooted in global divisions of labour and the differential valuing of human labour in the global North and South which is structured by imperialism and legitimised by ›race‹. Fair Trade is therefore not an alternative to neoliberalism, but simply a variation of it. Fair Trade advertising works to simultaneously erase and naturalise these structural inequalities through its relentless use of representations of ›happy‹ and ›productive‹ women workers, whose ubiquitous smiles implicitly testify to the ethical and moral nature of the product. In smiling these workers perform ›affective‹ labour which affirms the value of the Northern consumer's fair trade choice.[41] The consumer can feel good about his/her purchase. Yet smiling, as Marylyn Frye has noted »is often a requirement upon oppressed people [...]. If we comply, we signal our docility and our acquiescence in our situation. We need not, then, be taken note of. We acquiesce in being made invisible, in our occupying no space. We participate in our own erasure«.[42]

A study of advertising used by Oxfam for its ›Oxfam Unwrapped‹ charity gift-giving campaign[43] found that its audiences were constructed as

---

38 Cf. Kalpana Wilson: ›Race‹, Gender and Neoliberalism; id.: Race, Racism and Development.
39 Jo Littler: Radical Consumption, p. 15.
40 Fairtrade Max Havelaar: What is Fairtrade? (http://www.maxhavelaar.nl/faq/what-fair-trade?destination=english&backtitle=FAQ%27s).
41 Cf. Anandi Ramamurthy: Absences and Silences.
42 Marilyn Frye: Oppression and the Use of Definition, p. 2.
43 See Oxfam: Oxfam Unwrapped (http://www.oxfam.org.uk/shop/oxfam-unwrapped).

consuming subjects on several interlinked levels: as viewers sampling multiple images of the exoticised, racialised bodies and ›natural‹ surroundings of the women; as (potential) donors deriving gratification from observing (unobserved) the effects of their generosity; and as consumers in the North not only enjoying the undervalued product of the labour applied by ›poor women in the South‹ but using their leisure time to vicariously share the pleasure which these women are portrayed as deriving from their own labour.[44] Racialised and gendered exoticisation continues but is now increasingly incorporated into constructions of these women as hyper-industrious ›entrepreneurs‹.

This reinvokes and reformulates an earlier narrative: that of late colonial enterprises which were based on the acute exploitation of largely female labour. Tea advertising in the 1920s worked to provide legitimacy for the continuation of colonial rule in the context of growing demands for independence, using images of the Indian woman tea picker who was not only represented as alluring and sensual, but through her apparent contentment and productivity within an ordered environment symbolically affirmed the need for empire.[45] These images were also read in the context of discourses of the ›work ethic‹, individual responsibility and the ›deserving‹ and ›undeserving‹ poor which were deployed to extract ever greater surpluses from the working class in Britain and, via missionaries in particular, from its colonial subjects.

Regimes of representation work to evoke these continuities. Thus on the ›Cafedirect‹ website and on its tea packaging we find a quote from ›Mugisha Pauson, Tea picker, Mpanga, Uganda‹: »I like my work – I pick tea and put it in my basket. Believe it or not, I can smell the good quality tea leaves. Cafédirect has helped our community by giving us a fair price, so now I pick the tea with a big smile«.[46] This text and the accompanying smiling photograph, which have also been used on tea packaging, contain all the same elements as the colonial advertisements described here: labour and order producing contentment and a good quality product for the European consumer, and an explicit recognition of the benevolent role of the white man/company in making this possible. Perhaps the only factor which makes this stand out among contemporary development images of work is that Mugisha is a man. Like the Oxfam images, however, his portrayal is racialised in specifically gendered ways. Its construction of

---

44 Cf. Kalpana Wilson: ›Race‹, Gender, and Neoliberalism, p. 323.
45 Cf. Anandi Ramamurthy: Imperial Persuaders, p. 126.
46 Café Direct: Lydia Nabulumbi (http://www.memory4teachers.co.uk/channels/presentations/cafedirect/profile/Lydia%20profile.pdf).

the naively happy, close-to nature yet deliberately desexualized black man references a recurring trope which has been analysed extensively.[47]

As ›Fair Trade‹ has been mainstreamed, with major multinationals developing product lines which represent them as ethical and socially responsible, the imagery employed has diversified but continues to draw on racial tropes developed during the colonial period. The Fair Trade concept has been adapted to conform to the interests of transnational corporations like Nestlé, Unilever and Cadbury's and this is reflected in their advertising. The launch of Cadbury's fair trade Dairy Milk for example saw the firm focus on the representation of Ghana as a country rather than the representation of individual workers. This may be a result of the plight of Ghanaian cocoa bean farming which often does not provide enough for families to live on[48] as well as the fact that many of the farmers, as men, are not able to fit as effectively into the image of the industrious feminized worker from the South that has come to be the mainstay of Fair Trade advertising. In its portrayals of Ghanaian men the advertisement reinscribes racialised colonial representations of men in the global South as inherently ›lazy‹, irresponsible and preoccupied with sensual pleasure, now contrasted with women portrayed, as we have seen, as the ›good native‹ or ›deserving poor‹.

In 2009 Cadbury's teamed up with a popular Ghanaian singer, Tinny, to launch ›A Glass and a Half Records‹ with the song ›Zingolo‹ which they describe as celebrating »all things Ghana, its people, its rappers, its dancers, its cultural figures and, of course, its cocoa beans«.[49] The commercial begins with a tranquil scene in which a young man paints a publicity sign for ›Big Plant Cocoa Farm‹ when all of a sudden an enormous mask in the shape of a cocoa bean emerges from a garage to shake up the village. The hand-painted sign, which Cadbury's also uses as an aesthetic in partner print advertisements which profile the benefits of Fair Trade, they describe as culturally Ghanaian. It acts to inscribe Africa as inherently non-industrialised. The mask/bean – signifier of Cadbury's – spins after a pregnant pause as a song and drums begin to beat creating energy that sees cocoa beans pick themselves and gravitate towards the bean/mask attributing the capacity for transformation to Cadbury's as a Northern firm. As in dominant advertising narratives the labour of production is denied through the magical appearance of the beans that randomly fly out of the farm to adhere themselves to the mask, first to give it signs of masculinity (a beard and hair) and then to comically mimic the animals and people that it meets

---

47 Cf. Stuart Hall: The Spectacle of the ›Other‹; Richard Dyer: Heavenly Bodies.
48 Cf. David Gregory: Fairtrade Hopes for Cadbury Cocoa Farmers in Ghana.
49 Cf. Glass and a Half Productions: Cadbury Dairy Milk – Zingolo featuring Tinny.

to bring laughter. A sense of abundance is constructed by the popping and flying of cocoa beans that are larger than life with one bean ultimately exploding to reveal Tinny who then begins a song and dance routine on a roof top to which the villagers below join in. In narrative terms African masculinity is constructed as unproductive and embroiled in a world of sensual pleasure. The instigator of change is Cadbury's, nativised as bean/mask, that brings Africans their music through the sponsorship of Tinny, eventually flying into the sky transporting the beans.

What is significant about the imagery employed by Cadbury's Fair Trade launch is the adoption of a series of tropes that recall their advertising from the early 20th century when they first entered the West African cocoa trade. From 1906 onwards, the Quaker cocoa firms, (Cadbury's and Fry's) released a series of advertisements of the happy carefree ›Sambo‹ pouring abundant cocoa into the cups of Europe. These images acted to represent both firms' attitude towards colonial development in West Africa as well as to distance them from the controversy over slave-grown cocoa which emerged when labour conditions on the islands of São Tomé and Príncipe came to British public awareness in 1905 and 1906. Cadbury's and Fry's, as Quaker firms whose company images were built on philanthropy, wished to distance themselves from such practices and immediately looked for new sources of raw materials in West Africa where they were able to support their ideological position of what became known as a »dual mandate« for the coloniser, with »moral obligations« to train Africans to »take such responsibility as they are fit to exercise«, while at the same time undertaking the »material obligation« of developing the material resources of Africa »for the benefit of the people and of mankind in general«.⁵⁰ Cocoa growers in West Africa were small peasant farmers who sold their goods on the market rather than plantation producers. This system enabled Cadbury's to distance themselves from accusations of exploitation and uphold a policy of indigenous ownership of land while pursuing their own economic interests. As William Cadbury wrote in 1916 to the West African Lands Committee: »We would very much rather not have the responsibility. Let the natives bring it to the open market«. In one Fry's advertisement an African boy holds up an extra large cocoa bean which acts as a signifier of abundance and pours the product happily into the cups of European nations. Africa is structured as contentedly taking its place as the producer of raw materials, which are developed for ›mankind in general‹. The happy-go-lucky images of many of these advertisements also

---

50   Quoted from Anandi Ramamurthy: Imperial Peruaders, pp. 70 ff.; the following quotes are from ibid., pp. 83 (Cadbury) and 74 (Lugard).

suggest the African's lack of application to labour, as Lugard articulated: »it is misleading to cite the success of the [Gold Coast cocoa planters] as evidence of industry [...] when they are due primarily to an exceptionally favourable soil, climate and rainfall«. The new Cadbury's Fair Trade advertisement suggests the same forms of magical abundance and represents African men as unsophisticated and carefree individuals absorbed in a world rooted in pleasure. The image of a slightly vacuous looking African man (whose head shape is uncomfortably similar to the cocoa bean) inanely smiling finishes the advertisement to leave the representation of Africa as the abode of simple folk with simple pleasures, naturalizing and racialising its position within unequal structures of production and trade.[51]

The Appropriation of Movements for Social Justice

Whereas from the 1960s onwards, as we have discussed, language and images associated with movements for social justice were mobilised to sell particular commodities, today these terms and images are also being appropriated by international NGOS, frequently in partnership with corporates, for wider publicity campaigns which advance neoliberal development objectives and the interests of global capital. In this section, we look at two such recent, although very different, high profile campaigns – ›The Girl Effect‹ and ›Kony 2012‹.

›The Girl Effect‹ represents the rebranding of the Nike Foundation, which was established by the Nike Corporation in 2003 to fund projects involving adolescent girls in developing countries. Set up in partnership with the Population Council and the International Centre for Research on Women, it has gone on to establish partnerships with the World Bank and the UK Department for International Development (DfID). As argued elsewhere,[52] Nike's initiative was consistent with the ›feminisation of responsibility‹ for survival in the context of the ravages of neoliberal globalisation in the global South, further intensified in the period of global recession and crisis. The instrumentalisation of poor women is perhaps epitomised by the World Bank's slogan ›Gender Equality as Smart Economics‹.[53] But this represents a much wider consensus across development institutions, including the vast majority of NGOs. As a result of this consensus, while the concept of ›agency‹ is regularly mobilised in the

---

51 Cf. ibid., pp. 63-92.
52 Cf. Kalpana Wilson: ›Race‹, Gender and Neoliberalism.
53 World Bank: Gender Action Plan, 2007-2010; World Bank: World Development Report 2012.

construction by development institutions of poor women in the South as ›enterprising‹ subjects with limitless capacity to ›cope‹, movements which run counter to the neoliberal model, demanding the redistribution of resources, challenging the operation of markets, or confronting the violence of the ›democratic‹ neoliberal state, are rendered invisible.

The now celebrated video, ›The Girl Effect‹,[54] produced in 2008, marked the project's launch of the ›Girl Effect‹ brand and the removal of all reference to the Nike Foundation. This video is notable, particularly in the context of development, for what would become the signature style of the ›Girl Effect‹ publicity: its complete exclusion of images or speech, being based solely on an extremely pared down and simplified textual narrative in which individual capitalised words flash on an empty screen. This, along with a complete absence of any markers of place or culture, would appear to avoid some of the more obvious forms of objectification and exoticisation. In fact, there is a challenge to these processes implied in the invitation here to »imagine a girl living in poverty, no, go ahead, really, imagine her«. Yet paradoxically, as a result of its generality, it is also free to mobilise intertextual associations to deploy racialised tropes (familiar to the viewer from more explicit photographic images and texts used by NGOs and the media) quite extensively. Thus in the central sequence in the video, the word »girl« appears in the middle of a white screen and soon several tiny versions of the word »flies« are ›buzzing‹ around her. The word »baby« appears. A second later the word »husband« in very large letters falls on top of her, followed in quick succession by the appearance of »hunger« and »HIV«. This memorable chain of effects also serves to locate the causes of suffering (›hunger‹ and ›HIV‹) firmly and solely at the level of the local, the cultural (i.e. early marriage) and the individual, and in particular in the person (or concept) of the oppressive ›husband‹.

The role of the viewer as the powerful initiator of change, as responsible for releasing and directing the entrepreneurial agency, not in this case of individuals but of the »600 million girls in the developing world« is reaffirmed particularly strikingly here – the viewer is invited to »pretend that you can fix this« and as if at the click of a mouse, the ›girl's‹ ›burdens‹ (›flies‹, ›husband‹, ›baby‹ ...) fall away and the process of turning her into a microfinance entrepreneur who in turn banishes her community's poverty and generates global »stability« begins. The video is also marked by the speed with which the text appears and disappears and these processes of change are conveyed. This implicitly represents what is projected as

---

54   See http://www.youtube.com/watch?v=WIvmE4_KMNw; the following quotes are from ibid. (all letters are capitalised in the video).

the relative ›efficiency‹ of development initiatives which are directly corporate-led, and their compatibility with contemporary market-led globalisation. But it also works to construct the ›developing world‹ ›girl‹ as an ›investment‹ whose gendered and racialised propensity for labour can be instrumentalised to the point where her very life is speeded up: no sooner do we »put her in a school uniform« than we see her »get a loan to buy a cow« and »use the profits to help her family«. This is perhaps made clearest in the video's penultimate slogan: »Invest in a girl« we are urged, »and she will do the rest«.

In recent years, the focus on adolescent girls in the global South as the ›solution‹ to the ›problem‹ of development has been adopted and promoted much more widely by international development institutions. In 2007, UNICEF, UNIFEM and the WHO established the UN Interagency Task Force on adolescent girls. In 2008 the World Bank founded its Adolescent Girl Initiative, aimed at improving girls' and young women's economic opportunities. In 2010, the UK government announced that it would focus its development aid on girls and women.[55] Such interventions are increasingly represented as not only ›smart economics‹ (for which read beneficial for corporate capital) but also as an important weapon in the ›war on terror‹[56] and thus compatible with the contemporary imperialist project.

A striking aspect of the focus on adolescent girls has been the way in which ›girls‹ in the global North are directly addressed – primarily as consumers – by campaigns such as the ›Girl Effect‹ or the UN Foundation's ›Girl Up‹ campaign launched in 2010. »Via an extensive range of social media campaigns, ›roadshows‹ and merchandising promotions, girls in affluent societies, particularly the US, are hailed variously as the allies and saviours of their Southern ›sisters‹, using discourses of girl power and popular feminism«.[57] These campaigns reinforce racialised understandings of gender inequality which locate it exclusively in the global South: »First World girls are invited to endorse feminism but only in relation to the South. They themselves are seen as being the most empowered, socially connected and educated girls in history«. Further, whereas girls and women in ›developing‹ countries are increasingly represented as successfully saved from their earlier ›victim‹ status and transformed into hyper-entrepreneurial agents with an almost infinite capacity for labour, the capacity for collective and transformative, rather than entrepreneurial, agency is displaced onto apparently homogenous publics in the global

---

55 Rosalind Gill, Ofra Koffman: The revolution will be led by a 12-year-old girl.
56 Cf. Nicholas Kristof and Sheryl WuDunn: Half the Sky.
57 Rosalind Gill, Ofra Koffman: The Revolution Will be Led by a 12-year-old Girl; for the following quote see ibid.

North (and young people in particular). The latter are increasingly invited by development institutions using the language of ›revolution‹ to mobilise around agendas which are consistent with the needs of global capital.[58]

A particularly explicit example of these processes and their implications is the ›Kony 2012‹ video,[59] which went viral on the internet in March 2012.The video, produced by the US-based NGO Invisible Children, was part of a campaign for the arrest of Ugandan Joseph Kony, the leader of the armed group the Lord's Resistance Army, and his trial by the International Criminal Court for crimes against humanity, in particular, the abduction of thousands of children as soldiers. The video called for US military intervention in Central Africa to be stepped up in order to ›Stop Kony‹ and targeted young people in the global North to join a mass movement demanding this action.

Less than three weeks after being uploaded to the internet, ›Kony 2012‹ had been viewed by more than 84 million people through the targeting of superstars such as Rihanna and Oprah Winfrey who tweeted about it after being inundated by messages from teen fans. The video immediately generated intense controversy. Many commentators highlighted the fact that the video was heavily oversimplified and referred to a situation which had since changed drastically – Joseph Kony was no longer active in Uganda, and, it was argued, resources were more urgently needed to help ex-child soldiers to rebuild their lives than for the mission of capturing him. It was further pointed out that far from being reluctant to sustain a military presence in the region as the video suggests, the US administration had ongoing military involvement and significant strategic and economic interests in the area bordering Uganda, the DRC, the Central African Republic and Southern Sudan (the area where Kony has now fled), not least because of the existence of significant oil resources which are already being exploited by North American and British companies.[60] More generally, control over resources and governments in Africa has become, as the establishment of AFRICOM underlines, a geostrategic and economic priority for the US.[61]

The racism implicit in ›Kony 2012‹, which was seen as reproducing colonial narratives about Africa in which white people are constructed as having a moral obligation to intervene to rescue and ›save‹ black people from chaos, violence and irrationality was also highlighted.[62] Although the video is ostensibly about children in Uganda, the emotional core of the

---

58   Cf. Kalpana Wilson: Race, Racism and Development, pp. 187-197.
59   See http://www.youtube.com/watch?v=Y4MnpzG5Sqc.
60   Cf. F. William Engdahl: Invisible Children's Kony 2012 Video.
61   Cf. Tom Rollins: Kony 2012.
62   Cf. Teju Cole: The White Saviour Industrial Complex; ›Jessie‹: Kony 2012.

film is in fact the scene in which the white American filmmaker, Jason Russell, shows his five-year-old son a photograph of the ›bad guy‹ Joseph Kony, setting up a highly racialised dichotomy between the ›evil‹ black man and the innocent white child, who, once he understands the all-too-simple problem, can help to ›fix‹ it.

Building on this core dichotomy, the video (and another which followed in April 2012) appeals to Western teenagers to ›take action‹ by buying an ›action pack‹ of posters, bracelets and badges, or at least by ›sharing‹ the video. Consumption of merchandise as well as social media played an important role in participation in this ›movement‹ which critics argued had turned »the myopic worldview of the adolescent – ›if I don't know about it, then it doesn't exist, but if I care about it, then it is the most important thing in the world‹«[63] – into a justification for military intervention. In the narrative of ›Kony 2012‹, children in Uganda were ›invisible‹ until American high school and college students took note and made them ›visible‹, reproducing the colonial civilisational imperative.[64] The video goes on to deploy images of mass rallies of American youth dressed identically in ›Kony 2012‹ t-shirts shouting slogans and storming the White House and other symbols of state power. Meanwhile a voiceover intones a series of vague catchphrases about the power of social media, a »new generation of justice« and an end to »decisions made by the few with the money and the power«. This culminates in the disingenuous insistence that this is »a conflict where our national security or financial interests aren't at stake« which in turn allows the deployment of 100 US Army »advisors« in Uganda which had taken place in October 2011 to be hailed as a moral victory for »the people« who »demanded it, because it was right«.[65]

Both of the campaigns discussed in this section are marked by the increasing racialised construction of Northern publics as powerful collective agents with moral and civilisational obligations to intervene in the global South. The fact that the ›public‹ or even the favoured category of ›young people‹ in the global North is itself riven by conflicting interests and a highly unequal distribution of resources and power along lines of class, race and gender in particular, and that struggles taking place there are confronting the same forces which are ravaging the global South, is obliterated in this model. This actively reinforces the ›development/security‹ model of relations between people in the global North and South promoted by British and US governments, in which people in (or entering from) the South are identified primarily as a racialised threat to those in the North,

---

63 Kate Cronin-Furman, Amanda Taub: Solving War Crimes with Wristbands.
64 Cf. Dinaw Mengestu: Not a Click Away.
65 See http://www.youtube.com/watch?v=Y4MnpzG5Sqc (›Kony 2012‹).

which can only be neutralized through neoliberal forms of development dictated by these governments.

As we have argued in this chapter, racism in advertising and the wider questions of race and representation which it implies cannot simply be understood in terms of ›stereotypes‹ nor even is it enough to seek to understand these representations as the discursive products of colonial legacies. Racialised representations are shaped and re-shaped by political economy and changing strategies of global capital accumulation. We have seen how the targeting of markets in the global South as well as black communities in the global North led to changes in the tropes used in advertising, which however remained deeply racialised, drawing upon earlier representations. The languages and acts of resistance were absorbed into advertising rhetoric in order to trivialise or appropriate them. More recently the ›feminisation of survival‹ and capital's strategy of further intensifying the exploitation of women's labour in the global South under neoliberalism has led to changing gendered and racialised representations by development institutions and corporates. The promotion of fair trade and ›ethical consumption‹ has acted to normalise and legitimise global inequalities, generating – and allowing the Northern consumer to satisfy – a wider range of desires in the form of both actual consumption of goods and increased self-esteem. At the same time, understandings of ›race‹ have been both reshaped and reinscribed in attempts to counter sustained resistance. A key aspect of this has been the production of consumption-based models of social action which appropriate, depoliticise and redeploy representations of struggles for social transformation in ways that reproduce the racist and colonial ideologies of the civilising mission. However, even as these processes of appropriation occur, new forms of political organising and collective resistance inevitably challenge and expose them, opening up new possibilities for rethinking transnational solidarity.

References

Back, Les, Quaade Vibke: Dream Utopias, Nightmare Realities. Imagining Race and Culture within the World of Benetton Advertising. In: Third Text, 22, 1993, pp. 65-80.
Bristor, Julia M., Renée G. Lee, Michelle R. Hunt: Race and Ideology. African-American Images in Television Advertising. In: Journal of Public Policy & Marketing, 14, 1995, 1, pp. 48-59.
Buck-Morss, Susan: Hegel and Haiti. In: Critical Inquiry, 26, 2000, 4, pp. 821-865.
Chambers, Jason: Madison Avenue and the Color Line. African Americans in the Advertising Industry. Pennsylvania: University of Pennsylvania Press 2008.

Cherniavsky, Eva: Incorporations. Race, Nation and the Body Politics of Capital. Minneapolis: University of Minnesota Press 2006.
Cole, Teju: The White-Savior Industrial Complex. In: The Atlantic, 21.3.2012 (http://www.theatlantic.com/international/archive/2012/03/the-white-savior-industrial-complex/254843/).
Cronin-Furman, Kate, Amanda Taub: Solving War Crimes with Wristbands. The Arrogance of Kony 2012. In: The Atlantic, 8.3.2012 (http://www.theatlantic.com/international/archive/2012/03/solving-war-crimes-with-wristbands-the-arrogance-of-kony-2012/254193/).
Dyer, Richard: Heavenly Bodies. Basingstoke: MacMillan 1986.
Engdahl, F. William: Invisible Children's Kony 2012 Video. A Justication For More US AFRICOM Wars Over Oil. In: Global Research, 20.3.2012 (http://www.globalresearch.ca/invisible-children-s-kony-2012-video-a-justication-for-more-us-africom-wars-over-oil/29870).
Eze, Emmanuel C.: Hume, Race, and Human Nature. In: Journal of the History of Ideas, 61, 2000, 4, pp. 691-698.
—: Race and the Enlightenment. A Reader. Malden, MA: Blackwell 1997.
Frye, Marilyn: Oppression and the Use of Definition (http://zinelibrary.info/files/Frye.pdf – from id., The Politics of Reality. Essays in Feminist Theory. Trumansburg, NY: The Crossing Press 1983).
Gill, Rosalind, Ofra Koffman: ›The Revolution Will be Led by a 12-year-old Girl‹. Girl Power and Global Biopolitics. In: Youth Cultures in the Age of Global Media, ed. by David Buckingham, Sara Bragg, Mary Jane Kehily. Basingstoke: Palgrave Macmillan, forthcoming 2013.
Gilroy, Paul: The Black Atlantic. Modernity and Double Consciousness. London: Verso 1993.
Giroux, Henry A.: Benetton's ›World without Borders‹. Buying Social Change (http://www.csus.edu/indiv/o/obriene/art7/readings/benetton.htm – from: The Subversive Imagination. Artists, Society, and Social Responsibility, ed. by Carol Becker. New York: Routledge 1994).
—: Consuming Social Change: The ›United Colors of Benetton‹. In: Cultural Critique, 26, 1993/94, pp. 5-32.
Glass and a Half Productions: Cadbury Dairy Milk – Zingolo featuring Tinny [Full length – Official Version] 2009 (http://www.youtube.com/watch?v=hG-Kj9E1M6K4).
Goldberg, David T.: Racist Culture. Philosophy and the Politics of Meaning. London: Blackwell 1993.
Gregory, David: Fairtrade Hopes for Cadbury Cocoa Farmers in Ghana. BBC News, 31.8.2010 (http://www.bbc.co.uk/news/uk-england-11136797).
Hale, Charles: Neoliberal Multiculturalism. The Remaking of Cultural Rights and Racial Dominance in Central America. In: PoLAR, 28, 2005,1, pp. 10-19.
Hall, Stuart: The Spectacle of the ›Other‹. In: id. (ed.), Representation. Cultural Representations and Signifying Practices. London: Sage 1995. pp. 225-279.
Jaggar, Allison M.: Feminist Politics and Human Nature. Totowa, NJ: Rowman and Littlefield 1988.
James, Cyril Lionel Robert: The Black Jacobins. Toussaint Louverture and the San Domingo Revolution. London: Secker and Warburg 1938.

›Jessie‹: Kony 2012. Whiteness, Social Media and Africa. In: Racism Review, 15.3.2012 (http://www.racismreview.com/blog/2012/03/15/kony-2012-whiteness-social-media-africa/).

Kristof, Nicholas, Sheryl WuDunn: Half the Sky. Turning Oppression into Opportunity for Women Worldwide. New York: Vintage 2010.

Kempadoo, Kamala: Sexing the Caribbean. Gender, Race and Sexual Labor. London: Routledge 2004.

Kim Minjeong, Angie Y. Chung: Consuming Orientalism. Images of Asian-American Women in Multicultural Advertising. In: Qualitative Sociology, 28, 2005, 1, pp. 67-91.

Lenin, Vladimir Ilich: Imperialism, the Highest Stage of Capitalism. Peking: Foreign Languages Press 1975 [1st ed. 1916].

Littler, Jo: Radical Consumption. Shopping for Change in Contemporary Culture. Maidenhead: Open University Press 2009.

Luyt, Russell: Representation of Masculinities and Race in South African Television Advertising. A Content Analysis. In: Journal of Gender Studies, 2, 2012,1, pp. 35-60.

Melamed, Jodi: The Spirit of Neoliberalism. From Racial Liberalism to Neoliberal Multiculturalism. In: Social Text, 24, 2006, 4, pp. 1-24.

Mengestu, Dinaw: Not a Click Away – Joseph Kony in the Real World. In Warscapes (http://www.warscapes.com/reportage/not-click-away-joseph-kony-real-world).

Malefyt, Timothy de Waal, Brian Moeran: Advertising Cultures. Oxford: Berg 2003.

Mohanty, Chandra Talpade: Under Western Eyes. Feminist Scholarship and Colonial Discourses. In: Boundary 2, 12, 1986, 3, pp. 333-358.

Mösken, Anne Lena: Second Hand Scam. In: Exberliner, 31.1. 2012 (http://www.exberliner.com/articles/second-hand-scam/).

Nathanson-Moog, Carol: The Psychological Power of Ethnic Images in Advertising. In: Ethnic Images in Advertising. Philadelphia: The Balch Institute for Ethnic Studies 1984, pp. 19-22.

Nederveen Pieterse, Jan: White on Black. Images of Africa and Blacks in Western Popular Culture. Yale: Yale University Press 1992.

O'Barr, William: Culture and the Ad. Exploring Otherness in the World of Advertising. Boulder: Westview Press 1994.

Pires, Guilherme, P. John Stanton: Ethnic Marketing. Accepting the Challenge of Cultural Diversity. London: Thomson 2005.

Ramamurthy, Anandi: Absences and Silences: The Representation of the Tea Picker in Colonial and Fair Trade Advertising. In: Visual Culture in Britain, 13, 2012, 3, pp. 367-381.

—: Images of Industrialisation in Empire and Commonwealth During the Shift to Neo-Colonialism. In: Visual Culture and Decolonisation in Britain, ed. by id., Simon Faulkner. Aldershot: Ashgate 2006, pp. 43-70.

—: Imperial Persuaders. Images of Africa and Asia in British Advertising. Manchester: Manchester University Press 2003.

—: Spectacles and Illusions. Photography and Commodity Culture. In: Photography. A Critical Introduction, ed. by Liz Wells. London: Routledge 2008, pp. 253-256.

Rollins, Tom: Kony 2012. Don't be Fooled. In: New Statesman, 8.3.2012 (http://www.newstatesman.com/blogs/the-staggers/2012/03/africa-kony-uganda-military).

Ryan, Ted: The Making of ›I'd Like to Buy the World a Coke. In: Coca-Cola Journey, 1.1.2012 (http://www.coca-colacompany.com/stories/coke-lore-hilltop-story).

Sánchez Taylor, Jacqueline: Female Sex Tourism. A Contradiction in Terms? In: Feminist Review, 2006, 83, pp. 42-59.

Ward, Adrienne: What Role Do Ads Play in Racial Tension? In: Advertising Age, 63, 1992, 1, p. 35.

Waxman, Sharon: Benetton Laid Bare. In: Miami Herald, 8.2.1993.

Wilson, Kalpana: ›Race‹, Gender and Neoliberalism. Changing Visual Representations in Development. In: Third World Quarterly, 32, 2011, 2, pp. 315-331.

—: Race, Racism and Development. Interrogating History, Discourse and Practice. London: Zed Books 2012.

World Bank: Gender Action Plan, 2007-2010 (http://siteresources.worldbank.org/INTGENDER/Resources/GAPNov2.pdf).

—: World Development Report 2012. Gender Equality and Development. Washington DC: The World Bank 2011.

Studies

Buffalo Bill's ›Wild West‹
The Racialisation of the Cosmopolitan Imagination
Robert W. Rydell

Abstract: In the late Victorian era, few figures and fewer shows were better known on both sides of the Atlantic Ocean than Buffalo Bill and his Wild West. Often considered by scholars in terms of the show's racism and imperialism, this essay examines the intersection of both of these ideological formations with another, cosmopolitanism, and examines how, through its performances and representations in poster art, the Wild West, especially after it merged with Pawnee Bill's Great Far East spectacle, needs to be rethought in terms of modernisation, globalisation, and the commodity racism of its visual representations.

Between the late 1880s and the cusp of America's involvement in the First World War, Buffalo Bill's Wild West[1] made multiple tours of Europe (ranging north to south between Scotland and Italy and travelling west to east between Belgium and Hungary) and circumnavigated most of the United States. By the time of his death in 1917, when something like a state funeral took place for him in Denver, Colorado, Buffalo Bill and his wild west shows had become iconic representations of the American West for millions on both sides of the Atlantic.[2]

But, we need to rethink the significance of the Wild West less as a staging ground for nostalgic, escapist representations of the American frontier than as a staging ground for modernity, especially for promoting a new, modern cosmopolitan understanding of the world with long-dominant, but

---

1   Cody always insisted that his show was not a show and that it was an ›authentic‹ representation of the American West; he called it simply ›The Wild West‹.
2   Scholarly literature about Buffalo Bill is increasingly rich. The most comprehensive study is Louis Warren: Buffalo Bill's America. Other important overviews include Joy S. Kasson: Buffalo Bill's Wild West; Paul Reddin: Wild West Shows; and, Sarah J. Blackstone: Buckskins, Bullets, and Business. Two important interpretations are provided by Richard Slotkin: Buffalo Bill's ›Wild West‹ and the Mythologisation of the American Empire; and, Richard White: Frederick Jackson Turner and Buffalo Bill. On the show's importance for cosmopolitanism, see Jonathan D. Martin: ›The Grandest and Most Cosmopolitan Object Teacher‹. A useful introduction to issues in the study of cosmopolitanism is Garrett Wallace Brown and David Held (eds.): The Cosmopolitan Reader.

ever-evolving images that fixed expectations about how people racialised as ›others‹ were expected to perform on the world stage that this show did so much to construct. In ways both subtle and not so subtle, the show itself and the commodity advertising it generated tethered emerging, modern ways of thinking about the world in cosmopolitan, intercultural and multicultural, terms to older naturalised categories of race in order to advance the policies of both imperial and neo-imperial nation-states.

Political Biography

Before making the case that Buffalo Bill's Wild West needs to be considered in terms of its ideological innovations, it is useful to begin with a short biography of Buffalo Bill and short history of the show(s) that bore his name. Buffalo Bill was born William F. Cody in Iowa Territory in 1847. His parents were steadfast opponents of slavery and not just opposed to its expansion into the western territories. After moving to Kansas, Cody's father was stabbed after giving an anti-slavery speech and died shortly thereafter. During the American Civil War, Cody joined a US cavalry regiment and subsequently worked as a ›scout‹ and hunter for railroads, supplying railroad workers with bison meat. In one year alone, by his own estimate, with the help of his trusty gun (which he named Lucretia Borgia after a popular opera based on a Victor Hugo libretto), he killed some 4,000 bison, earning him the nickname Buffalo Bill that would stay with him for the rest of his life.

In 1869, Cody's exploits as a buffalo hunter came to attention of Ned Buntline, the *nom de plume* of a popular dime novelist. Buntline wrote a story about Cody's shooting prowess that transformed Buffalo Bill into an overnight sensation and propelled him onto the New York stage for a short career as an actor performing plays about his own life. Then, with the outbreak of wars against the Indians on the upper plains following the Battle of the Little Big Horn, Cody resumed his role as an army scout. Three weeks after Custer's death at the Battle of the Little Big Horn or, as Native Americans refer to it, the Battle of Greasy Grass, Cody killed, or contributed to the killing, of Cheyenne chief Hay-o-Wei and scalped him, shouting: »The first scalp for Custer«.[3] By now Cody was totally in tune with the theatrical possibilities of his life, and he immediately set to work writing an autobiography and his own dime novels, but he knew that the real money was in theatre.

---

3   Joy Kasson: Buffalo Bill's Wild West, p. 38.

The problem was how to capture the expanse of American West and the drama of killing Indians on Broadway. The stage was just too small. Probably influenced by rodeos and P. T. Barnum's efforts to launch an outdoor rodeo drama in the 1840s, Cody hit upon the idea for a show that, in 1883, he incorporated as ›Buffalo Bill's Wild West, America's National Entertainment‹. It played to full houses in Madison Square Garden. But Cody and his public relations team were not satisfied. In 1886, Cody's manager, Nate Salsbury, had the good fortune to meet the despondent promoters of an American international exhibition that had been scheduled to open in London that same year. The problem was that the organisers of this spectacle had lied about the support of political and business leaders in both England and the US. And, to make matters worse, when the show's opening looked like it would conflict with the British Government's colonial exhibition about India, the show's promoters were in a real bind. As they struggled to keep their plans alive, they traveled to Washington, D.C. and were getting nowhere until, by chance, they met with Cody's manager, Salsbury, whose chief claim to fame before the Wild West was as a performer and producer of blackface minstrel entertainment. Over dinner, Salsbury and the organisers of the American Exhibition, struck a deal – they agreed to make ›Buffalo Bill's Wild West‹ the star attraction at their exhibition that they would reschedule to open in 1887.

When the ›State of Nebraska‹ steamship left New York's docks, it attracted, thanks to Salsbury's work with New York newspapers, a great deal of attention. As well it should. Its entourage included »83 saloon passengers, 38 steerage passengers, 97 Indians, 180 horses, 18 buffalo, 10 elk, 5 Texan steers, 4 donkeys, and 2 deer«.[4] That the troupe performed blackface shows on board has not been discussed often enough and probably should be because it tells us something about Cody's ›Wild West‹ being born in the wider context of racist popular entertainments (it is worth nothing that Salsbury, in 1895, organized ›Black America‹, an outdoor minstrel show that featured about 500 African American performers).[5]

As the steamship made its way across the Atlantic, Cody's publicity team in London began plastering the city with billboards announcing the show's arrival. Once it was set up outside the Earl's Court in London's East End, the encampment became the hot spot for London's smart set. The prime minister made it a point to meet Cody and several of the Indians. Then, just four days before the opening of the show, the Prince of Wales, renowned ladies' man, showed up for an advance preview. He was

4   Quoted in Robert W. Rydell, Rob Kroes: Buffalo Bill in Bologna, p. 106.
5   Richard W. Etulain: Telling Western Stories, p. 17; see also, Roger Allan Hall: ›Black America‹.

so impressed that he returned to the palace to tell his mother, one Queen Victoria, that she really should attend a performance. She went one better. She *commanded* a performance – one that took place on May 11th and made news across the Empire.

What happened was this: When the show began with a rider carrying an American flag into the arena, the Queen supposedly stood up (which meant everyone else in the audience stood as well). As Cody recalled the moment: »All present were constrained to feel that here was an outward and visible sign of the extinction of that mutual prejudice, amounting sometimes almost to race hatred, that had severed [England and the United States] from the time of George the Third to the present day. We felt that the hatchet was buried at last and the Wild West had been at the funeral«. At this moment, the Wild West, a form of American mass culture, had become an instrument of foreign policy both in England and the United States.

Before heading home to the US, Cody booked a return engagement – this time to the European continent. It began with a stint at the 1889 Paris Universal Exposition. From Paris, the Wild West headed south. Somewhere enroute, Cody renamed the show. It was now ›Buffalo Bill's Wild West and Congress of Rough Riders of the World‹. And it included equestrian acts from the Middle East. The show traveled as far south as Rome, where the ›Wild West‹ performers received a special blessing from the Pope![6]

Over the next two decades, the Wild West traveled the United States and Europe, becoming a virtual-reality show with its themes constantly updated to reflect current events. A couple of examples should suffice. In 1898, the show advanced the cause America's war with Spain by taking as its theme ›Westward the Course of Empire‹ and included this paean to the moral worth of the rifle: »The bullet is the pioneer of civilization, for it has gone hand in hand with the axe that cleared the forest, and with the family Bible and school book. Deadly as has been its mission in one sense, it has been merciful in another; for without the rife-ball we of America would not be to-day in the possession of a free and united country, and mighty in our strength. And it so has been in the history of all people, from the time when David slew Goliath, down through the long line of ages until in modern times science has substituted for the stone from David's sling the terrible missiles that now decide the fate of nations«.[7]

---

6   The preceding summary of Buffalo Bill's life is drawn from Robert W. Rydell, Rob Kroes: Buffalo Bill in Bologna, pp. 29-34, 105-119.
7   Quoted in Jack Rennert: 100 Posters of Buffalo Bill's Wild West, p. 9.

During the run-up and immediate aftermath of the war with Spain, the Wild West shaped the cultural context for depicting and remembering that war with specific intertextual references. Teddy Roosevelt, long an admirer of the show, probably took the name ›Rough Riders‹ from the Wild West and Cody returned the favour with a poster depicting Roosevelt's ›charge‹ up San Juan Hill and by including members of the Rough Riders in the performances for his 1899 season.[8]

Contested Readings of the Show

To suggest that the Wild West played a constitutive role in shaping American political culture does not seem like an overstatement. When, however, scholars have turned their attention to the actual performances that took place there is little agreement about how to read them, especially with respect to performances by Native Americans. During its thirty-year run, the show employed hundreds of Native Americans, mostly, but not exclusively Sioux. They were paid for their performances, entered into individual contracts that earned them more money than they would have received on reservations, and were generally well-treated by Cody even to the extent that he would pay the expenses home for at least some of the Indian performers who became ill while they toured Europe. The nub of disagreement among scholars, however, is not whether Buffalo Bill was, as he claimed, »a friend of the Indians«,[9] but the degree to which Indian performers, men, women, and some children, used the show to preserve their own cultural identities and advance their own economic well being, becoming what historian Lester George Moses calls professional »show Indians«. As Moses puts it: »Buffalo Bill saw the employment of Indians in the shows as a method to ease the transition of a proud and capable people to the cultural demands of the majority«.[10] Liminal to the core, the performative spaces of the ›Wild West‹ afforded room for native performers to negotiate at least some of their terms for their survival during an era in American history that was bounded by government policies that alternated between ethnic cleansing and forced assimilation.

This argument has the advantage of giving Indians agency apart from the Pine Ridge Agency, Crow Agency, and other ›agencies‹ set up by the government to eradicate their cultures. But, for all of the growing evidence

---

8 Richard White: Frederick Jackson Turner and Buffalo Bill, pp. 50 ff.
9 This phrase recurs in many popular accounts of the showman. See, for instance, ›New York Times‹, 20.9. 1987 (›Opinion‹).
10 Lester George Moses: Wild West Shows and the Images of American Indians, p. 8.

we have about the Indian performers (we know many of their names and tribal affiliations and have a growing archive of portrait and collective photographs and motion picture images),[11] we do not have evidence that the Indian performers scripted the shows in which they participated. And the contracts that the Indians signed left them little room to manoeuvre.

Take for instance the 1905 contract between Buffalo Bill and his then partner, circus impresario James Bailey, and Dreaming Bear and her two children. Under the terms of the contract, the Wild West would pay Dreaming Bear $10 per month, but $4 was held in trust by the showmen until the end of the season and would only be paid after Dreaming Bear and her children returned to the Pine Ridge Reservation. The contract further stipulated that Dreaming Bear's travel expenses would be paid along with »needful medical attendance« and that the Wild West would »protect [Dreaming Bear] from all immoral influences and surroundings« and that she would agree »to keep sober«. Dreaming Bear, the contract made clear, would be supplied with »proper food and raiment, except one set of Indian Clothes, Head Dress, moccasins, etc.«

An identical contract was issued on the same date to Casey Red Shirt with the only difference occurring in the pay: Red Shirt would receive $21 per month. In both contracts, the most salient language appeared in the opening lines with the clear statement that the performer would »accompany the exhibition [...] for exhibition purposes in Europe, the object being to give public exhibitions of American Frontier Life« and that the performer »agrees to do whatever in reason and justice may be required of him while in the services of the [show], and which may be necessary and incident to such exhibition, not inconsistent with the laws of morality and the ordinary rules of propriety«.[12] If this was not exactly indentured servitude, it certainly was not a model of »free agency«.[13]

The upshot was that Indians were hired to perform in and not script the shows. And there is no evidence that, whether they were hired to do so or not, they ever had a hand in scripting the narratives of the performances. The result was that Indians, while certainly ›making do‹ on the road, enacted often twice-daily performances of the conquest of the American frontier by whites that reinforced dominant white views of Indians as savages who were likely doomed to extinction. Whatever psychological benefits they derived from mock attacks on white travellers racing around the arena in the Deadwood Stage or from surrounding hapless setters in

---

11 See, for instance, Michelle Delaney: Buffalo Bill's Wild West Warriors.
12 [Contracts], 9 March 1905, Buffalo Bill Papers, McCracken Research Library, Buffalo Bill Historical Center [cited hereafter as BBHC], MS. 6, Business Series.
13 Lester G. Moses: Wild West Shows and the Images of American Indians, p. 175.

log cabins, Indian performers, day in and day out, enacted narratives that Cody and his managers intended to reinforce white supremacist fantasies of savagery and of the ›vanishing Indian‹.

Why did Indians perform with Buffalo Bill in these enactments? Moses is surely right to argue that the conditions of the shows were better than on the reservations. And he is surely right to argue that the shows provided Indians with an opportunity to preserve their cultural identities – their languages, their sacred beliefs, and their music – at precisely the time the federal government and Indian reformers were assaulting all of these underpinnings of native cultures. Moses has the support of other scholars, for instance, Vine Deloria, who argues that the show »provided a platform for displaying natural ability that transcended racial and political antagonisms and, when, contrasted with other contemporary attitudes towards Indians, represented one that was amazingly‹ sophisticated and liberal«.[14] But the performances, with so much of their stagecraft informed by dominant white supremacist values, had the effect of reinforcing, through patterns of repetition, the very racism that the ›Wild West‹ and other forms of popular entertainment were designed to perpetuate and instill in mass audiences.

One could, of course, argue that Indian performers were engaged in ›ironic‹ engagement with dominant racist values. Or, one could argue that the involvement of Indians in enacting narratives of ›savagery‹ paralleled what some African American entertainers did in order to survive as performing artists when they composed music and lyrics for one of the most offensive (and popular) musical genres of the later Victorian era on both sides of the Atlantic, the ›coon song‹. When asked about his hit song of 1896, ›All Coons Look Alike to Me‹, African American composer Ernest Hogan later admitted that »the song caused a lot of trouble in and out of show business, but it was also good for show business because at the time money was short [... and] [t]hat one song opened the way for a lot of colored and white songwriters«.[15] African American poet Paul Laurence Dunbar likely would have agreed. He collaborated with African American composer Will Marion Cook on an operetta, ›In Dahomey‹, probably based on the Dahomeyan Village at the 1893 fair, that helped both men secure a living, but was no less demeaning of African Americans and likely exacerbated Dunbar's alcoholism and precipitated his early death.[16]

Why did Native American and African American performers collaborate with the white managers of wild west shows and white publishers

---

14 Vine Deloria, Jr: The Indians, pp. 53 f.
15 Ernest Hogan quoted in Maurice Peress: Dvorak to Duke Ellington, p. 39.
16 Cf. John Bush Jones: Our Musicals, Ourselves, pp. 33 ff., Jeffrey P. Green: ›In Dahomey‹ in London in 1903.

of ›coon songs‹? Any answer is complicated, but surely must be tied to understanding just how oppressive racism – both as ideology *and* practice – was for people of colour. For Native Americans, the implementation of racist attitudes meant ethnic cleansing; for African Americans it meant lynching. To be sure, performers had choices. Indians, for instance, could have chosen not to perform and risk enduring the full brunt of the government's assimilationist policies – and starvation – on the reservations. And some may well have chosen to perform in the shows and ›act out‹ resistive strategies in their performances (which some doubtless did when they encircled and threatened the Deadwood Stage and settlers' cabin). Whether such repetitive enactments of resistance (and defeat at the hand of Buffalo Bill and white military units who always rode to the rescue) were empowering is worth carefully considering, especially in light of the experience of African American artists with music that became »soundtracks of empire«.[17]

There is another possibility with respect to the appeal of the ›Wild West‹ for Native Americans – one that is closely linked to the increased globalisation of the show in the 1890s and the opening decades of the twentieth century. Quite simply, as it became increasingly cosmopolitan and multicultural in its representation of different cultures as part of its efforts to promote western imperialism, the ›Wild West‹ afforded in its living spaces for performers from around the world the possibility of intermingling with people with different degrees of access to power in their own countries. In the living spaces of the show where performers ate, played, slept, and conversed, ample opportunities existed to find openings in the seams of dominant racist and imperial ideologies. Importantly, these seams ran along the loosely stitched points of intersection between performers of different cultures who, by the early 1890s, had transformed the ›Wild West‹ into »the Congress of Rough Riders of the World«.

For example, for the 1893 ›Wild West‹ exhibition that was held a short walk from Chicago's World's Columbian Exposition, Cody's managers assembled skilled riders, including, as historian Joy Kasson has noted, »Mexican vaqueros, Syrian and Arabian horsemen, Russian cossacks, Argentinean gauchos, and military units from Germany, England, and France«.[18] Over the next two decades, troupes of Zouaves, Hawaiians, Filipinos, Cubans, Persians, Sikhs, Africans, and Japanese performed in what, by design and in effect, became a virtual imperial reality show, translating the imperial news of the day into outdoor theatre. For instance,

---

17 For further analysis of these issues, see Robert W. Rydell: Soundtracks of Empire.
18 Joy Kasson: Buffalo Bill's Wild West, p. 111.

the Boxer Rebellion inspired a performance in Buffalo Bill's ›Wild West‹ called ›The Rescue at Pekin‹ where the walls surrounding the city were scaled by performers representing an alliance of European colonial powers (along with Sikh allies) and American military units who, in turn, routed the Chinese insurgents, played, in this case by Native Americans with their hair braided in pigtails.[19]

Herein lies a story worth telling and one hinted at by one of the Native American performers, Black Elk, who, in 1887, joined the Wild West when it traveled to England. According to Black Elk, when Cody's agents arrived at the reservation seeking performers to journey overseas, Black Elk, having lived and fought through the horrors of the warfare on the Upper Plains that would culminate in 1890 with the massacre of Indians at Wounded Knee, South Dakota, determined that the ›Wild West‹ afforded an interesting opportunity. »I thought I should go«, he recalled, »because I might learn some secret of the Wasichu that would help my people somehow«. »Maybe«, he reflected, »if I could see the great world of the Wasichu, I could understand how to bring the sacred hoop together and make the tree to bloom at the center of it«. When Queen Victoria visited the show at Earl's Court, she underscored what many Indians already knew, namely that divisions existed among whites about how to treat the Indians. »If I owned you Indians, you good-looking people«, Black Elk recalled her telling the assembled Indians, »I would never take you around in a show like this. You have a Grandfather over there who takes care of you [...], but he shouldn't allow this, for he owns you, for the white people to take you around as beasts to show to the people«.[20] Black Elk was likely not alone in realising that the seams in the racist canvas of the Wild West were not exactly a tightly closed-stitch.

Indeed, as historian Louis Warren has noted, life on the road for Wild West performers involved multiple transgressions of multiple borders. Black Elk evidently fell in love with an English woman during the show's 1887 tour and hoped she would return to the US with him. Another performer, Luther Standing Bear fell in love and married Louise Rieneck who had been his nurse in a Vienna hospital when the performer was recovering from injuries incurred during a show.[21] And, although performers tended to dine with members of their own ethnic groups, there were ample opportunities for actors from around the world to socialise and interact. These interactions were not always positive as, for instance, when a cowboy used a wire rope to lasso some of the African boys who, along with their par-

---

19 Paul Reddin: Wild West Shows, p. 135.
20 John G. Neihardt: Black Elk Speaks, p. 182.
21 Cf. Louis A. Warren: Buffalo Bill's America, pp. 390-396.

ents, acted in the show. But the show featured cowboys who, themselves, were bi-racial descendents of white Americans and Sioux or other Native American tribes. The same held for the gauchos, descendents of Spanish and indigenous populations of Latin America, who joined the show in the early 1890s. In ways never intended by the show's managers, the ›Wild West‹, in the daily lives of performers, reflected the reality of a potentially restive and resistive population of subalterns who refused to think of themselves simply as colonial subjects, objects, or victims.[22]

The Cosmopolitan Challenge and the ›Power of the Poster‹

Given these realities, both the performers and the show's message had to be carefully managed. On both counts, the show's organisers proved up to the challenge. To chaperone the indigenous performers when they left their living quarters to visit towns, Cody and his managers relied on one of the cowboy performers who had served in the Civil War as a union soldier. The show's management also relied on translators and indigenous impresarios like the West African John Tevi who had worked with French colonial promoters to organise Dahomeyan Villages at world's fairs since at least the 1893 World's Columbian Exposition.[23] The Dahomeyans' armed resistance to French imperialism could not have been lost on Cody's management team both in terms of being an attraction in a show dedicated to colonial conquest in outposts of empire and as a potential problem along the lines of the anti-colonial meetings that took place at French world's fairs around the turn of the century when performers from the colonies took to meeting together to compare notes about colonial oppression and resistance.[24]

To forestall any sympathies that the »artful deceptions«[25] of performers might elicit from the show's audiences, Cody and his management team developed their own brand of artistry through graphic designers who produced thousands of posters and billboards that contained the unruly cosmopolitanism of performers in formulaic repetitions of racist stereotypes, making available to passers-by, at a glance, the assertion that the emergence of an increasingly globalised world would be one in which people could be expected to live up to and enact their racialised identities.

---

22 Both Lester George Moses: Wild West Shows and the Images of American Indians, pp. 277 ff. and Louis A. Warren: Buffalo Bill's America, pp. 397-416 make these points.
23 Cf. Robert W. Rydell: Africans in America.
24 Mabel O. Wilson: Negro Building, p. 115.
25 The phrase is from Louis A. Warren: Buffalo Bill's America, p. 397.

To put this in slightly different terms, distilling the old wine of racism into new bottles labeled cosmopolitanism became fundamental to the task of ideological innovation within the ›Wild West‹. To rebrand the show as a cosmopolitan commodity and make it seem relevant for understanding rapidly changing global events, Cody and his management team turned to their stable of highly talented lithographers.

Coming to the ›Wild West‹ as they did through theatre, Cody and his managers had always understood the »power of the poster«, to borrow a phrase from Margaret Timmers.[26] Indeed, by the middle of the nineteenth century, any theatre impresario understood the value of plastering public places with ›bill-stickers‹. The value of poster-art only increased with the advent of Jules Cheret's high-speed printing presses that enabled the mass production of color lithographs. Cody and his associates were certainly familiar with the medium and its associated technologies, but, as Jack Rennert has insisted, the relationship between the lithographers and Cody was much closer than one might think. Cody always insisted on extremely high-quality productions that would make his posters stand out on walls and fences otherwise plastered with billboards.[27] So attentive was Cody to the artistry that went into the design of the ›Wild West‹ posters that one American artist, Max Bachmann, inscribed a print to Cody, commending Buffalo Bill for being »the pioneer of realism in American art«.[28]

Cody, Rennert notes, personally knew many artists and designers who understood the value of a contract for the Wild West for their own careers and economic well-being. To negotiate the contracts and assure the quality of the productions, Cody relied on his general agent, Louis E. Cook. Cook, in turn, worked with about a dozen design firms, sometimes using multiple firms to generate posters (generally single sheets) and billboards (generally multiple sheets) for a single ›Wild West‹ season. The returns could be lucrative: the show distributed as many as 500,000 posters in a single season. And they could be visually overpowering in terms of their sheer dimensions – one billboard produced for the 1899 season contained over 168 individual sheets and measured 9 feet tall by 143 feet wide! Usually two weeks before the show arrived in a town, an advance team would set up stands to accommodate the larger boards and put brush and paste plastering posters everywhere possible within two hundred miles of the town where a performance would take place. This was true on both sides of the Atlantic. As one English newspaper complained in a ditty about the show: »I may walk lit, or ›bus‹ it, or hansom it; still | I am faced by the features

26 Margaret Timmers (ed.): The Power of the Poster.
27 Catherine Haill: Pleasure and Leisure, p. 70.
28 Quoted in Jack Rennert: 100 Posters of Buffalo Bill's Wild West, p. 4.

of Buffalo Bill, | Every hoarding is plastered, from East-end to West, | With his hat, coat, and countenance, lovelocks and vest«.[29]

Plastered around towns and the countryside, Wild West posters caused circus managers to complain about the lack of space for their own advertisements. And, because of their scale and design quality, as Rennert explains, a ›Wild West‹ poster »would surely attract the attention of every single individual who came within sight of it. In fact, the billboards became tourist attractions in their own right and their sheer size gave them an undeniable force« as imperial commodities.[30]

So, how exactly did this »undeniable force« operate? Margaret Timmers offers an explanation, insisting: »Above all, [posters] communicate through the accessibility and adaptability of their graphic vocabulary. Posters address us in everyday contemporary language, and appeal to us with directly compelling imagery. Through the distillation process which is part of their creative form, they have the ability to embody complicated thoughts and messages with a concentration of imagery akin to poetry«.[31] At a glance, visitors could gain insights into what to expect when the show came to town – and what to expect in an increasingly cosmopolitan world fraught with imperial conflict and natural forces needing to be tamed. And what they could expect, at least as far as the posters suggested, was a world that, for all of its changes and upheavals, could still be understood by adhering to fixed racial categories made visible and essentialised through the artistry of poster designers. More than this, these posters constituted a performative dimension in their own right, for, as Anne McClintock explains in her work about imperial and racist commodities: »Commodity racism became distinct from scientific racism in its capacity to expand beyond the literate, propertied elite through the marketing of commodity spectacle«.[32] Posters enacted representations of racial difference, making categories of race legible, all the while occluding all references to contemporary forms of colonial labour whether on Indian reservations or in formal or informal colonies of western imperial powers. Falling into the category of what McClintock terms »commodity jingoism«, the posters became part of the common currency of visual images that aestheticised and modernised categories of human difference in racist terms.

Take, for instance, the 1898 lithograph produced by the Courier Company in Buffalo, New York with its masthead, ›Buffalo Bill's Wild West and Congress of Rough Riders of the World‹, and subtitle: ›Wild Rival-

29 Quoted in ibid, p. 5.
30 Ibid., pp. 4 f.
31 Margaret Timmers (ed.): The Power of the Poster, p. 8.
32 Anne McClintock: Imperial Leather, p. 209; for the following quote see ibid.

Buffalo Bill's ›Wild West‹

Fig. 1: Posters reflected and advanced the ›Wild West's‹ efforts to racialise the imagination

ries of Savage, Barbarous and Civilized Races‹ (see fig. 1).³³ As Rennert describes it, the poster shows »a kind of summation« of previous posters produced by the Courier Company that »had featured individual national horsemen and now show them together in one scene«, showing »from left to right, the South American Gaucho, the American Cow-boy, the Mexico Vaquero, the Cossack, the American Indian, and the Arab Horseman« riding across the plains with Buffalo Bill and Annie Oakley at the head of the pack. What makes this poster work visually, Rennert writes, are the »well-delineated facial expressions – both of horse and rider«.³⁴ What makes its message clear is that the different riders, including the sea-green-hued American Indian, are identified specifically in the subtitle as ›races‹.

No less emphatic in its deployment of racial categories to contain a world in motion was the ›Race of Races, the Show of Shows‹ produced in 1895 by the Springer Lithographic Company to advertise Buffalo Bill's show after Cody took on as his partner circus owner James A. Bailey and developed one of the first traveling shows to rely on electrical lighting. Although the masthead ›Lighter than Day‹ certainly evokes the show's emphasis on electric lights, the narrative flow of the poster – from Indian

---

33 ›Buffalo Bill's Wild West and Congress of Rough Riders of the World; Wild Rivalries of Savage, Barbarous and Civilized Races‹, poster, Library of Congress, Prints and Photographs Division.
34 Jack Rennert: 100 Posters of Buffalo Bill's Wild West, p. 11.

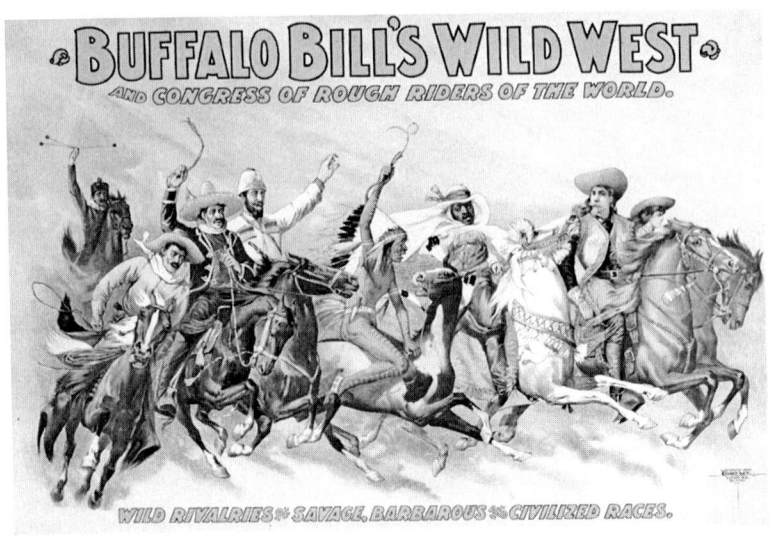

*Fig. 2: By the late 1880s, the Wild West
was advancing imperial narratives in the form of commodity spectacles*

attacks on the Deadwood Stage, to the slightly menacing depiction of the Middle Eastern rider seeming to cut off the others, to the reassuring panel depicting the Indians being routed by the U.S. cavalry – reinforces the impression of the modern world as ›race of races‹ requiring the vigilance of Buffalo Bill astride his horse with his gun at the ready.[35]

There are, of course, multiple examples of similar renditions of racial profiling. The 1899 Courier Company poster advertising ›Buffalo Bill's Wild West and Congress of Rough Riders of the World‹ carries the subheading, ›The Real Sons of the Soudan, Whose Brawn and Muscle Have Amazed the World‹ (see fig. 2).[36] The show promised »marvelous horsemanship, athletic achievements, gun spinning and pyramid building« – veritable exotic whirling dervishes – all the while being superintended, the poster suggested, by Buffalo Bill depicted off to the right standing tall in his saddle.[37]

The artistic deployment of racial categories, sometimes subtle, sometimes dramatic, also appeared in the posters advertising performances that promised to make sense out of contemporary world events. Posters depicting performances within the Wild West shows of Cuban insurgents'

---

35 Cf. ibid.
36 ›Buffalo Bill's Wild West. The Real Sons of the Soudan‹, poster, Library of Congress, Prints and Photographs Division.
37 Jack Rennert: 100 Posters of Buffalo Bill's Wild West, p. 11.

victory over Spanish soldiers had to navigate the boundaries of Cuban and Spanish racial identities and did so by drawing subtle distinctions between representations of Spanish soldiers and civilians as cowardly, shadowy racial degenerates unable to withstand the assaults of machete-wielding Cubans who were depicted in the American popular press of the mid-1890s as »screaming with the voice of Indians« as they charged Spanish troops.[38]

Wild West poster artists drew on these popular accounts to make clear that in the contest between ›savagery‹ and ›degeneracy‹, savagery held the upper hand. As if to underscore the usefulness of racial categories for mapping the world, the programme for the 1900 season offered this racial explanation of the origins of the South American Gauchos who joined the ›Congress of Rough Riders‹. »The Gauchos are the descendants of the early colonizers of the South American wilds«, the programme noted. »The fiery Hispanian temperament [sic], the infusion of native Indian blood, together with the wild lonely life on the ocean-like pampas, are the conditions responsible for the production of the Gauchos«. »The civilization that the Spanish colonists took with them to the Llanos gradually became subdued by the savagery of the new situation«, the programme further explained, »until their descendants, the Gauchos, were as wild and ferocious as the aborigines, the Indians«. The result, the programme added, was the creation of what amounted to a new breed, »a near approach to the mythical centaur«, carrying the Gaucho's association with the »wild equines« to »even a more intense degree than any of the equestrian races« that the programme had earlier identified as »the North American Indian, the Cowboy, the Vaquero, the Cossack, and the Prairie Scout«.[39]

The naturalisation of race suggested by these descriptions was nothing new in the graphic designs that Cody used to promote the Wild West. Since the show's beginnings, animals and natural landscapes had featured prominently in the performances themselves as well as in the show's advertising. Images of cowboys riding or saddling bucking mustangs and steers were as commonplace as landscapes of soaring mountain peaks or spreading prairie grasses that provided backdrops for renditions of mock battles between cowboys and Indians. Because his show was billed as an ›authentic‹ representation of the American West, one could simply regard these images as part of the naturalistic décor and leave it at that. But very little in the show was innocent of intention or effect. It is worth remembering that, according to historian Jonathan Spiro, at precisely the same time that this show was reaching its apex of popularity, ›old stock‹ American

---

38 John Lawrence Tone: The Machete and the Liberation of Cuba, p. 10.
39 Quoted in Jack Rennert: 100 Posters of Buffalo Bill's Wild West, p. 8.

elites who traced their ancestry and wealth back to the ›Mayflower‹ were beginning to raise concerns about the degeneracy of ›trophy‹ big game animals in the American West.⁴⁰ Many of the same individuals, Madison Grant, Henry Fairfield Osburn, and George Bird Grinnell to name a few, »suddenly realized that *Homo sapiens* was itself an endangered species«. Led by Madison Grant, they spearheaded the development of a new movement intended to unite concerns about ›breeding‹ with racial degeneration. That movement, of course, was eugenics.

Coined by Francis Galton in 1883, the same year Buffalo Bill first incorporated his show, eugenics promoted the ›science‹ of race betterment and took hold on both sides of the Atlantic by the beginning of the twentieth century among elites worried about racial degeneracy and about the deterioration and extinction of the largest and best of the wild animal populations of the United States. With mounting concerns in the United States about, as M.I.T President Francis Walker argued, »the *replacement* of native by foreign stock«,⁴¹ the American eugenics movement succeeded in securing federal immigration restriction laws, culminating in the 1924 National Origins Act, as well as in passing state laws that promoted the sterilisation of the ›unfit‹ and prohibited sexual intercourse between people of allegedly different racial backgrounds.

To my knowledge, there is no evidence that Cody actively promoted the eugenics programme per se, but his efforts to profile different ›racial types‹ enacting fantasies of racial conquest against backdrops depicting the vanishing frontier and vanishing people (like Indians) and animals (like bison) helps make it possible to understand why, in 1920, three years after Cody's death, an article appeared in ›Eugenical News‹ purporting to detail »The Traits of Buffalo Bill«. These included Cody's own »pioneer stock«, his »lively visual imagination«, and, above all, that »love of excitement and danger [that] is part of the instinct of fighting, which is elemental, since it is useful in securing the desired mate«.⁴² Could Buffalo Bill have served as a poster child for the eugenics movement?

As this article made clear, as far as the eugenicists were concerned, he was a contender. But however useful his life story may have been (bearing in mind that his adventurousness would have seemed problematic to eugenicists after the First World War in which Europe's allegedly superior races got caught up in the spirit of adventure and slaughtered each other!), Cody's more important contribution to shaping the cultural landscape in

---

40 Cf. Jonathan Spiro: Defending the Master Race, 2009; for the following quote see ibid., p. 58.
41 Quoted in ibid., p. 98.
42 Traits of Buffalo Bill, pp. 17 f.

which ideas about eugenics took root had less to do with his »personal traits« than with »his lively visual imagination« that saw cosmopolitanism in terms of fixed racial categories.

Cosmopolitanism and Racism

This juxtaposition of cosmopolitanism and racism, loosely linked in the show's programmes since 1899, became absolutely explicit in 1908/1909 when Cody's Wild West merged with Gordon Lillie's Great Far East and became the ›combined shows‹, traveling around the United States until 1913.[43] Within a year of its creation, the show was not only being billed as »An Oriental Spectacle«, but as a »Great Drama of Cosmopolitan Life« that would »entertain while educating the spectator through the medium of animated pictures and scenes typical of the Wild West and Far East«.[44] What could spectators expect to learn? The poster, »Pawnee Bill's Great Far East Combined with Buffalo Bill's Wild West« (see fig. 3),[45] offers some clues. With its subtitle, »An Oriental Vision for the First Time Presented on the American Continent«, the poster mirrors a scene right out of world's fair midways with their ›Cairo Street‹ representations. Instead of providing the usual depictions of Indians and cowboys set against western American landscapes, the artist has substituted the Great Pyramid and a caravan of exoticised representations of dark-skinned people from Africa, the Middle East, and South Asia traveling on elephants and camels in the company of a British lancer galloping hurriedly to catch up with a white woman on horseback being accompanied by an African wearing a fez. Riveting this eye-catching procession to the theme of the ›Wild West‹ is the heroic figure of Gordon Lillie, ›Pawnee Bill‹, whose confidence speaks volumes about who is in charge of the ›Orient‹. Lest anyone think the poster bore no relationship to the performances, one newspaper insisted that »[t]he various scenes and incidents illustrated on the bill boards and in the advertisements will be faithfully executed«.[46]

Programmes, complete with descriptions of each act, helped fill in the picture for audiences: »From the entree of the various groups of horsemen until the thrilling finish, the audience is entranced with the ever-changing acts, varied and pleasing and at all times authentic illustrations of the

---

43   Cf. Jonathan D. Martin: ›The Grandest and Most Cosmopolitan Object Teacher‹, pp. 92-123, cuts off the story in 1899.
44   Cf. ›Butte Miner‹, 28.8.1910 (advertisement).
45   ›An Oriental Vision for the First Time Presented on the American Continent‹, poster, Buffalo Bill Historical Center, Cody, Wyoming, USA: 1.69.2738.
46   ›Arizona Republican‹, 4.10.1910, p. 8 (›Buffalo Bill to Retire‹).

Fig. 3: By 1909, the Buffalo Bill and Pawnee Bill Combined Show had merged narratives about the ›Far West‹ with the ›Far East‹ had become an imperial road show that was advertised as being ›cosmopolitan‹

types and scenes depicted. The Great Far East, presenting the men and scenes of the Eastern Hemisphere, is introduced in the same arena with historical Wild West displays. These two half-world features are, in reality, a world-including exhibition intended to instruct, entertain, and amuse the multitudes. The picturesque conglomeration of strange and unfamiliar people, drawn from the Oriental nations, includes reckless Arabs, whose tireless steeds traverse the sands of Sahara; the Japanese ›little brown men of the Orient‹, termed also ›the Yankees of the East‹, whose soldiers and horsemen moved against the vanquished Russian; the mysterious Hindoo Faklirs from India, the Whirling Dervish of Egypt, and the picturesque natives of the South Sea Islands«.[47]

---

47   Buffalo Bill's Wild West Combined With Pawnee Bill's Great Far East. Magazine of Wonders and Daily Record [1909]. In: BBHC, MS6: William F. Cody, Reel 5.

To make clear that this pageant of orientalism moved along a vertical axis of racial hierarchy as well as a horizontal axis of performance skills, programmes for the show insisted that this »dream of the Orient« revealed »[a]n ideal panorama of the Far East, presented in spectacular form with genuine natives who enact the characters which they represent«. »The Hindu Fakirs«, the programme insisted, »are really Hindu Priests. Actually they gather at Simali, in the Himalaya Mountains of India and perform sacred rites which in reality are these same mysterious performances. Among the tests presented at Simali is Hindu Levitation; the suspending in mid-air of a human form, unaided by perceptible supports. The Australian Boomerang Throwers are the lowest type of humanity, but little removed from the dumb beast in the matter of intelligence«.[48]

However much the show may have been a »great drama of cosmopolitanism«, this »world-including exhibition« made clear that the world should and must be experienced in terms of permanent racial categories rooted in nature. This was the message in the 1910 advertisement which announced that the show would be »Holding the Mirror of Nature for Reflections of Oriental Pageantry and Splendors«. The world, in other words, might be becoming more intercultural, but nature's mirror of racial categories remained useful, indeed essential, for understanding – and containing – it. For all that the show set in motion in the arena through thrilling performances of horsemanship, acrobatics, and gunplay, when the dust settled, ›race‹, however contested by the show's subaltern participants, still stood as a seemingly reliable guide for predicting how people would conduct themselves in a world becoming ever more interconnected.

To cut to the chase, sociologist Stuart Hall had it right when, writing about inferential racism and repetition in the mass media, he insisted: »Dominant definitions connect events, implicitly or explicitly, to grand totalizations, to the great syntagmatic views-of-the-world: they take ›large views‹ of issues: they relate events to the ›national interest‹ or to the level of geo-politics, even if they make these connections in truncated, inverted or mystified ways. The definition of a hegemonic viewpoint is a) that it defines within its terms the mental horizon, the universe, of possible meanings, of a whole sector of relations in a society or culture; and b) that it carries with it the stamp of legitimacy – it appears coterminous with what is ›natural‹, ›inevitable‹, ›taken for granted‹ about the social order«.[49] This was precisely the work of ideological innovation in the Wild West and its posters.

48 Ibid.
49 Stuart Hall: Encoding/Decoding, p. 60.

By the time Buffalo Bill died in 1917, the Wild West had reached a trans-Atlantic audience of some fifty million. Posters and other forms of advertising, not to mention over 500 dime novels published in the United States alone, reached countless more at once creating and confirming expectations about the show's content. How should we assess its influence on the way people thought about race? This essay has been an exercise in worrying about recent readings of the show that have increasingly emphasised the show's performers and performances as enacting meanings tied to cultural preservation (in the case of American Indians) and promoting greater intercultural understanding (as in the case of the other performers in the show). Without meaning to suggest that these readings are completely wrong, I have sought to recast the show in light of the ways it increasingly engaged its spectators in imaging the modern, cosmopolitan world as racialized to its core.

The genius of Cody and his artists was to devise robust visual forms through performances and posters that replicated older racial categories, naturalised them as permanent, and conjoined them with both imperialism and cosmopolitanism in making modernity seem much less threatening. Visitors could leave the arenas where they saw the Wild West and Far East performed and understand that racism and cosmopolitanism were compatible and, in the case of the show, mutually reinforcing. To be sure, there were crosswinds of resistance that swept across the show's performative spaces, but the show's primary ideological innovation lay in helping audiences imagine that they could grasp, understand, and even be entertained by colonial frontiers, whether in the United States or elsewhere around the globe, that held out the prospect for the eventual victory of ›civilisation‹ over ›savagery‹.[50]

References

Blackstone, Sarah: Buckskins, Bullets, and Business. A History of Buffalo Bill's Wild West. Westport: Greenwood Press 1986.
Delaney, Michelle: Buffalo Bill's Wild West Warriors. A Photographic History by Gertrude Kasebier. New York: Collins 2007.
Deloria, Jr., Vine: The Indians. In: Buffalo Bill and the Wild West, ed. by Peter H. Hassrick, Richard Slotkin, Vine Deloria, Jr., Howard R. Lamar, William Jud-

---

50 I am particularly grateful to Mary Robinson and Sean Campbell and the staff at the Buffalo Bill Historical Center in Cody, Wyoming for their assistance in helping me secure material, both visual and textual, for this essay. I am also grateful to Kiki Leigh Rydell for her insights.

son, and Leslie A. Fiedler. New York: Brooklyn Museum of Art 1991, pp. 45-56.

Etulain, Richard: Telling Western Stories. From Buffalo Bill to Larry McMurtry. Albuquerque: University of New Mexico Press 1999.

Green, Jeffrey P.: ›In Dahomey‹ in London in 1903. In: The Black Perspective in Music, 11, 1983, 1, pp. 22-40.

Haill, Catherine: Pleasure and Leisure. Posters for Performance. In: The Power of the Poster, ed. by Margaret Timmers. London: V&A Publications 1998, pp. 26-70.

Hall, Roger Allan: ›Black America‹. Nate Salsbury's ›Afro-American Exhibition‹. In: Educational Theatre Journal, 29, 1977, 1, pp. 49-60.

Hall, Stuart: Encoding/Decoding. In: Media Studies. A Reader, ed. by Sue Thornham. New York: New York University Press 2010 (1980), pp. 51-61.

Jones, John Bush: Our Musicals, Ourselves. A Social History of the American Musical Theatre. Hanover: Brandeis University Press 2003.

Kasson, Joy: Buffalo Bill's Wild West. Celebrity, Memory, and Popular History. New York: Hill and Wang 2000.

Martin, Jonathan D.: ›The Grandest and Most Cosmopolitan Object Teacher‹. Buffalo Bill's Wild West and the Politics of American Identity, 1883-1899. In: Radical History Review, 66, 1996, pp. 92-123.

McClintock, Anne: Imperial Leather. Race, Gender and Sexuality in the Colonial Contest. New York [et al.]: Routledge 1995.

Moses, Lester George: Wild West Shows and the Images of American Indians, 1883-1933. Albuquerque: University of New Mexico Press 1996.

Neihardt, John G. (ed.): Black Elk Speaks. New York: Pocket Books 1975 (1932).

Peress, Maurice: Dvorak to Duke Ellington. A Conductor Explored America's Music and Its African American Roots. New York [et al.]: Oxford University Press 2003.

Reddin, Paul: Wild West Shows. Urbana: University of Illinois, 1999.

Rennert, Jack: 100 Posters of Buffalo Bill's Wild West. New York: Darien House 1976.

Rydell, Robert W.: Africans in America. African Villages at America's World's Fairs (1893-1901). In: Human Zoos, ed. by Pascal Blanchard Gilles Bosch, Nanette Jacomijn Snoep. Liverpool: Liverpool University Press 2008, pp. 286-293.

—: ›Soundtracks of Empire‹. In: European Journal of American Studies [Online], special issue, 1, 2012, document 7 (http://ejas.revues.org/9712;DOI:10.4000/ejas.9712).

—, Rob Kroes: Buffalo Bill in Bologna. The Americanization of the World, 1869-1922. Chicago: University of Chicago Press 2005.

Slotkin, Richard: Buffalo Bill's ›Wild West‹ and the Mythologization of the American Empire. In: Cultures of United States Imperialism, ed. by Amy Kaplan, Donald E. Pease. Durham: Duke University Press 1993, pp. 164-181.

Spiro, Jonathan: Defending the Master Race. Conservation, Eugenics, and the Legacy of Madison Grant. Burlington: University of Vermont Press 2009.

Timmers, Margaret (ed.): The Power of the Poster. London: V&A Publications 1998.

Tone, John Lawrence: The Machete and the Liberation of Cuba. In: Journal of Military History, 62, 1998, pp. 7-28.
Traits of Buffalo Bill. In: Eugenical News, 5, March 1920, 3, pp. 17-18.
Warren, Louis: Buffalo Bill's America. William Cody and the Wild West Show. New York: Alfred A. Knopf 2005.
White, Richard: Frederick Jackson Turner and Buffalo Bill. In: The Frontier in American Culture. An Exhibition at the Newberry Library, ed. by James R. Grossman. Berkeley [et al.]: University of California Press 1994, pp. 7-65.

›Fun Without Vulgarity‹?
Commodity Racism and the Promotion of Blackface Fantasies
Michael Pickering

Abstract: Blackface minstrelsy was one of the first forms of popular entertainment in Britain to become fully commercialised, not only in the grand-scale shows staged in London and large provincial towns and cities, but also through such adjunct products as sheet-music. As a form of commercial popular entertainment it endured in Britain for 150 years, and even after the heyday of the stage minstrel show was able to migrate successfully into such mass media as phonography, radio, film and television. This chapter examines blackface minstrelsy in Britain as a form of commodity racism. Such racism is usually associated with material products like soap and jam, but in its promotion and marketing minstrelsy was itself a form of commodity racism deeply involved in selling what it produced and in that process increasing the circulation and perpetuation of racial stereotypes and racist notions. The purpose of the chapter is to consider how blackface minstrelsy as commercial entertainment operated as a vehicle for racial stereotyping and how such stereotyping operated through the popular aesthetics in which minstrelsy resonated.

In early 2009, the daughter of the former British Prime Minister, Margaret Thatcher, was censured for referring to the French-African tennis star, Jo-Wilfried Tsonga, as looking like a golliwog. Her repeated use of the word golliwog occurred in the backstage green room of the BBC programme ›The One Show‹, and when the story leaked, the BBC offered an unreserved apology. Carol Thatcher herself refused to comment, despite the fact that the producers of the show tried over five days to persuade her to add to their own apology. She was reported as wishing to maintain »a dignified silence«. Thatcher was subsequently sacked from the programme, but not from the BBC. Her sacking irked the newly elected Conservative mayor of London, Boris Johnson, who referred to her comments as only »a bit offensive«.[1]

I begin with this story for several reasons. First of all, Carol Thatcher's refusal to offer a full apology, and Johnson's opinion that she should not

---

1   Cf. ›Daily Mirror‹, 7.2.2009; for the quotes see ›Guardian‹, 6.2.2009.

have been sacked but merely taken aside and quietly reprimanded, show that neither public figure regard the use of the term golliwog as derogatory and demeaning; it is instead only »a bit offensive«. Many people in Britain share this view. Support for it might be expected in rightwing newspapers like the Murdoch-owned tabloid ›The Sun‹, but the BBC received 2245 complaints about her being axed from the show, only 60 of these agreeing with the action.² Secondly, the racist term used by Thatcher is widely known in connection with a child's doll, and it is this connection that is sometimes used to claim that the term is innocuous or, as Thatcher's spokesperson averred, a word only to be taken as lighthearted fun – one meant as a joke in a private conversation.³ This relates to the third reason for starting with this case, which is that this racist term not only derives from the name for a child's doll, but also extends back to the long show-business tradition in Britain of blackface minstrelsy. This tradition lasted from the early nineteenth to the late twentieth century, and usually but not invariably involved white men blacking up their faces and hands, and donning wigs and costumes, in an impersonation of black men (and sometimes women). Even in its last days on television and the provincial stage, during the late 1970s and 1980s, it was still considered by some to be ›harmless fun‹. Reasserting the close historical links between the golliwog and blackface minstrelsy connects with a final reason for mentioning this anecdote about a celebrity's ill-judged remarks. This is that in part via this reference and in part via others, minstrelsy is closely connected with the development of commodity racism. Examining this form of racism and its relation to the blackface tradition is the purpose of this chapter.

Before beginning to do this it would be helpful to add further comment and elaboration to the various points made so far as this will provide some of the contextual breadth that is often missing from the reporting of such controversies as that involving Carol Thatcher, and also prepare the stage for what is to follow. Starting with the claim of innocuousness, this attains currency not only because of its reference to a children's toy but also because of its association with other commodities that have long laid claim to the symbolic collateral of childhood innocence. The most well-known of these are the use of a golliwog as a brand icon for Robertson's jam and marmalade, and the appearance of golliwogs in children's fiction, particularly that written by the English author, Enid Blyton.

---

2   Ibid. For ›The Sun‹, see for example Garry Bushell's tirade against ›political correctness‹ and the liberal, middle-class »clueless clods« who run the BBC in his TV commentary section: ›Garry Bushell on the Box‹, ›The Sun‹, 15.4.1998.
3   ›Daily Mirror‹, 7.2.2009.

James Robertson & Sons took the golliwog as a commercial trademark in the early twentieth century, using it on their jam-jar labels and price lists as well as in their advertising. It proved enormously popular, with customers from the late 1920s exchanging coupons from the labels for badges and brooches of golliwogs playing various sports such as golf and football. Towards the end of the twentieth century, it was estimated that since 1910 the company had despatched more than twenty million of them.[4] As a promotional tool and means of ensuring consumer loyalty, the scheme was hugely successful. During the final three decades of the twentieth century, despite increasing criticism by African-Caribbean groups and growing awareness in Britain of the negative impact of such imagery on black people, the firm proved recalcitrant, resorting to such tactics as dropping the second syllable of the term and calling their icon a golly, as if this would quite remove the racist sting; giving him new occupational identities such as astronaut rather than the stereotypical roles of sportsman or musician; and claiming that while they sold 250000 golly badges to collectors each year, they received few letters of complaint about the golliwog image. According to Robertson's brand director, the »feedback has consistently been that for the vast majority of people, the golly is a positive thing that they like«.[5] Such claims were often made by this company, but it is not difficult to find evidence that the golly was not always regarded as an inoffensive nurseryland character, as for example was the case when Robertson planned a golliwog castle, with giant-sized gollies, for Liverpool's international garden festival in the early 1980s. This was judged »an outrageous insult« to the black people of Toxteth and the plan was duly abandoned.[6]

This form of commodity racism constitutes one particular line through which the golliwog became a pervasive presence in British culture. The other most significant one, beside that associated with the rag doll itself, occurred in stories written for children. While Enid Blyton's use of this character is perhaps the best known, it can be traced back to *The Adventures of Two Dutch Dolls*, a child's book illustrated by Florence Upton,

4 ›Daily Mail‹, 22.6.1999.
5 BBC News, 23.8.2001; see http://news.bbc.co.uk/1/hi/business/1505411.stm [23/2/2013]. The same recalcitrance was shown by the chain of heritage shops, Past Times, who until 1994 sold large metal-plate and smaller fridge magnets of the golliwog, and apparently only stopped doing so for commercial rather than ethical reasons (Tony Kushner: Selling Racism, pp. 75 f.; see Raphael Samuel: Theatres of Memory, pp. 86 f., 98 f. for more on this company). This would appear to be true as well of Robertson's eventual decision in 2001 to switch from the racist symbol of the golly to new promotional characters based on drawings by Quentin Blake in the stories of Roald Dahl. At the time of writing, golly fridge magnets and Robertson's badges are still available on eBay, and Amazon continue to sell golliwog dolls.
6 ›Glasgow Herald‹, 1.5.1984.

with the story in verse written by her mother, Bertha, published in 1895.[7] This is where the golliwog first appeared. The Uptons published twelve more volumes featuring this trio, but the golliwog outlasted the two other characters and developed a much broader career, in part because the Uptons failed to copyright their creation. This happened particularly with the mass manufacturing of golliwog dolls, which became widely sold in Britain, Europe, the United States and Australia, but according to Florence Upton's biographer, the golliwog also appeared on wallpaper, china and pottery, paperweights, postcards and jewellery. During the interwar period, de Vigny of Paris even marketed a perfume in a golliwog-shaped bottle with sealskin hair on the stopper.[8] In the first Upton book, the golliwog was described as »a horrid sight«; it was intended to be seen as ugly, and

Fig. 1: The Upton Golliwog

Fig. 2: The Upton Minstrel

initially at least, meant to be scary. This is borne out by the visual image of the white dolls' first encounter with him: they are shown as alarmed and frightened, while he is depicted as grotesque, with pop eyes, thick lips and wild unruly hair (see fig. 1).

Once the female dolls come to know him, though, he is seen to be endearing and gallant, whereas the golliwogs featuring in Enid Blyton's mid-twentieth century children's stories were represented as mean-spirited, rude, untrustworthy and prone to theft. Here again is the minstrel ancestry of the golliwog, for the two most common blackface stereotypes are the sentimentalised happy-go-lucky plantation hand and the vain urban

7 The full text of this book is reproduced as an ebook at http://www.gutenberg.org/files/16770-h/16770-h.htm [23/2/2013].
8 Norma S. Davis: A Lark Ascends, pp. 102 f.

dandy or ›coon‹, with the golliwog clearly inheriting the vividly coloured, mock-gentlemanly attire of the latter. Minstrelsy also commonly portrayed the black male as a born thief, a stereotypical attribution perpetuated by Blyton. In one of her Noddy stories, a golliwog asks the hero for help, and then steals his car.[9]

In light of all this, it is naïve either to deny or downplay the offensiveness involved, regardless of the golliwog's particular manifestations or the fact that, even in his first appearances, his minstrel derivation made him »the caricature of a caricature«.[10] Those who dismiss anti-golliwog protest either fail to recognise the racist toxicity involved, perceiving the golly simply as a historical curiosity or object of heritage, or claim that the Upton creation was never intentionally racist in the first place. Taking this second point first, blackface associations were apparent even with the golliwog's debut representation, not only in his own appearance but also through the inclusion of a banjo-playing minstrel in the first Upton volume (see fig. 2).[11]

Racial stereotyping may have been more blatant in Enid Blyton's children's fiction, but the Upton golly has clear minstrel roots. Turning to the first point, the golliwog also has continuing racist associations; if that is not so, why are golliwog stalls a regular feature at BNP festivals as well as still being widely sold elsewhere, and how is it that the soft doll can be used as a racial taunt in a dispute between neighbours?[12] The most powerful testimony comes perforce from black people because unless you have had the term golliwog hurled at you as a form of abuse from school playground days onwards, »it is unlikely you will understand why a small doll causes such a big fuss«. In making this point, Hannah Pool's view of the Thatcher controversy was that it reminded her exactly of such abuse, for even though the golliwog was originally male, the term has been used to taunt both girls and boys of African-Caribbean origin, and it continues to cause controversy and distress.[13]

The continuing offensiveness of the term connects with one of the key points I am pursuing in this chapter, which is that stereotypes, including those involved in commodity racism, may have a much longer lifespan or more durable legacy than the cultural form or product with which they

---

9   Cf. David Pilgrim: The Golliwog Caricature. Jim Crow Museum of Racist Memorabilia, Ferris State University, available at http://www.ferris.edu/news/jimcrow/golliwog [23/2/2013].
10 Ibid.
11 http://www.gutenberg.org/files/16770-h/16770-h.htm [23/2/2013]; see p. 45.
12 See Hannah Pool: ›I'll Tell You Why A Small Doll Causes Such A Big Fuss‹, ›Guardian‹, 11.10.2011; also ›Daily Mail‹, 24.10.2011.
13 ›Guardian‹, 6.2.2009; Tony Kushner: Selling Racism, p. 81; and see ›Manchester Evening News‹, 1.8.1998 for the story ›School Mums in Golly Row‹.

were historically associated.[14] If this is clear for the golliwog, it can also be shown to be the case with the cultural form from which it was derived. In devoting the rest of the chapter to this task, I shall focus principally upon the sheet music covers, programmes, posters and promotional images associated with British blackface minstrelsy, and I shall do so because these were all adjunct forms of commodity racism. The racist stereotyping involved will become clear as we move from example to example, while the focal commodity on offer was the minstrel show itself. This is a deliberate point of emphasis because, although it is widely recognised that minstrelsy was the originating source in advertising or branding certain well-known household goods, minstrelsy itself was a commodified form of popular entertainment, and sheet music was a vehicle not only for selling the songs and tunes associated with it, but also for selling minstrelsy to the British public.

Sheet Music and Stereotypes

There were many kinds of minstrel act and show. These included amateur entertainments in blackface along with seasonal, charity and semi-professional manifestations of the form, most of which showed either minor or incidental degrees of profit motivation. While these were all influential in helping racism to spread and more particularly, helping certain racial stereotypes about black people to become more and more entrenched, the greatest influence in this respect was professional stage minstrelsy. Metropolitan minstrelsy, and the minstrel shows performed in the theatres of the expanding industrial towns and cities, became increasingly commercialised in the second half of the nineteenth century, with the incentive to garner substantial financial returns growing steadily in importance. This was part of a broader movement in popular music and popular theatre involving their transformation into lucrative branches of business and commerce, with market success becoming held as a key index of popularity as such.

The legacy of this transformation remains strong, across all areas of musical entertainment, and while commodity racism is now regarded as distasteful and offensive, it was driven by the same business imperatives and entrepreneurial dealings that prevail in the contemporary cultural industries. Minstrelsy was at the forefront of this revolution in the commercialisation of popular entertainment. Among its many consequences was

---

14 For an attempt to develop a historical understanding of stereotyping as well as a broad conceptual engagement with it, see Michael Pickering: Stereotyping.

the professionalisation of songwriting as well as of acting and performing, and with this came the sea-change whereby song itself became a highly profitable commodity. As Derek Scott has noted, the »commodification of music was at its most visible in the sheet music trade«, and this made music publishing »the most important musical money-making enterprise of the new commercial age«.[15]

In the world of entertainment, popular music in particular is a volatile and unpredictable cultural product, making it difficult to know in advance where market success may favour any specific song or piece of music. There is a continual tension between attempts to forge market success and the vagaries of custom and popular taste. Business and industry may try to manipulate consumer demand, and various tactics such as song-plugging and the introduction of a ›hook‹ are long-established, but the market for popular music and popular entertainment more broadly remains unstable despite the huge profits that have been derived from selling songs, along with the singers who transmit them to a broad public. This was just as true for the mass production and distribution of sheet music in the Victorian and Edwardian periods as it has been subsequently, for sheet music then was »the economic heart of the music industry«.[16] For this reason music and theatre entrepreneurs used whatever means were available to them to help their products reap the greatest rewards possible. Since racism was inherent in blackface minstrelsy as a cultural form, this meant that, for this particular branch of popular entertainment, using racism to encourage its market success was an obvious commercial step.

The racism was there from the start, as for example in the grotesque figure of Jim Crow, the persona of Thomas Dartmouth Rice whose success, following his initial metropolitan appearances at the Surrey and Adelphi theatres in 1836, sparked off the long-enduring love of minstrel entertainment in Britain. The English copperplate engraving reproduced in figure 3 follows the better-known New York illustration, with the same stance involving right hand on hip and left hand flung upwards as an integral feature of the cavorting dance steps which accompanied Rice's song and act, as does the peculiar admixture of dandy city attire and rural plantation costume.[17] This relates to the already mentioned, most prevalent male stereotypes of early blackface minstrelsy – the ragged slave and the mock-gentleman (see fig. 4 for the latter).

---

15   Derek B. Scott: Sounds of the Metropolis, p. 24.
16   P. David Marshall: Celebrity and Power, p. 150.
17   For the New York version, see Sam Dennison: Scandalize My Name, p. 46; for Rice's reception in Britain and the ensuing Jim Crow craze, see Michael Pickering: Blackface Minstrelsy in Britain, pp. 7-13.

These are symbolically conflated in the Jim Crow illustration with the waistcoat, cravat and jacket with lace cuffs in the upper half of the figure and the torn and patched trousers and busted-open shoes of the lower half, the connection rather than opposition between the two being signified by the torn bottom-part of the jacket which remains an aspect of the upper half but is at the same time suggestive of the lower. The conflation may be said to connote the doomed attempt of any aspiration by the black man for upward social mobility, a dimension of the visual meaning of this image that is confirmed by the background additions made to the English engraving (which are not in the New York version). The alligator, frog and lizard link the black to the animal kingdom, while the simian connection in particular is made clear by the inclusion of two circus-type monkeys, one of them in a tailcoat and fancy hat with a feather in it, the other sporting a rather exotic umbrella.[18] These link with the upper-half portion of the figure in the illustration in making a mockery of the sartorial pretensions of the Zip Coon-type stereotype, but it is the stereotypical conflation which is the most notable feature of this and other depictions of Jim Crow, for the dandy and plantation caricatures became separated in later minstrelsy, with the former later transmuting into the dangerous ›coon‹ stereotype and the latter descending into the Old Black Joe or pious Uncle Tom stereotype. The engraving reminds us of how such stereotypes were intertwined in racial ideology.[19]

Rice's act involved the construction of Jim Crow as a comic character, and one aspect of blackface racism that endured into the days of radio minstrelsy and beyond is the demeaning portrayal of the black as a figure of fun. Hand-in-hand with this was the sentimentalised pathos and nostalgia that were either associated with the burdensome sorrows of the slave or an unrequited yearning for life on the old slave plantation. Clearly these were different, and it is worth noting that although racism was inherently characteristic of minstrelsy's representations of black people and black culture, it was not necessarily pro-slavery. Indeed, in early minstrelsy anti-slavery songs were a distinct sub-genre, with songs like Lucy Neal, saddening

---

18 The two monkeys in the engraving for the song-sheet cover were presumably meant to be illustrations of the ›ring tail'd monkey‹ and the ›rib nose baboon‹ of the Original Jim Crow song sung by Rice; see Sam Dennison: Scandalize My Name, p. 52.

19 The visual conflation is integral to two other English sheet-music covers of the »celebrated nigger song«, as the promotion on one of these phrased it. These were published by B. Williams in Cloth Fair, Smithfield, and Charles Jeffereys & Co, Frith Street, London, but neither contain the reptilian and simian references, the former showing Rice on stage at the Surrey, the latter relating to his performances at the Adelphi but depicting him dancing on the shoreline of a southern river (see Mander and Mitchenson Collection, Bristol University).

›Fun Without Vulgarity‹? 127

Fig. 3: Jim Crow   Fig. 4: Zip Coon

audiences with its slave's lament of forced separation and the narrator's broken heart, being hugely popular in England, and some minstrel song composers, like the Englishman Henry Russell, being openly opposed to the ›peculiar institution‹.[20]

Uncle Tom's Cabin, a massively popular novel in Britain, was also incorporated into minstrelsy as well as being adapted into a theatrical melodrama. This was not only because of its anti-slavery stance but also because of its similar racial stereotypicalities and its reproduction of the dual mode of comicality and sentimentality that was pivotal to minstrelsy's appeal.[21] A quite distinct, if not entirely unrelated form of sentimentality infused the songs that portrayed plantation life as intrinsically happy and carefree, a place where »de darky hab no troubles« and »de beauties ob creation will nebber lose dere charm«.[22] This was of course a gross historical travesty, but one that was crucial in advancing the stereotypical notion of the black as naturally indolent, workshy, hedonistic and inclined to sing and dance at the drop of a straw hat: »We darkies lead a merry life, | Free

20 Derek B. Scott: Sounds of the Metropolis, p. 167.
21 Michael Pickering: Blackface Minstrelsy in Britain, pp. 23 f., 31.
22 Negro and American Songs, pp. 57 f. The quotations are taken from ›Ring de Banjo‹ by Stephen Foster, who is perhaps the best-known exponent of plantation song; for Foster, see Charles Hamm: Yesterdays, chapter 10, and Ken Emerson: Doo-Dah!

from thoughts of sorrow; | Far remov'd from care and strife, | Heedless of tomorrow«.[23]

References to black labour were few, although occasionally they occur in early minstrel songs, one widely known example from the 1840s being ›Dance, Boatman, Dance‹ (see fig. 5). This song, known also as ›De Boatman's Dance‹ is attributed to Dan Emmett of the Virginia Minstrels, a four-man minstrel troupe consisting of banjo, violin, tambourine and castanet bones and one of the first to appear in Britain during the 1840s. The association with Emmett is obliquely made on this sheet-music cover; the primary association goes to the English troupe ›The Ohio Niggers‹ as well as to their singer Mr Sharp, probably John W. Sharp, musical director of the Vauxhall Gardens, and to the arranger W. West, who was one of the earliest British minstrel songwriters.[24] The scene depicted on the cover draws on the notion of black hedonism as the figures in the background exemplify a life of habitual singing and dancing as an all-night revel comes to an end and the sun begins to rise, the personified image of which links with the lines in the chorus: »O dance all night till broad daylight | an go home with de gals in the morning«.

The song is somewhat unusual in that it has rather bawdy undertones, while the sheet music cover is, as it used to be phrased in polite society, highly suggestive. This kind of visual detail, compositionally at the centre of the illustration, doesn't appear on later minstrel music covers. Black female sexuality was rarely used within later minstrelsy as an overt component of its commodity racism. It is not only this which makes it noteworthy, for we need also to consider how the song intimately combines work and pleasure. Seeing these as one and the same in the stereotype of the happy-go-lucky ›negro‹ reinforced the antithesis that was opening up between work and leisure in Britain at this time, the one becoming the realm of necessity, the other cleaved away from it as the realm of pleasure. The song opposes this separation, but only at the expense of mythologising black folk culture and adding to the construction of a racialised black Other.

This construction is at the same time gender-differentiated. The two main figures on the music cover are the Ohio river-boatman celebrated in the title of the song, who is involved in his work ferrying people on the water, and a female partygoer who is departing the hop with its home-made music. She makes her lascivious intentions abundantly known through her decolletage, such an ample display of heaving bosom being almost an ab-

---

23 Fifty Songs Sung by the Ethiopians, p. 3.
24 Michael Pickering: Blackface Minstrelsy in Britain, pp. 11, 55.

errant feature even of the more robust examples of early minstrelsy. The two figures are clearly ›lubstruck‹ as they gaze into each others' eyes and prepare to sail away to a scene of early morning amorous sport. The image confirms the stereotypical notion of avidity in black female sexuality

Fig. 5: *An early minstrel song-sheet cover conjoins the themes of work and leisure while highlighting black sexuality as the key feature of its commodity racism.*

while also inciting a complementary blackface fantasy in an exoticised blending of work and pleasure that clearly resounded as alternative to the increasing alienation of labour in industrialising Britain. Alternative, yes, but permissible only via the process of ›othering‹ black people and culture in the American South. This was central to minstrelsy's portrayal of African-American people. It set up a pattern of romantic primitivism that has beset the way black music and culture has been thought about ever since. This pattern is entirely compatible with commodity racism, for as Richard Middleton has noted, romantic primitivism is bound up with the historical development of capitalism itself: »ideologically, in capitalism's need for an Other, to refresh its ›spirit‹ of non-productive time, to energise and justify its own contrasting drive to ›civilisation‹, and at the same time to prove its liberalism; economically, in capitalism's need for ›raw materials‹, natural, human and cultural, to feed the expanding machinery of commodification«.[25]

Anglicising Blackface Entertainment

Certainly the romantic primitivism of examples like this was part of what attracted people to minstrelsy in its initial phases, but the primitivism had to conform to the anglicisation of blackface entertainment in the years following its general establishment in the 1840s. Among other things, this involved a move towards greater refinement and respectability, these qualities being realised in the addition of an orchestra and the use of this to introduce musical elegance and polish; increased emphasis on ›darky‹ sentimentalism; rejection of any instance of blueness or profanity; and even in some cases the aristocratic adoption of court dress, as for example with the Coloured Opera Troupe.[26]

As a general rule of thumb, it can be said that the more genteel the minstrel entertainment on offer, the less blatant or overt the racism, at least in an outwardly manifest sense, and this was true also of visual representations of the Dixie idyll, partly because plantation pastoralism was cross-class in appeal, and partly because its widespread appeal depended on sympathetic identification and the projection of longing onto a mythical faraway land. This remained true well into the twentieth century, as is clear from the front covers of two collections of plantation songs published by Chappell & Co in the late nineteenth century, and W. Paxton & Co Ltd in 1935. The first of these (see fig. 6) presented three such songs, ›My Dusky Soudern Bride‹, ›Way Down The Ohio‹ and ›De Little Black Coon‹. It shows that late-Victorian writers and composers of considerable renown were hardly averse to producing songs in this genre. George Sims was a journalist, dramatist and novelist as well as song writer, perhaps most famous today for ›Christmas Day in the Workhouse‹, while Ivan Caryll was a composer of operettas and musical comedies as well as being musical director of the Gaiety and Lyric theatres. The illustration in the top-left-

---

[25] Richard Middleton: Studying Popular Music, pp. 168 f.
[26] For more on the anglicisation of minstrelsy, see Michael Pickering: Blackface Minstrelsy in Britain, chapter 1. The distinction between polite and plebeian forms of minstrelsy occurred early on in Britain, with blackface entertainers like The Great Mackney performing to both sets of audience in the 1840s (see ibid: pp. 13 f.).

hand corner is stereotypical Deep South pastoral, with a singer leaning on an old rustic fence of wooden palings and accompanying himself on the banjo – the archetypal minstrel instrument – as he serenades his ›dusky soudern bride‹ by the light of a crescent moon.

The second example (fig. 7) brought together some of the most celebrated songs of this genre, written and composed by the most celebrated exponents of such song, Stephen Foster and James Bland. A clear element of continuity with ›Dance, Boatman, Dance‹, despite the ninety years or

Fig. 6 & 7: Two British minstrel song collections both utilise as their selling point the myth of the Deep South plantation as a carefree, joyous location of unfettered music-making.

so between them, lies in the ruralist fantasy they cater in, with the various downhome characters crooning in the cane brake under the moonlight, or raising their arms and greeting the morning sun with a song in their hearts, but the later emphasis, particularly in the Paxton collection, is entirely on a generalised romanticism designed to appeal visually to the widest possible range of music consumers, and help sell this particular musical commodity.

Along with this rule of thumb, we need to recognise a broader pattern of development, for while the empathy invoked by anti-slavery songs was later revived in the favourable British reception of black spirituals, during the later nineteenth century there occurred an increasing hardening and wider acceptance of racist ideas and attitudes. This continued steadily as Britain approached the period of ›high‹ imperialism. Throughout the whole Victorian period, white British people realised in part a sense of their own racial superiority through its black inversions, but this was not a static realisation, for there was clearly a shift from an earlier ethnocentric response to Africans and those of the African diaspora to a more stridently racist attitude. This is too starkly put, for although we can see this transition occurring over the later nineteenth century, we need to avoid proposing too neat a version of it. The change was not straightforwardly from an object of pity to a figure of fun, for what was Rice's stage character if not a figure of fun? We need also to remember the longer lineage of the ›noble savage‹ conception, and the genuine sympathy for the sufferings of slavery both before and after the American Civil War, as for example in British responses the Fisk Jubilee Singers.[27] The transition is nevertheless clear enough, and as might be expected, such a development was reflected in sheet music covers and other items of minstrelsy promotion, with the visual portrayal of blacks becoming a vehicle of racist ridicule in a much more disdainful manner. So, for example, the social pretensions of urban blacks continued to be seen as absurd, for their alleged racial inferiority compared with the white middle- and upper-classes rendered any imitation of polite society on their part inutile. Contrary to the self-help ethos that was integral to Victorian bourgeois thought, blanket assumptions about black racial characteristics made commentators »less willing to recognise the abilities of individual blacks«, with some suggesting »that even ›a self-improved Negro‹ could not rise to the elevated status of a gentleman«.[28] Alongside this continuity, and as evidence of its increasing entrenchment

Fig. 8: This sheet-music cover relies not only on stereotypical notions associated with black dress-style but also uses grotesque physical distortion as a commercial ploy.

---

27 See Michael Pickering: Blackface Minstrelsy in Britain, pp. 118 ff., and chapter five more generally; Michael Pickering: ›A Jet Ornament to Society‹; Doug Seroff: The Fisk Jubilee Singers in Britain.
28 Douglas A. Lorimer: Colour, Class and the Victorians, p. 15.

in race-thinking, the graphic presentation of black ostentation and swagger became more and more grotesque. This is clearly apparent in the illustration accompanying the music for ›New York Nigger Quadrilles‹ (see fig. 8), arranged by an established British writer and composer of minstrel songs, W. H. Montgomery, and published in London by Jefferys.

In line with the general development of Victorian minstrel sheet music, the facial features – compared, say, to the English Jim Crow figure in figure 3 – have become more exaggerated, not only in the mouths and eyes, but also in the sideways direction of the woman's eyes, a way of looking that became characteristic of minstrelsy and added even further to the visual ridicule. In further contrast to figure 3, which depicted a white man in blackface mocking a black man, here we have a complete racist fabrication of a ›black‹ couple mocking themselves. It is because of this that exaggeration is the leitmotiv of the illustration, as for example in the outsize nature of the jewellery, the excessive decoration in the dress, and the long phallic suggestiveness of the banjo with which the man is serenading his sweetheart. The mock-aristocratic nature of their foppery is summarised by the portrait on the wall behind them: the same over-the-top headgear, in a picture displaying her own resplendent charms, only emphasises the overweening folly of her vanity.

The potential consumer of this sheet music was middle- and upper-class, for it was retailed at half a crown, roughly half an agricultural labourer's weekly wage at the time.[29] It was obviously intended that those from these social strata would be the ones to enjoy being regaled with this example of racial mimicry and mockery. The quadrille is a type of square-dance that was popular in the nineteenth century, containing four sections of thirty two bars each, plus a final section, with operatic tunes commonly being adapted for the music. Performed by four couples, it was imported from elite Parisian ballrooms by English aristocrats in the early nineteenth century, and throughout the century usually associated with polite social circles. There was historically a slave association with this dance because it was taken at the same time into British colonial holdings in the Caribbean, becoming an element of social entertainment among planters, with slaves used to provide music for their parties. Black people themselves adopted, and altered, the dance, and the sheet-music cover may be alluding historically to this mimicry and mocking it, in what amounted to a double mocking, though ironically slaves had themselves used the quadrille to mock the high-falutin ways of the planters.

---

29   A. Wilson Fox: Agricultural Wages in England and Wales During the Last Fifty Years; Charles Stewart Orwin, B. I. Felton: A Century of Wages and Earnings in Agriculture.

The high price of the music for these quadrilles reminds us of the cross-class appeal of minstrelsy and its associated products. Even though sharing many common features and with a continual two-way flow of performers across the Atlantic, as already noted minstrelsy developed in Britain and North America in different ways, with refined musical arrangements and vocal harmonising distinguishing the more upmarket shows in Britain. In large part due to its aura of cultural refinement, the British minstrel show acquired a reputation as a form of wholesome family entertainment, a show to which even a clergyman could take his wife and offspring without fear of offence or embarrassment. Its popularity from the 1840s to well into the twentieth century extended across all existing social and cultural divides in Britain, though there were nevertheless different strains of minstrelsy, with some songs being entirely compatible with drawing-room ballads, and their performance being socially distinct from the street entertainment provided by minstrel buskers, or the cockney blackface ›business‹ found in gaffs and singing saloons.[30] Despite this cultural range, minstrelsy was never regarded as morally dubious or aesthetically debased, unlike the music hall, and what this accrued for its socially varied audiences was not cultural capital, but racist symbolic capital.[31] White people generally felt confirmed in their sense of superior racial stock, with minstrelsy making it seem that the essentialisation of difference between »a naturally cultivated nature and a naturally natural nature« was based not so much in social class or status, but in biology and biological inheritance.[32]

This does not mean that class discourse was never a dimension of blackface entertainments – it was clearly there, for example, in the differentiation between Mr Interlocutor and the two cornermen clowns, Tambo and Bones, with part of the fun being in the comic provision of punchlines by the clowns – or that such entertainments didn't promote ruling-class interests. By contributing to the growing racism in Britain, »many came to accept the idea of a paternalistic Pax Britannica, notions of ›responsible governments‹ abroad, and then the need for imperialist expansion and the scramble for Africa«.[33] Among other things as well, the social heterogeneity of audiences and consumers of minstrel products helped increase the growing wealth of the music-publishing industry, which in general terms across the period from 1800 to 1914 »may well have witnessed a fifty to

---

30 Michael Pickering: Blackface Minstrelsy in Britain, pp. 55-69.
31 I take this term from Anja Weiß: Racist Symbolic Capital, p. 48 et passim; see also the paper by Wulf D. Hund in this volume.
32 Pierre Bourdieu: The Field of Cultural Production, p. 236.
33 Derek Scott: The Singing Bourgeois, p. 83.

one hundred fold increased in production«, with London becoming a centre of minstrel sheet-music production equal to that of New York.³⁴

Music publishers like Hopwood and Crew, and Charles Sheard, with his ›Musical Bouquet‹ series, carried minstrel as well as music-hall songs into middle-class parlours and church halls. As one bit of advertising puffery from Hopwood and Crew had it, their minstrel songs »had taken such a permanent hold in the esteem of the musical public, ever welcomed and highly appreciated in the drawing room, and the greatest favourites with teachers in Class Instruction«. While there was »unmistakable evidence [...] of the British embourgeoisement of American minstrelsy« in this commodification of minstrel song and music, it was also the case that different markets were being catered for, with one publisher, Davidson, selling ›Negro Songs‹ at three pence each in his series the ›Musical Treasury‹, which was styled as »the original and only genuine music for the million«.³⁵ It was also the case that sheet music could become de-commodified even when prices were high. So, for example, one of the songs included in ›Popular Plantation Songs‹ (fig. 7), ›So Early in De Morning‹, was published in the mid-nineteenth century in an up-market London edition by Metzler & Co. It sold at two shillings, and was intended for a genteel clientele, yet the song wasn't confined to performance in the homes of the rich or well-off, for we know that it entered into oral tradition around this time and was assimilated into the repertoires of both male and female working-class singers. In the early-twentieth century, the song was transcribed from the singing of Mrs Pitt, of Eastleach in Gloucestershire, by Alfred Williams, who differed from most folk-song collectors of this period in taking account of the full breadth of people's repertoires, rather just the select examples of it that have become idealized in the folk music canon. In his annotation to the song, he notes that it was popular in the upper Thames valley around the 1860s and onwards, »especially around Sherborne, where it was a great favourite of the girls and women at work in the fields«.³⁶ This suggests that the same song could be sold as a musical commodity at different prices, and also pass into circulation in alternative ways, some of which, after its initial marketing, may not have involved exchange value of any kind.

---

34 Dave Russell: Popular Music in England, p. 134; see Derek B. Scott: Sounds of the Metropolis, p. 155.
35 Derek B. Scott: Sounds of the Metropolis, pp. 156 f. In general terms prices for sheet music did not fall significantly until the 1870s. For further reasons behind the high prices prior to this, see Cyril Ehrlich: The Music Profession in Britain since the 18th Century, p. 108.
36 Alfred Williams: Folk-Songs of the Upper Thames, p. 178.

It also shows that minstrel songs could acquire a value in use that was not intended in their initial commodity marketing, this particular example having been adapted by female agricultural labourers as an accompaniment to their physical labour. If its commercial dimension quite disappeared in this way, the question this raises is what happened to its racism as a plantation song? The song, like all plantation songs, was a travesty of the brutal realities of slave labour in the Deep South, purveying instead the racial stereotype of the blithely contented black slave or labourer, yet this in itself does not preclude identification by female agricultural workers in Gloucestershire with African-American field-hands in South Carolina. There is evidence of British workers in other manual occupations identifying closely with the exploited lives and sorrows of African-American people – the Welsh coalminer, Bert Lewis Coombes (1893-1974), for example, felt an unbidden wave of empathy run through him on hearing in the pub next door a gramophone record of Paul Robeson singing ›Old Man River‹ as he was dressing himself for his night-shift down the pit – so there is no reason why this did not apply to female farm-hands as well.[37]

Quite what this identification amounted to is difficult to say, for the song wavers between criticism of the ›massa‹, the slave-owner, (»Massa neath the shade would lay | While we poor niggers toiled all day«) and praise for him now he is dead (»Of all the massas he was the best«). This was a conventional trope in the plantation song, and what we take for criticism today may be nothing other than straightforward empirical observation, but it is difficult to avoid feeling that some expression of resentment was not present when the ›massa‹ was transposed to the English farmer, whose own existence is starkly contrasted with that of the field-hands. The comparison between the farmer and »we poor niggers« was implicit in the singing of the song in the context of their open-air labour. That is where Mrs Pitt learned the song, and so it is with reference to that context that the song should be historically understood.[38]

Show Business and Spectacle

This particular example suggests that we need to attend to the ways in which the racism of the minstrel commodity could, to a certain extent at least, diminish according to social context and the social relations pre-

---

[37] Bert Lewis Coombes: These Poor Hands, pp. 258 ff.
[38] Cf. Alfred Williams: Folk-Songs of the Upper Thames, p. 178; a newly recorded version of the song by Laura Hockenhull is available on the CD allied with Marek Korczynski, Michael Pickering, Emma Robertson: Rhythms of Labour.

vailing in any specific set of circumstances. At the very least, such racism was not semantically all of a piece across different contexts and relations. Along with this, it is important to emphasise that the pleasures of minstrelsy for its socially varied audiences did not solely lie in the affirmation it appeared to provide for their racist symbolic capital, for even though blackface entertainments were perhaps the most important vehicle of racist caricature and stereotyping of the nineteenth and early twentieth centuries, contributing in a very significant way to the inferiorisation of black people, its cultural attractions were manifold. It was not only the sheer variety of different acts and the different elements of the minstrel show, but also, for large-scale versions of this new form of commodified entertainment, the visual spectacle that was involved.

As I have argued elsewhere, British minstrelsy's popularisation of racism and the widespread acceptance of black racial stereotypes which it facilitated, was made possible precisely because it was hitched to an entertainment vehicle which brought with it a range of attractions and delights.[39] Spectacle was central to these for the audiences of the grand shows mounted by the main metropolitan companies that developed from the 1860s, both catering for and at the same time exploiting the commercial opportunities offered by the changing leisure patterns and retail revolution of the late nineteenth century.

It is vividly palpable in this poster for the Moore and Burgess Minstrels, one of the two main minstrel companies in London, run by Fred Burgess, their English business manager, and George Washington Moore, an American who settled in Britain and was responsible for organising everything to do with the entertainment itself.[40] Their headquarters from 1865 to the early years of the twentieth century was the smaller of the two halls that comprised the prestigious St James's Hall, Piccadilly (the larger hall was occupied by the London Philharmonic Society). As the poster shows, the intended theatrical effect was a sense of grandeur and magnificence, this being created by the large number of performers arranged in three successive horseshoe tiers, the addition of a (white, or non-masked) conductor as well as Mr Interlocutor in the centre of proceedings, baroque stage architecture set off by resplendent curtains and fake palms, the centerpiece inclusion of a harp among the other musicians playing wind and string instruments as well as one man on cymbals, and finally the smart livery of striped trousers, cummerband and bowtie – itself far removed

---

39   Cf. Michael Pickering: Blackfacing Britain.
40   For Moore, see Michael Pickering: Blackface Minstrelsy in Britain, pp. 30 ff.

from the ragged plantation costume of other minstrel representations.[41] The poster provides clear evidence of the refined character of the entertainment (see fig. 9). This is not only suggested by the addition of a harp, but also the legend ›fun without vulgarity‹, and the circular cutaway which

*Fig. 9: Moore & Burgess Minstrels poster
illustrating their dual appeal of refinement and spectacle.*

shows the entrance to St James's Hall frequented by top-hatted gentlemen. Comic antics and buffoonery were certainly part of the show, for no minstrel show was complete without them, and these along with stump speeches are indicated by the three additional images at the top of the poster, but the general emphasis was nevertheless on elegance, refinement and grand-scale display combining to produce »an entertainment at which no sensible person can take offence«.[42]

Self-evidently, being sensible, and so considered reasonable, fair-minded and judicious, is a historically variable quality, for minstrelsy as a cul-

---

41   The Moore & Burgess Minstrels appeared in formal evening attire for the first half of the show, after which they put on more comic forms of dress, but starting in this way set the social tone for the whole evening, after which the audience were softened up sufficiently for the more burlesque aspects of the entertainment.
42   Moore & Burgess Minstrels, p. 79.

tural form is now regarded as offensive, whereas in the last years of the nineteenth century, when this opinion was aired, good sense included acceptance of racist ideas and attitudes. The question of offence registered then in a different discourse, one of moral acceptability and good manners rather than inter-ethnic tolerance and what we now refer to as multiculturalism. The distinction is important because it did not extend – or only partially extended – to sensitivity towards how black people were being represented, or to being sensible of the gross distortions involved in these representations. For this reason, although Derek Scott is right to identify George ›Pony‹ Moore as being »without the grotesqueness found in many of the American burnt cork caricatures« when he performed in blackface, this does not mean that the Moore & Burgess Minstrels did not indulge in any general grotesquerie of representation. That is certainly clear in the cartoonish images of blacks they produced in order to provide members

Fig. 10: Annex to Moore & Burgess Minstrels programme, listing the last trains out of London, depicts various minstrel characters engaged in ›blackface fun‹.

of their audience with times of late trains they could catch following an evening being entertained in St James's Hall (see fig. 10). The images of minstrels shown are engaged in a variety of clownish antics or stances, the facial features are nothing if not grotesque, while semiotically the link with later golliwog images hardly needs any special pleading.

Conclusion

Commodity racism is usually associated with advertisements for material products like jam, oats, rice or shoe polish, but as a branch of newly commercialised popular entertainment, minstrelsy was itself a form of commodity racism in the selling and promotion of its products. The consequence of this was an increase in the circulation and perpetuation of black racial stereotypes. For this reason, advertising and commodified blackface entertainment are historically closely allied, with early forms of marketing and branding drawing freely on the racial stereotypes that were the common coin of minstrelsy. Race-based trademarks like the golly were derived from blackface imagery and discourse. At the same time, minstrelsy meant a good deal more than any particular example of imperialist advertising. Its racialised Other had to appeal beyond the exchange value of the commodity to which it belonged; it also had to produce, and resonate within, a range of pleasures and attractions in popular aesthetics. Only then was its success assured.

I have tried in this chapter to show, in some measure at least, how this operated through minstrelsy's avowedly commercial products of song sheet cover, poster and programme. What these examples of minstrel ephemera demonstrate with regard to commodity racism is that racism provided the binding force that brought the exchange value of the product and the aesthetic values of the entertainment into unification when otherwise they would have had no necessary compatibility at all. It was not then the racism in itself which was responsible for activating the ideology it conveyed, but the popular entertainment through which it was smuggled in. Even with its more genteel versions, whether on the metropolitan stage or on song albums intended for middle-class drawing rooms, any diminution of racism was only in an outwardly overt manner, and at times it wasn't apparent at all, as is clear with the upmarket ›New York Nigger Quadrilles‹ example. The racist dimension in minstrelsy was certainly variable, but this was more to do with its ability both to be believed in its depiction of blacks and to be seen as only make-believe. The outward overtness of its racist representations was thus to do with whether and where the stress fell upon sentimental refinement or comic vulgarity, or on realist detail rather than imaginative diversion. For this among other reasons, trying to understand the popular appeal of minstrelsy is not tantamount to condoning its racism, but it does require us to consider what constituted blackface fun and ask why minstrel acts and shows were taken as fun, accepted as pleasure, and embraced with such popularity. Without an attempt to answer this question our historical understanding of it will be limited.

Part of it is to do with minstrelsy's remarkable cultural stretch – bringing into the blackface fold entertainments as diverse as acrobatics and dancing dogs, stump speeches and Shakespearian burlesque – and part to do with making ›blackness‹ safely known and knowable, the ›blackness‹ which is, as Zadie Smith has recently put it, »what white people fear and adore and want and dread«.[43] Minstrelsy annulled the fear and dread, at least temporarily, and elaborated upon the adoring and desiring; it made a pleasing spectacle out of ›black‹ bodies and faces, and presented audiences with alluring fantasies of black character and culture. It was because of, not despite, doing such things that it reinforced a sense of white superiority and the need for white colonial possession and imperial control. Ideology is most effective when it is invisible as ideology, and blackface minstrelsy was crucial in making racist ideology invisible as ideology because it was disguised as sentiment and fun. Ideology and entertainment in minstrelsy were a self-reinforcing circle because if black people were really like that, as they were shown and represented, then that justified the fun and sentiment, while the fun and sentiment produced and helped perpetuate the various stereotypical notions about blacks which proved so durable. The basic difference then between how these were expressed in minstrelsy and how they were articulated in colonial discourse was only a matter of formality, as was made clear by Lord Lugard, the British soldier, mercenary and colonial governor, who regarded black people as »happy, thriftless, excitable [...] lacking in self-control, discipline and foresight [...] full of personal vanity, with little sense of veracity, fond of music [...]. His thoughts are concentrated on the events and feelings of the moment, and he suffers little apprehension for the future [...]. He lacks power of organisation, and is conspicuously deficient in the management and control alike of men and business [...]. He is prone to imitate anything new in dress or custom«.[44] All of these stereotypical notions were abundant in minstrel entertainment, but they were accepted and seen as credible because they were made acceptable by the heterogeneous abundance of the entertainment.

Minstrelsy made of the black what the white was not, at least in his or her own idealised self-image. What was denied to whites was projected onto blacks – and that of course was the whole significance of the black-

---

43 Zadie Smith: On Beauty, p. 242.
44 Frederick J. D. Lugard: The Dual Mandate in British Tropical Africa, pp. 69 f., 88.

face mask, making of the white performer what he was and could not be in the moral and social order of Victorian Britain.[45] Minstrelsy was meant to be, and commercially advertised itself as, respectable – fun without vulgarity – but this was always somewhat disingenuous, for minstrelsy took its audiences outside of their own self-arrogated respectibilities and allowed them an interval of unrespectable, disorderly, non-rational recreation. As Nathan Huggins so astutely noted: »White men put on black masks and became another self, one which was loose of limb, innocent of obligation to anything outside itself, indifferent to success [...]. The verisimilitude of this persona to actual Negroes [...] was at best incidental. For the white man who put on the black mask modeled himself after a subjective black man«.[46] Acting out the racial fantasy of the white-fabricated black enabled minstrelsy to make vulgarity respectable, transform it into what could be seen as sentimental or comic, as harmless entertainment – the very grounds on which many argued for the retention of ›The Black and White Minstrel Show‹ on television when the BBC finally realised that the historical tide had turned and the very act of its impersonation of black men had become widely regarded as offensive. This is the view that has been inherited with allied blackface forms like the golliwog, which has leant itself to a term considered by some as at best only »a bit offensive«, or able to be used, as Carol Thatcher allegedly used it, just as a joke. That is not the case and that is why it backfired, with the various people who were there in the green room of ›The One Show‹ complaining about it and making it a public affair. It is when the use of such terms or the telling of jokes that are offensive to their targets does backfire that we can see the perpetrators of comic racism not as amusing but as themselves the comic object.

References

Bourdieu, Pierre: The Field of Cultural Production. Cambridge: Polity 1993.
Coombes, Bert Lewis: These Poor Hands. The Autobiography of a Miner Working in South Wales. London: Gollancz 1939.
Davis, Norma S.: A Lark Ascends. Florence Kate Upton, Artist and Illustrator. London: The Scarecrow Press 1992.
Dennison, Sam: Scandalize My Name. Black Imagery in American Popular Music. New York: Garland 1982.

---

45 For extensive critical treatment of the blackface mask in British minstrelsy, see Michael Pickering: Blackface Minstrelsy in Britain, chapter 4.
46 Nathan Irwin Huggins: Harlem Renaissance, pp. 253 f.

Ehrlich, Cyril: The Music Profession in Britain since the 18th Century. Oxford: Clarendon Press 1985.
Emerson, Ken: Doo-Dah! Stephen Foster and the Rise of American Popular Culture. New York: Simon and Schuster 1997.
Fifty Songs Sung by the Ethiopians. London, n.d.
Fox, A. Wilson: Agricultural Wages in England and Wales During the Last Fifty Years. In Journal of the Royal Statistical Society, LXVI, 1903, pp. 273-257.
Hamm, Charles: Yesterdays. Popular Song in America. New York [et al.]: Norton 1979.
Huggins, Nathan Irwin: Harlem Renaissance. New York: Oxford University Press 1971.
Korczynski, Marek, Michael Pickering, Emma Robertson: Rhythms of Labour. Music at Work in Britain. Cambridge: Cambridge University Press 2013.
Kushner, Tony: Selling Racism. History, Heritage, Gender and the (Re)production of Prejudice. In Patterns of Prejudice, 33, 1999, 4, pp. 67-86.
Lorimer, Douglas A.: Colour, Class and the Victorians. English Attitudes to the Negro in the Mid-Nineteenth Century. Leicester: Leicester University Press 1978.
Lugard, Frederick J. D.: The Dual Mandate in British Tropical Africa. Edinburgh [et al.]: Blackwood 1922.
Marshall, P. David: Celebrity and Power. Minneapolis [et al.]: University of Minnesota Press 1997.
Middleton, Richard: Studying Popular Music. Milton Keynes [et al.]: Open University Press 1990.
Moore & Burgess Minstrels. Strand Musical Magazine, 4, July-December 1896, pp. 78 f.
Negro and American Songs. London, n.d.
Orwin, Charles Stewart, B. I. Felton: A Century of Wages and Earnings in Agriculture. In: Journal of the Royal Agricultural Society of England, 92, 1931, pp. 231-257.
Pickering, Michael: ›A Jet Ornament to Society‹. Black Music in Nineteenth-Century Britain. In: Black Music in Britain, ed. by Paul Oliver. Milton Keynes [et al.]: Open University Press 1990, pp. 16-33.
—: Blackface Minstrelsy in Britain. Aldershot [et al.]: Ashgate 2008.
—: Blackfacing Britain. In: Racism and Modernity. Festschrift for Wulf D. Hund, ed. by Iris Wigger, Sabine Ritter. Berlin [et al.]: Lit Verlag 2011, pp. 236-256.
—: Stereotyping. The Politics of Representation. Basingstoke [et al.]: Palgrave Macmillan 2001.
Russell, Dave: Popular Music in England. Kingston [et al.]: McGill-Queen's University Press 1987.
Samuel, Raphael: Theatres of Memory. London: Verso 1994.
Scott, Derek B.: Sounds of the Metropolis. The 19th-Century Popular Music Revolution in London, New York, Paris and Vienna. Oxford [et al.]: Oxford University Press 2011.
—: The Singing Bourgeois. Songs of the Victorian Drawing Room and Parlour. Milton Keynes [et al.]: Open University Press 1989.
Seroff, Doug: The Fisk Jubilee Singers in Britain. In: Under the Imperial Carpet, ed. by Rainer Lotz, Ian Pegg. Crawley: Rabbit Press 1986, pp. 42-54.

Smith, Zadie: On Beauty. London: Penguin 2006.
Weiß, Anja: Racist Symbolic Capital. A Bourdieuian Approach to the Analysis of Racism. In: Wages of Whiteness and Racist Symbolic Capital, ed. by Wulf D. Hund, Jeremy Krikler, David Roediger. (Racism Analysis | Yearbook 1). Berlin [et al.]: Lit Verlag 2010, pp. 37-56.
Williams, Alfred: Folk-Songs of the Upper Thames. London: Duckworth 1923.

From Œcumene to Trademark
The Symbolism of the ›Moor‹ in the Occident
Malte Hinrichsen

Abstract: Against some recent publications, this chapter portrays the occidental image of the ›moor‹ as undergoing a chequered history of representations. Emerging as a sanctified knight in late medieval iconography and visually included in a Christian realm opposing Muslim enemies, the ›moor‹ of the Middle Ages was all but a racist stereotype. Noble families like the Tuchers of Nuremberg incorporated portrayals of a dark-skinned saint in their coat of arms, while art and literature allowed for black characters to be chivalrous and gallant. With the establishment of transatlantic slavery, the ›moor's‹ noblesse was reduced to his extravagant oriental appearance, while he was attributed the social role of a servant in equivalence to the African slave in the colonies. Eventually, when Enlightenment thought fostered scientific justifications for plantation slavery, the ›moor‹ like the ›negro slave‹ was classified as racially inferior. Thus, in 1855, as the Tucher family started to promote beer with the ›moor's head‹, this heraldic figure was long emptied of its initial positive attributions. Amidst other advertising ›moors‹ of the 19th century, it both benefited from and contributed to the popularisation of racism. The preservation of the trademark symbol during the Nazi era, when other traditional representations of ›moors‹ were abandoned, further illustrates that a commodified and racialised image of the black had overwritten an icon of intercontinental œcumene.

Around 1900, the term ›Mohr‹ was the »advertisers' synonym for ›black«« in German commodity culture.[1] When, in 2009, the Austrian ice-cream producer ›Eskimo‹ started to promote its newly launched dessert ›Mohr im Hemd‹ with the Austro-English slogan »I will Mohr«, this aroused massive protests by social activists, arguing that the term ›Mohr‹ bears pejorative connotations and perpetuates racist stereotypes for people of colour.[2] Yet as the company then stopped its contested campaign, this again provoked an outcry by Austrians who attacked anti-racist organisations

---

1   David Ciarlo: Advertising Empire, pp. 414, 213 ff. Throughout the text, I will apply the English term ›moor‹ for all general considerations and refer to translations like the German ›Mohr‹ when the discussed example requires linguistic specification.
2   Cf. Claus Pirschner, Claudia Unterweger: Will i mohr?

for challenging their traditional and supposedly innocent designations for confectionary.³

Despite this reactionary backlash, products and companies in the German-speaking world are increasingly confronted with allegations of racism, when they fail to abandon ›traditional‹ racist trademark symbols or launch new campaigns perceived as lacking in racial sensitivity.⁴ Building on the achievements of the civil rights movement in the United States, where racist representations in advertising have been publicly criticized since the 1960s, anti-racist organisations in Germany have started to draw attention to racist promotion, and more specifically to the continuous presence of commodified ›moors‹ in popular culture.

A considerable part of this criticism derives from recent publications of German Critical Whiteness Studies, which include lexical collections of racist vocabulary and, among other things, attempt a deconstruction of the term ›moor‹.⁵ The respective articles similarly assess the etymological and historical devaluation the notion contains and chronicle a supposedly uninterrupted tradition of its usage by racist whites.⁶ Allegedly originating in the Greek and Latin words for ›foolish‹, ›godless‹ and ›black‹, ›moor‹ is said to have first been used as a derogatory designation for Muslims, interwoven from early on with racialised perceptions of skin colour. Through constant reproduction it has made its way from medieval religious persecutions to the everyday racism of the 20th century, not least giving the name to Germany's most prominent advertising figures.

Following these interpretations, activists in Berlin since the early 2000s fought for the renaming of the local ›Mohrenstraße‹ due to its racist and colonialist references.⁷ Surprisingly, their purpose was opposed by a scholar of German colonial history, who publicly advocated a different reading of the controversial term ›moor‹ as an initially neutral designation deriving from pre-racist discourses on Africans. When the ›Mohrenstraße‹ was given its name around 1700, he argues, it lacked derogatory connota-

---

3   Cf. Michael Möseneder: Bevorzugung statt Wortstreit. For a similar controversy in Switzerland see Regina Bendix: Of Mohrenköpfe and Japanesen, p. 15.
4   Cf. Malte Hinrichsen: Racist Trademarks, pp. 88-97. For contemporary examples see www.meinjulius.at dealing with the famous Meinl-Mohr in Austria, the initiative ›No Mohr‹ against the racist advertising of Austrian Mohrenbräu, or the activities of der-braunemob.de, which critically address German everyday racism.
5   For an introduction to Critical Whiteness Studies in Germany see Maureen M. Eggers, Grada Kilomba, Peggy Piesche, Susan Arndt (eds.): Mythen, Masken und Subjekte.
6   Cf. Ulrike Hamann: Das M-Wort; Susan Arndt, Ulrike Hamann: Mohr_in. A critical assessment of these collections in general and the lemmata on ›moors‹ in particular can be found in Wulf D. Hund: Vor, mit, nach und ohne ›Rassen‹, pp. 748-752, 757.
7   Cf. Joshua K. Aikins, Christian Kopp: Straßennamen mit Bezügen zum Kolonialismus in Berlin, pp. 16 f.

tions and merely recalled the visit of an African delegation on the court of Frederick William of Brandenburg, the ›Great Elector‹.[8]

Analysing the prominent example of the Tucher-Mohr, this chapter will contribute to the aforementioned controversies by following the figure through its chequered history, from its emergence in the family's coat of arms around 1300 to its commodification on beer mats and other merchandising products. Against this backdrop, the Tucher trademark symbol of today is one that exemplifies both the racism of contemporary advertising *and* the complex development of a racist stereotype.

Origination

Since Greek and Roman antiquity, dark-skinned Africans had been subjected to xenophobic discriminations with their complexion as an »exciting interest«, but these were neither systematically justified nor characterised by a common stereotypical image of the black.[9] The black ›moor‹, as an artistic device with recurring features and attributes, entered the stages of European iconography and literature in the High Middle Ages, namely during the Staufer era when the Holy Roman Empire was fighting Muslims in Palestine, while at the same time the royal court moved to multiethnic Sicily, where the kings took several Africans into their service.[10] At this time, when Jew-hatred resulted in numerous pogroms being added to the itinerary of crusaders, the image of the black was a complex setting far from racist stereotyping.[11]

By the time of the crusades, the German term ›mor‹ (as the Middle High German precursor of the later ›Mohr‹) was applied to both Muslim Arabs (the later ›Maure‹) and Africans, which might have inspired some of today's inaccurate interpretations.[12] While the former were almost uni-

8 Cf. Ulrich van der Heyden: Gröblicher Rufmord an von der Gröben; Joshua K. Aikins, Chandra-Milena Danielzik, Matti Steinitz: Wie weiß ist der Elfenbeinturm? See also Peter Martin: Schwarze Teufel, edle Mohren, p. 86.
9 Robert Miles: Racism, p. 12. For a discussion of ancient discourses on skin colour see still Frank M. Snowden: Before Color Prejudice. Cf. also Benjamin Isaac: The Invention of Racism in Classical Antiquity; Miriam Eliav-Feldon, Benjamin Isaac, Joseph Ziegler (eds.): The Origins of Racism in the West.
10 Cf. Hans W. Debrunner: Presence and Prestige, pp. 18-23.
11 The persecutions of Jews in Europe accompanying the first crusade are discussed in Jeremy Cohen: Sanctifying the Name of God. Most medieval references to so-called ›hellemoren‹ (transl.: *hell moors*) made use of the dark colour on a merely symbolical level as a general marker for the evil and uncanny, cf. Andreas Mielke: Nigra sum et formosa, p. 84; Sylvia Hahn: Das Rätselraten um den Mohren, p. 19.
12 Cf. Andreas Mielke: Nigra sum et formosa, pp. 82 f.; see also Andrea Polaschegg: Der andere Orientalismus, p. 75. For English and Portuguese connotations of the respective terms see Emily C. Bartels: Making More of the Moor, pp. 434 f.; Josiah Blackmore: Imagining the Moor in Medieval Portugal, pp. 28 ff.

formly portrayed as demonic and hostile, images of the latter were increasingly influenced by the iconography of Christian blacks, that embodied the universality of the Catholic Church and made little of the Islamic

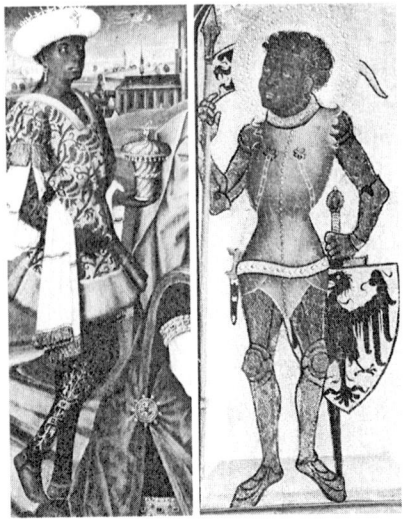

Fig. 1 a & b: From the 13th century, Christian icons as one of the three Magi (left) and St. Maurice (right) were depicted with dark complexion.

threat.[13] The black Magus, Prester John and Saint Maurice formed a trinity of images, which positively depicted Africans as faithful representatives of distant Christian peoples (see fig. 1 a & b).[14] Although their skin colour functioned as a marker of difference, the common creed established a connection between Europe and Africa that bridged the Muslim empire and seemed to »imply that all races are equal before God, and that the Christian mission is universal«.[15]

According to Allison Blakely, the emergence of Africans in religious painting of the late Middle Ages is »not surprising«, since perceptions of

13 Cf. Henri Baudet: Paradise on Earth, pp. 13-20; Paul Kaplan: Black Africans in Hohenstaufen Iconography. Eckhard Breitinger, African Presences and Representations in the Principality/Markgrafschaft of Bayreuth, p. 110, finds even earlier evidences for the veneration of »dark-skinned« St. Augustine.
14 Fig. 1a: Detail of Friedrich Herlin the Elder's ›Adoration of the Magi‹ (1462), reprinted in Jean Devisse, Michel Mollat: The Image of the Black in Western Art, II, 2, p. 136 (mirror-inverted); Rainer Kahsnitz, Achim Bunz (eds.): Die großen Schnitzaltäre, p. 55. Fig. 1b: Detail of an altarpiece in Brandenburg (ca. 1370-80), reprinted in Jean Devisse, Michel Mollat: The Image of the Black in Western Art, II, 2, p. 169.
15 Paul Kaplan: Black Africans in Hohenstaufen Iconography, p. 29 – note that the term ›race‹ did not exist in the contemporary discourse of that time.

reality were frequently translated to biblical allegories.[16] Thus, increasing contact with Africa affected the blackening of existing icons, especially of those that traditionally embraced oriental characters. The three Magi, for example, were portrayed with foreign exoticised clothing since the 8th century to bear witness to their distant homelands.[17] Inspired by blacks employed by emperor Frederick II, German and Italian artists began to include black attendants to the Magi's entourage, and from the late 13th century onwards frequently depicted one of them as African himself.[18]

The chronicle of the Tucher, the famous ›Tucherbuch‹ of the late 16th century, traces the family's coat of arms back to an »Æthiopum gens« that once defended faith and fatherland like the Tuchers protect their hometown of Nuremberg[19] (see fig. 2).[20] This comparison is widely interpreted as a direct reference to Saint Maurice, a legendary »duke of the moors«, who allegedly led the Theban Legion against rebellious Gauls and became

Fig. 2: Dating at least from the 14th century, the Tuchers' coat of arms was famously redrawn for the Tucherbuch of 1591.

a martyr.[21] Emerging as the patron saint of the Holy Roman Empire, he was initially depicted as a white European knight until he frequently acquired a dark complexion in the 13th century.[22] As a symbol for the Chris-

16 Allison Blakely: Blacks in the Dutch World, p. 83.
17 Cf. Joseph L. Koerner: The Epiphany of the Black Magus, pp. 10 f.
18 Cf. Paul H. D. Kaplan: The Rise of the Black Magus in Western Art, pp. 7-11.
19 Das Große Tucherbuch, f. 24v.
20 Fig. 2: Detail of Jost Amman's drawing of the Tuchers' coat of arms in Das Große Tucherbuch, f. 24r, reprinted in Peter J. Bräunlein: Von Mohren-Apotheken und Mohrenkopf-Wappen, p. 225; Ludwig Grote: Die Tucher, fig. 100.
21 As »herzoge der Môre« Mauritius is addressed in the ›Kaiserchronik‹ of 1160, cited in Peter Martin: Schwarze Teufel, edle Mohren, p. 35.
22 For the visual history of the black St. Maurice see Gude Suckale-Redlefsen: Mauritius.

tian piety of distant peoples, he became the icon of the Wendish Crusade and early mission in Eastern Europe.[23] Thus, spreading most notably in Central Europe's border regions, he was soon portrayed in countless coats of arms of the regional clergy and nobility.[24]

Coats of arms, as »specific sets of markings« to be »applied to armor, horse trappings and banners«, were among the earliest references to black characters in (Central) European culture.[25] Intimating the intercontinental trade networks of noble families and the heroism of St. Maurice, ›moors‹ like the one on Herdegen Tucher's helmet in the early 15th century lacked derogatory connotations[26] (see fig. 3).[27] Rather they represented the belief that chivalry was not (as yet) restricted to physical appearance or geographic origin, but was an expression of Christian faith and noble descent. The ›moor‹ figure could even be identified with members of the family, as a church window created in celebration of the pilgrimage of Hans Tucher in 1481 illustrates. The depiction of the ›moor‹ with a sweaty headscarf is reminiscent of the patriarch's crossing of the desert and highlights the representative function of the heraldic figure.[28]

In Central Europe, where visual portrayals of blacks in heraldry and religious paintings were most popular, they were soon accompanied by literary portrayals of African virtue. According to Andreas Mielke, there »was barely a major text in German medieval literature in which no ›moors‹ appeared«. In his study, he gives examples for the pre-racial image of Africans in Middle High German writing and especially focuses on Wolfram von Eschenbach's ›Parzival‹ and its positive black character Feirefiz.[29]

Additional evidence for the late medieval belief in a fundamental commonality of dark-skinned ›moors‹ and fair Europeans can be found in various illustrations of the miraculous deeds of the Saints Cosmas and Damian, whose story in the Legenda Aurea was among the most popular religious

23 Cf. Jean Devisse: The Image of the Black in Western Art, II, 1, p. 153.
24 Cf. Gude Suckale-Redlefsen: Mauritius, pp. 50-53. Exemplarily, the background of the ›moor‹ of Freising, which was, e.g., featured in the papal coat of arms of Benedict XVI is examined in Sebastian Anneser, Friedrich Fahr, Norbert Jocher, Norbert Knopp, Peter B. Steiner (eds.): Der Mohr kann gehen. See also Jean Devisse, Michel Mollat: The Image of the Black in Western Art, II, 2, pp. 7-58.
25 Gude Suckale-Redlefsen: Mauritius, p. 51; Peter J. Bräunlein: Von Mohren-Apotheken und Mohrenkopf-Wappen, p. 220.
26 Cf. Peter Martin: Schwarze Teufel, edle Mohren, pp. 52-55.
27 Fig. 3: Sketch of Herdegen Tucher and Berthold Nützel, reprinted in Peter Martin: Schwarze Teufel, edle Mohren, p. 334; Ludwig Grote: Die Tucher, fig. 66.
28 Cf. Randall Herz (ed.): Die ›Reise ins Gelobte Land‹ Hans Tuchers des Älteren, plate 31.
29 Andreas Mielke: Nigra sum et formosa, p. 83 (if not specifically marked, quotations from non-English sources are my translations). In contrast to abovementioned scholars, who superficially understand Feirefiz as early evidence for anti-black attitudes of the 13th century, Mielke interprets the black knight as the real hero of Wolfram's epic, ibid., pp. 99-108. See also Wulf D. Hund: Rassismus (1999), pp. 29-32.

From Œcumene to Trademark

Fig. 3: In the 15th century, the Tucher-Mohr represented the chivalrous and religious qualities of the family.

texts of the Middle Ages.[30] One biographical episode in particular inspired artists across Europe: the transplantation of the necrotic leg of a European cleric with the black leg of a deceased Ethiopian ›moor‹.[31] Depicting the surgery as a peaceful and clean ceremony, with the black limb seamlessly attached to the white torso, painters of the 15th century delivered an image of human integrity that overshadowed outward differences.[32]

Objectification

Images of the thaumaturgic abilities of Cosmas and Damian outlived most representations of heroic blacks, but not without fundamental changes to their implicit messages. Since the emergence of the transatlantic slave trade, images of Africans tended to concentrate on their position as slaves and domestic servants.[33] For the visual culture of the legendary organ

---

30 Cf. Anneliese Wittmann: Kosmas und Damian, p. 12.
31 Cf. Gerhard Fichtner: Das verpflanzte Mohrenbein, p. 87.
32 In Georg Schreiber: Medizin und Charisma, the author interprets the application of a ›moor‹'s leg as a reference to »primitive vigours« and »magical energies« attributed to the African. Furthermore, he argues that the desecration of the grave would not have been acceptable with a Christian. Since the early textual and visual sources give no evidence for a pagan religion of the ›moor‹ and, on the contrary, emphasise the recentness of his death as the reason for choosing his leg, this interpretation seems to be biased by later developments of racial theories.
33 For early representations of slavery in Renaissance Italian sculpture see Lorenz Seelig: ›Ein Willkomme in der Form eines Mohrenkopfs von Silber getriebener Arbeit‹, pp. 82-85.

donation this meant that the black was no longer depicted as a dignified decedent, but as a living spare parts repository whose suffering does not interfere with the moral righteousness of the operation (see fig. 4 a & b).[34] Thus, a late 16th century Spanish relief shows the sacred physicians intently operating on their patient, while the ›moor‹, alive but distorted with pain, holds his mutilated leg.[35]

This representation of the ›moor‹ as a dehumanised and therefore acceptable victim of physical violence marks a break in the European iconography of the black, at a time when transatlantic slave trade induced the emergence of skin colour racism.[36] Blacks increasingly became »objects« in European art, although, as David Goldberg interprets the »shift from religiously to racially conceived identity« in Hieronymus Bosch's ›Garden of Earthly Delights‹, they could remain »enchanting and enticing«.[37] During this process, as Winthrop D. Jordan asserts, the exaggerated colour of black »became so generally associated with Africa that every African seemed a black man« and was represented as »pitchy black« in visual culture.[38] Essentially, Africans were »marked [...] with a natural badge of pigmentation« that enabled their pictorial exploitation as a side-effect of their large-scale commodification on the slave markets.[39]

In Renaissance art, from the Mediterranean via Britain to France and Central Europe, the impact of slavery was most distinctly reflected when court painters portrayed their patron's »most remarkable acquisitions: a black slave and a fair mistress«.[40] Images of dark-skinned domestic slaves as the representatives of an »ethnic specialization« to the »occupational roles allocated to blacks in western society«, entered the stage as symbols of luxury and still were not obviously offensive.[41] However, the emerging »stereotype of the docile Negro which was taking hold in the West and would live on for centuries«, developed into the co-existence of two black

34   Fig. 4a: Fernando del Rincon, ›Miracle of the Black Leg‹ (late 15th century), reprinted in Jean Devisse, Michel Mollat: The Image of the Black in Western Art, II, 2, p. 206; Marie-Louise David-Danel: Iconographie des Saints médecins Come et Damien, plate 13. Fig. 4b: Relief from Valladolid (mid-16th century), reprinted in Jean Devisse, Michel Mollat: The Image of the Black in Western Art, II, 2, p. 207; Marie-Louise David-Danel: Iconographie des Saints médecins Come et Damien, plate 14.
35   Cf. Marie-Louise David-Danel: Iconographie des Saints médecins Come et Damien, p. 49.
36   The shift of European slave trade to Africa is frequently connected to the development of racist thought. Cf. for example Wulf D. Hund: Rassismus (2007), p. 73; Imanuel Geiss: Geschichte des Rassismus, p. 88; Audrey Smedley: Race in North America, pp. 142-146. For a reference to assumed skin colour racism in Muslim slave societies see Egon Flaig: Weltgeschichte der Sklaverei, pp. 124-138.
37   David T. Goldberg: Racist Culture, p. 24.
38   Winthrop D. Jordan: White over Black, p. 5.
39   Ivan Hannaford: Race, p. 167.
40   Gary Taylor: Buying Whiteness, p. 41.
41   Jan Nederveen Pieterse: White on Black, p. 124.

stereotypes, which George Fredrickson diagnosed for the later American slave society as a »sharp and recurring contrast between ›the good Negro‹ in his place and the vicious black out of it«.[42] In Europe, this dualism

Fig. 4 a & b: From the 15th to the 16th century, the image of the ›moor‹ reflected the fundamental changes in European perceptions of Africans.

was, at least partially, linguistically fostered by the division of ›moor‹ and ›negro‹.[43]

Whereas the external African slave overseas was increasingly depicted as a »violent, treacherous and dangerous being«, blacks in Europe were similarly reduced to subservient roles, but equipped with »Moorish, in the sense of Arabic, costume«.[44] Images of these court servants, thus, represented »a form of orientalism« and redefined the symbolism of ›moors‹ »as oddities to be incorporated in a life-style that was always ostentatious, often bacchanalian and not infrequently bizarre«.[45] Represented in Oriental trappings, the African servant in Europe remained part of traditional

---

42 Allison Blakely: Blacks in the Dutch World, p. 113; George M. Fredrickson: The Arrogance of Race, p. 215.
43 Although the ambiguity of the term ›moor‹ led historians to general assumptions about differing complexities, ›negroes‹ and ›moors‹ were not initially distinguished through their skin colour, cf. Peter Martin: Schwarze Teufel, edle Mohren 81-89.
44 Madge Dresser: Slavery Obscured, pp. 58 f.; Jan Nederveen Pieterse: White on Black, p. 124.
45 Jan Nederveen Pieterse: White on Black, p. 124; Walter Rodney: Africa in Europe and the Americas, p. 584. In his study on images of blacks in the works of William Hogarth, David Dabydeen interprets this redefinition as a degrading continuation of the iconography of black saints. Thus, he assesses the »image of the black Magus attending Madonna in an attitude of human equality« to be »debased into the image of

discourses on ›moors‹, while ›negro‹ became a synonym for ›slave‹ in the colonies.[46] Equally disfranchised, this division enabled the integration of the former in domestic slavery, while the latter measured the death toll for the emerging plantation economy.

From its outset, transatlantic slavery had also influenced the visual culture of heraldry. In 1471, the Portuguese merchant Fernão Gomes re-

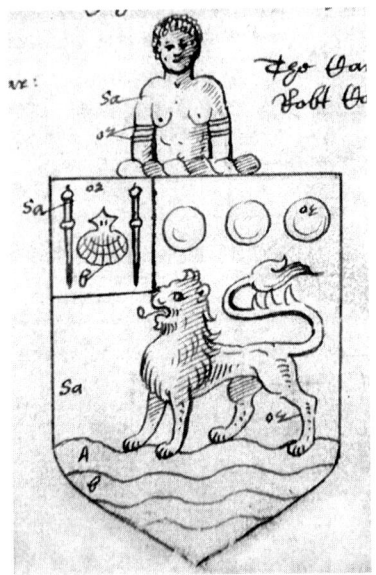 

Fig. 5: By the 16th century, transatlantic slavery had influenced not only the representations of Africans, but also the applications of coats of arms.

Fig. 6: In the early 16th century, Albrecht Dürer, like many of his contemporaries, had incorporated a ›moor‹ to his personal coat of arms and portrayed the Tucher-Mohr.

ceived slave trade rights for the West African Gold Coast and was further »rewarded with [...] a coat of arms showing ›the heads of three negroes wearing collars and pendants of gold‹«, which is still exhibited on Lisbon's Praça Império.[47] Similarly in England, slave trader John Hawkins' coat of arms of 1568 »celebrates the trade he pioneered in England since

    the black slave-servant attending the secular mistress«, David Dabydeen: Hogarth's Blacks, p. 36.
46 For the »concept of the Negro slave«, cf. Markéta Křížová: Frontiers of Race, Frontiers of Freedom. See also Malte Hinrichsen: Racist Trademarks, pp. 14-34.
47 Kim F. Hall: Things of Darkness, p. 19, citing Pierre Vilar: A History of Gold and Money, p. 53.

it includes a naked and bound African slave«[48] (see fig. 5).[49] In central Europe at that time, the traditional motif of the ›moor's head‹ was increasingly superseded by portrayals of ›aboriginal‹ blacks, dressed in loincloth or entirely naked. With headdress or turban, some of these figures referred to imagined inhabitants of the Americas or East India, though always emphasizing the otherness of the (›noble‹) ›savages‹.[50]

Furthermore, in the age of discovery the primary use of these crests was no longer for identification in battles, but for the labelling of property, so that coats of arms were frequently engraved in collars, which marked slaves as the possession of their masters.[51] Those collars along with the unmistakeable pigmentation, were common features of representations of slaves in Europe and overseas.[52] Although their »sartorial elegance [...] belie[d] the sordid reality of the servitude of naked and manacled blacks in the colonies«, the slave status of ›moors‹ in domestic service was undisputed.[53] In visual culture of the 16th and 17th century, the sacred or knightly ›moors‹ of the late Middle Ages had become subjected to an ideology of Western superiority that eradicated older perceptions of potentially ›equal‹ others.

While from the early 16th century this iconography of African slavery was most noticeable in the Mediterranean and on the British Isles, the Franconian Tuchers had their family emblem drawn by Albrecht Dürer, who himself bore a ›moor‹ in his coat of arms[54] (see fig. 6).[55] As long-distance traders in fabrics, spices and dyes with contacts to Spain and Italy, however, the Tuchers must have witnessed the rise of the transatlantic slave trade from the start.[56] As early as 1536, members of the Tucher fami-

---

48 Claire Jowitt: The Culture of Piracy, p. 102.
49 Fig. 5: John Hawkins' coat of arms, reprinted in Claire Jowitt: The Culture of Piracy, p. 103; Kim F. Hall: Things of Darkness, p. 20.
50 Cf. Hans-Ulrich von Ruepprecht: Der Mohr als Wappenfigur, p. 52. Some pictorial evidence is given in Mira A. Schnoor: Der Mohr im Wappen. For the concepts of ›good‹ and ›noble savages‹ cf. Jan Nederveen Pieterse: White on Black, pp. 30-39. For Africans as ›noble savages‹ see Urs Bitterli: Die Entdeckung des schwarzen Afrikaner, pp. 79-96. See also Ter Ellingson: The Myth of the Noble Savage.
51 Cf. David Bindman, Henry L. Gates, Jr.: Preface to The Image of the Black in Western Art, p. xviii; Susan Dwyer Amussen: Caribbean Exchanges, p. 223.
52 Cf. Susan Dwyer Amussen: Caribbean Exchanges, p. 215.
53 David Dabydeen: Hogarth's Blacks, p. 114.
54 Cf. Eckhard Breitinger: African Presences and Representations in the Principality/ Markgrafschaft of Bayreuth, p. 124.
55 Fig. 6: Albrecht Dürer, ›Wappen der Scheurl und Tucher‹ (1512), reprinted in Christian Kuhn: Generation als Grundbegriff einer historischen Geschichtskultur, p. 191.
56 Cf. Philippe Braunstein: Wirtschaftliche Beziehungen zwischen Nürnberg und Italien im Spätmittelalter, pp. 387, 395. For the trade network of the Tucher family see Ludwig Grote: Die Tucher, pp. 28-40. The role of the slave market in the Renaissance Mediterranean is exemplarily discussed in Sergio Tognetti: The trade in black African slaves in fifteenth-century Florence.

ly were involved in the slave-trading activities of Lazarus Nürnberger and other German merchants and, thus, contributed to the changing image of their coat-of-arms motif.[57] In 1589 at the latest, when the first black slaves were brought to Nuremberg, the Tuchers must have noticed that heraldic chivalry and sanctity were not conceded to most dark-skinned Africans.[58] Around two centuries later, as the exploitations of Africans were further rationalized and the science of human races was at the heart of intellectual discourse, the Tucher family still had first-hand accounts on the philosophy of modern racism.

Racialisation

When Georg Wilhelm Friedrich Hegel gave his Berlin Lectures on the ›Philosophy of History‹ and assessed that the »Negro [...] exhibits the natural man in his completely wild and untamed state«, he had married Marie von Tucher, whose family's coat of arms seemed only superficially untouched by the fundamental changes in the European perception of dark-skinned Africans.[59] Hegel's emphasis on nature signalled that the ›negro‹ was no longer distinguished through (the lack of) culture and religion, but rather along biologically determined racial parameters.[60] In the early 19th century this was no exceptional opinion but rather built on scholarly inquiries that involved most great minds of the time. In actual fact, the »great philosophers and statesmen of the eighteenth and nineteenth century [...] all endorsed the hierarchical division of humanity into superior and inferior races«.[61]

Since 1750 at the latest, racial hierarchies systematised established prejudices and suggested the natural inferiority of coloured races to European whites. Philosophers like Hume and Kant supported these biological classifications with reflections on the mental and cultural deficiencies of

---

57   Cf. Rolf Walter: Oberdeutsche Kaufleute und Genuesen in Sevilla und Cadiz (1525-1560), p. 27.
58   Cf. Peter Martin: Schwarze Teufel, edle Mohren, p. 46; Lorenz Seelig: ›Ein Willkomme in der Form eines Mohrenkopfs von Silber getriebener Arbeit‹, p. 93.
59   Georg W. F. Hegel: Vorlesungen über die Philosophie der Geschichte, p. 90. Transl. cited in Babacar Camara: The Falsity of Hegel's Theses on Africa, p. 85. Hegel's racism is discussed in Sander L. Gilman: On Blackness without Blacks, pp. 93-102; Charles Simon-Aaron: The Atlantic Slave Trade, pp. 507-522; Gudrun Hentges: Schattenseiten der Aufklärung, pp. 244-271.
60   This can be interpreted as part of a discursive shift that took place in 18th century Enlightenment thought. As Snait Gissis: Visualizing ›Race‹ in the Eighteenth Century, pp. 52 f., asserts, »the social became observed and analyzed through the natural – explained on the basis of natural (e.g., geographical, geological, climatic) conditions«.
61   Howard Winant: The World is a Ghetto, p. 28.

the degraded peoples.[62] Africans occupied a central role in these Enlightenment discourses on human inequality and their scientific devaluation corresponded to a linguistic shift. In 1784, Samuel Thomas Soemmerring published the first edition of his observations on human inequality in a treatise »about the physical difference of the moor from the European«, but already by the second edition of the very next year the word ›moor‹ was replaced by ›negro‹.[63]

As reflected in the case of Angelo Soliman, by the late 18th century even the most noble ›moors‹ were consigned to the racial inferiority of ›negroes‹.[64] Brought to Europe in early infancy, Soliman received academic training and worked as an educator. He married an Austrian noblewoman and became a reputable member of the local Freemason's lodge. After his death, however, he was not treated according to the social status he had achieved, but to the racial classification he was given. Scientists of the natural history collection used his skin to produce a taxidermic model and equipped it with feathers and glass beads to »display uncivilized Africa«.[65] While his social advancement suggests that Soliman was given the chance to prove his abilities, his post mortem exhibition seems the inevitable purpose of an African body during the rise of the European racial sciences.

This process of scientifically defining people of African descent as ›negroes‹ was fostered by Petrus Camper, who provided the aesthetic scheme to identify their inferior beauty as in-between that of humans and animals.[66] Not only Hegel esteemed Camper's ›facial angles‹, an imaginary line from forehead to front teeth, as a »very significant distinction between the human and animal appearance«.[67] That this concept not only enabled the differentiation of humans, but also provided the blueprint for forthcoming portrayals of Africans can be witnessed in countless images of racialised blacks.

62 Cf. Emmanuel C. Eze (ed.): Race and the Enlightenment. See also the respective essays in Andrew Valls (ed.): Race and Racism in Modern Philosophy.
63 Samuel T. Soemmerring: Über die körperliche Verschiedenheit des Mohren vom Europäer; id.: Über die körperliche Verschiedenheit des Negers vom Europäer.
64 Cf. Sünne Juterczenka: ›Chamber Moors‹ and Court Physicians, pp. 173-174; Iris Wigger, Katrin Klein: ›Bruder Mohr‹, pp. 83-91; Philipp Blom: Solimans Körper, Angelos Geist, p. 15.
65 Heather Morrison: Dressing Angelo Soliman, p. 375. Cf. also Philipp Blom: Straussenfedern, Muscheln und Glasperlen; Sünne Juterczenka: ›Chamber Moors‹ and Court Physicians; Iris Wigger and Katrin Klein: ›Bruder Mohr‹, pp. 105-111. For the racist symbolism of feathers in 18th century anthropology see Felicity Nussbaum: The Limits of the Human, p. 140.
66 Cf. David Bindman: Ape to Apollo, pp. 201-209; George L. Mosse: Die Geschichte des Rassismus in Europa, pp. 49 f.; Wulf D. Hund: Die Körper der Bilder der Rassen, pp. 17-21. See also Miriam C. Meijer: Race and Aesthetics in the Anthropology of Petrus Camper.
67 Georg W. F. Hegel: Vorlesungen über die Ästhetik, p. 387. Cf. Gudrun Hentges: Schattenseiten der Aufklärung, p. 251.

Soon, these representations included a new application to the Tuchers' coat of arms ›moor‹. When the family took over the Nuremberg Royal Brewery in 1855, they introduced the »Moor's Head as a trade mark for the firm«, which then became »well known in all parts of the world«.[68] However, a comparison between the traditional and the trademark emblem reveals that not the medieval portrait of St. Maurice featured on beer mats and bottles, but rather Hegel's and Camper's ›negro‹ with his characteristic sloping forehead (see fig. 7e). Exaggerated lips and the posture of his head round off the African stereotype and emphasise how by the 19th century racial science had entirely overwritten early European representations of blacks.

Simultaneously, racialized images of Africans were increasingly utilised as symbols for the economic superiority of the European empires. Just one year before Tucher started to promote beverages with their redefined ›moor‹, the reopened Crystal Palace in London exhibited industrial produce, colonial riches and, not least, models of African natives to the general public.[69] Visitors to these fairs and to later ethnological expositions were not only assured of their belonging to a wealthy and civilised country, but also to the preeminent race of mankind. This strategy of ideologically including people from all strata of society within the culture of imperialism was adopted by the young advertising industry and colonial imagery led to the early »›racialisation‹ of brand identities«.[70] »Commodity racism«, as Anne McClintock notes, »became distinct from scientific racism in its capacity to expand beyond the literate, propertied elite«.[71]

In Germany, so-called ›Völkerschauen‹ toured cities and towns from the 1850s and enabled the development of a »popular racism, which spread rapidly, taking root throughout Europe«.[72] By the late 19th century there »was hardly a product, which was not at least temporarily advertised with Asians or Africans«.[73] The success of American minstrel shows disseminated ideas of comical blacks, imperial propaganda provided seemingly ethnological images, and portraits of eroticised dark-skinned females played on the sexual connotations of race. Depictions of oriental black

---

68 Freiherrlich von Tuchersche Brauerei A.-G., back page.
69 See the article by Wulf D. Hund in this volume.
70 Anandi Ramamurthy: Imperial Persuaders, p. 15. See also Malte Hinrichsen: Promoting Racism.
71 Anne McClintock: Imperial Leather, p. 209.
72 Pascal Blanchard, Nicolas Bancel, Sandrine Lemaire: From Scientific Racism to Popular and Colonial Racism in France and the West, p. 104. See also Nana Badenberg: Mohrenwäschen, Völkerschauen; Anne Dreesbach, Helmut Zedelmaier (eds.): ›Gleich hinterm Hofbräuhaus waschechte Amazonen‹.
73 Stefanie Wolter: Die Vermarktung des Fremden, p. 52. For the following see ibid., pp. 61-81; David Ciarlo: Advertising Empire, pp. 217-225.

›moors‹, however, as the alleged ›historical‹ branch of racist advertising, were always at the centre of promotional activities and remain the most persistent trademark stereotype in German commodity culture.

Commodification

Particularly around the First World War, when the »conventions of racialization were so widely established in consumer culture that it is nearly impossible to find images of blacks that do not deploy them«, German marketers promoted their products with advertising ›moors‹.[74] In sharp contrast to overtly racist propaganda of that time, childlike blacks with fez and exaggerated physiognomies were featured in ads for cocoa, coffee or tobacco and functioned as »intelligible [...] confidant, that in some way belonged to German culture and tradition«.[75] Chocolaty sweets were named after ›moors‹ and the Sarotti-Mohr of 1918 became the »most visible black figure in German popular culture«.[76] Similarly in Austria, coffee retailer Julius Meinl established a black servant as its trademark symbol, evoking fantasies of Orient and luxury.[77] Even earlier and parallel to the Tucher family, Vorarlberg brewer Josef Mohr had introduced the ›moor's head‹ from his family's coat of arms as the new emblem for his brewery, a symbol that was maintained by the following owners down to the present day[78] (see fig. 7 a-f).[79]

The Tucher trademark was among this range of popular advertising ›moors‹, when other traditional representations of Africans were attacked under the racist regime of National Socialism. As »persons of alien blood«

74 David Ciarlo: Advertising Empire, p. 291.
75 David Ciarlo: Rasse konsumieren, p. 148. In the 1920s, Sarotti could even play on erotic connotations of chocolate and blackness, while the black soldiers occupying the Rhineland were publicly accused of abusing German women and staining their racial purity, cf. Malte Hinrichsen: Racist Trademarks, pp. 72 ff., and for the nexus of chocolate and blackness ibid., pp. 47-52.
76 Jan Nederveen Pieterse: White on Black, p. 158. See also Joachim Zeller, Heiko Wegmann: ›Mohren‹.
77 Cf. Raymond Bachollet, Jean-Barthélemi Debost, Anne-Claude Lelieur, Marie-Christine Peyrière: Négripub, p. 77.
78 Manuela Meyer, Bettina Fleischanderl: Es ist eben mehr als nur ein Logo.
79 Fig. 7a (clockwise from top left): Ludwig Hohlwein, advertisement for Riquet tea (ca. 1924), reprinted in Hermann K. Frenzel (ed.): Ludwig Hohlwein. Fig. 7b: Advertisement for Sarotti chocolate (1928), reprinted in Rita Gudermann: Der Sarotti-Mohr, p. 59. Fig. 7c: Advertisement for Meinl coffee (1918), reprinted in Raymond Bachollet, Jean-Barthélemi Debost, Anne-Claude Lelieur, Marie-Christine Peyrière: Négripub, p. 77. Fig. 7d: Beermat of Mohrenbräu, reprinted in Jan Nederveen Pieterse: White on Black, p. 190. Fig. 7e: Tucher trademark symbol, reprinted in Peter J. Bräunlein: Von Mohren-Apotheken und Mohrenkopf-Wappen, p. 227. Fig. 7f: Trademark for Nietzschmann & Hildebrandt (1910), reprinted in David Ciarlo: Advertising Empire, p. 292.

blacks and their offspring were stripped of citizenship with the Nuremberg laws of 1935 and in political propaganda »racist depictions of blacks provided a secondary racial Other«.[80] Public portrayals of blacks like the traditional emblem of Coburg, which directly referred to St. Maurice, were replaced in tribute to the fascist government.[81] Advertising figures such

Fig. 7 a – f: In the early 20th century, the Tucher-Mohr was among a multitude of advertising ›moors‹ that played on established stereotypes and commodity racism.

as the Sarotti-Mohr, however, were left unchanged and could even be applied for wartime propaganda.[82] Whereas references to heroic Africans as St. Maurice challenged the Nazis' ›Untermenschen‹-ideology, racialised advertising ›moors‹ did not endanger the racial purity of the Third Reich. Now was the time for the Tucher family to remove any last doubts about the meaning of their trademark symbol.

In 1938, as the National Socialists had already replaced some of the public coat of arms showing ›moor's heads‹, the Tucher brewery pub-

80 Clarence Lusane: Hitler's Black Victims, p. 106; David Ciarlo: Advertising Empire, p. 323.
81 Cf. Hubertus Habel: Die Abschaffung des Coburger ›Mohrenkopf‹-Stadtwappens 1934.
82 Rita Gudermann: Der Sarotti-Mohr, pp. 93-104. Cynically, this company's first biographer became one of the main advocates of the enforced sterilisation of so-called ›Rhineland bastards‹ in Nazi Germany, cf. Hans Macco: Die Entstehungsgeschichte der Schokoladenfabrik Sarotti; id.: Rasseprobleme im Dritten Reich. See also Robert W. Kestling: Blacks under the Swastika, p. 89.

lished an advertising booklet to clarify that for their symbol the »designation ›negro's head‹ is wrong« and, thus, »there is no reason to alter this old trademark«.[83] Besides the fact that the family's coat of arms was only used for the brewery from 1855, this argument implicitly built on the racist Nazi interpretation of the black figure and perverted the historical development

Fig. 8: In 1938, when images of blacks were affected by Nazi racism, the Tuchers further commodified their ›moor‹ and secured its continuity as a racist trademark.

of the ›moor‹ into a racist image. Abolishing authentic testimonies of medieval representations of Africans, the Nazis confirmed black stereotypes of commodity culture that were recognisable as being racially inferior, socially subordinate and economically exploited. By defining their symbol amidst other advertising ›moors‹, the Tucher brewery, thus, secured its continuity, but approved an interpretation of its trademark figure that completely abandoned its initial messages of œcumene and tolerance.

This ultimate conversion of the Tuchers' emblem is pictorially supported with a dark-skinned turbaned child on the top of the trademark symbol (see fig. 8).[84] In revealing feather trimming, this figure recalled the exoticism of savagery and the luxurious connotations of the black servant. Lifting a Bavarian beer mug, furthermore, this black character was now

83 Freiherrlich von Tuchersche Brauerei A.-G., back page.
84 Fig. 8: Tucher trademark symbol as introduced on the front page of an 1938 advertising brochure. Freiherrlich von Tuchersche Brauerei A.-G., front page.

closely identified with the product to be sold and had nothing in common with the ›moor‹ that once personified pilgrim Hans Tucher on a stained-glass window in the late 15th century. The racialised ›moor‹ of Tucher's 1855 trademark symbol was not only racialised but also commodified in a double debasement.

The 1938 Tucher advertising combined the two most ubiquitous images of ›moors‹ in European commodity racism: the childlike, oriental servant and the ›moor's head‹. Originating in medieval representations of African nobility and their heraldic expression, both images had long become readily identifiable as symbolic references to the allegedly racial inferiority of blacks. Whereas the former in his servile appearance offered not only beverages and sweets but also the imagination of consumable advancement, the latter, frequently with exaggerated colour and physiognomy, was used as the trademark emblem for »items ranging from safety pins to champagne«.[85] Thus, the ›turbaned black‹ in the Tucher advert celebrates the German art of brewing, while the ›moor's head‹ passively represents the brewery. The heraldic Tucher-Mohr, once a representation of sanctified Africans worshipping the Christian God, remained a means of advertising and was assisted by a black servant worshipping Bavarian beer.

Nowadays, Tucher's ›moor's head‹ can be purchased on promotional items ranging from aprons to flip-flops.[86] More than five centuries after Herdegen Tucher wore his family's emblem on helmet, shield and caparison, the present-day German beer-drinker can dress himself with the Tucher-Mohr from head to toe. Where the former referred to a legendary knight of African descent to underline his fighting strength, the latter, at best, signalises his affinity to a certain brewery and secures its commercial business with what Americans might call ›black memorabilia‹. From its emergence as a proud representative of faith and kingdom, the ›moor‹ became a servant, a racialised ›negro‹ and a merchandise caricature.

The case of the Tuchers' coat of arms illustrates how the global history of anti-black racism fundamentally altered the meaning of images. When, in 1855, the Tuchers introduced the ›moor‹ as the trademark symbol for their brewery, Africans had long been constructed as naturally inferior. Against this backdrop, commercial applications even of the most traditional ›moors‹ cannot simply be accepted as a reference to an innocent history. The advertising ›moors‹ that were among the few undisputed representations of blacks in times of overt racism, survived because of their

---

85   Dana S. Hale: Races on Display, p. 28.
86   See the Tucher shop http://www.tucher.de/shop/ts8/index.php?CUR_ID=101.

conscious or unconscious foundation on racist ideology. As Charles Mills stated, you can be »beneficiaries« of the ›Racial Contract‹ although you are not »signatories to it«.[87]

However, critical race theory should not content itself with righteous intentions. It also needs to provide scientific validation for its claims. Unhistorical interpretations of the ›moor‹, for example, are needlessly vulnerable to scholarly critique and distract from the complexity of racist stereotyping. To argue that the history of the ›moor‹ is one of continuous skin-colour racism, concedes an almost natural quality to this mode of discrimination. Following this stereotype through the stages of its cultural, social and scientific construction is not only academically sound but also increases the prospect of its happy demise.

References

Archival Sources

Das Große Tucherbuch. Eine Handschrift zum Blättern. Stadtarchiv Nürnberg, E 29/III Nr. 258. Ed. and digitised by Michael Diefenbacher. Augsburg: Haus der Bayerischen Geschichte 2004.
Freiherrlich von Tuchersche Brauerei A.-G. Nürnberg: ca. 1938. Stadtbibliothek Nürnberg, Nor. 2525.4.

Literature

Aikins, Joshua K., Christian Kopp: Straßennamen mit Bezügen zum Kolonialismus in Berlin. Berlin: Berliner Entwicklungspolitischer Ratschlag, 2008. In: http://ber-ev.de/download/BER/03-positionen/f-kolonial/2008-11-13_dossier-kolonialistische-strassennamen.pdf [19.04.2012].
—, Chandra-Milena Danielzik, Matti Steinitz: Wie weiß ist der Elfenbeinturm? Ein Rechtsstreit am Otto-Suhr-Institut für Politikwissenschaften der FU Berlin. In: HUch, Sonderausgabe Rassismus, 2008/9, pp. 7-9.
Amussen, Susan Dwyer: Caribbean Exchanges. Slavery and the Transformation of English Society, 1640-1700. Chapel Hill: University of North Carolina Press 2007.
Anneser, Sebastian, Friedrich Fahr, Norbert Jocher, Norbert Knopp, Peter B. Steiner (eds.): Der Mohr kann gehen. Der Mohr im Wappen des Bischofs von Freising und die Säkularisation 1803. Lindenberg i. Allgäu: Fink 2002.
Arndt, Susan, Ulrike Hamann: Mohr_in. In: Wie Rassismus aus Wörtern spricht. (K)Erben des Kolonialismus im Wissensarchiv deutsche Sprache, ein kritisches Nachschlagewerk, ed. by Susan Arndt, Nadja Ofuatey-Alazard. Münster: Unrast 2011, pp. 649-653.

---

[87] Charles W. Mills: The Racial Contract, p. 11.

Bachollet, Raymond, Jean-Barthélemi Debost, Anne-Claude Lelieur, Marie-Christine Peyrière: Négripub. L'image des Noirs dans la publicité. Paris: Somogy 1992.
Badenberg, Nana: Mohrenwäschen, Völkerschauen. Der Konsum des Schwarzen um 1900. In: Colors 1800/1900/2000. Signs of Ethnic Difference, ed. by Birgit Tautz. Amsterdam: Rodopi 2004, pp. 163-184.
Bartels, Emily C.: Making More of the Moor. Aaron, Othello, and Renaissance Refashionings of Race. In: Shakespeare Quarterly, 41, 1990, 4, pp. 433-454.
Baudet, Henri: Paradise on Earth. Some Thoughts on European Images of Non-European Man. New Haven [et al.]: Yale University Press 1965.
Bendix, Regina: Of Mohrenköpfe and Japanesen. Swiss Images of the Foreign. In: Journal of Folklore Research, 30, 1993, 1, pp. 15-28.
Bindman, David: Ape to Apollo. Aesthetics and the Idea of Race in the 18th Century. London: Reaktion 2002.
—, Henry L. Gates, Jr.: Preface to The Image of the Black in Western Art. In: The Image of the Black in Western Art, 4 Vols., new ed., vol. 1, ed. by David Bindman, Henry L. Gates, Jr. Cambridge, Mass. [et al.]: Belknap Press of Harvard University Press 2010, pp. vii-xix.
Bitterli, Urs: Die Entdeckung des schwarzen Afrikaners. Versuch einer Geistesgeschichte der europäisch-afrikanischen Beziehungen an der Guineaküste im 17. und 18. Jahrhundert. Zürich [et al.]: Atlantis 1970.
Blackmore, Josiah: Imagining the Moor in Medieval Portugal. In: Diacritics, 36, 2006, 3-4, pp. 27-43.
Blakely, Allison: Blacks in the Dutch World. The Evolution of Racial Imagery in a Modern Society. Bloomington [et al.]: Indiana University Press 1993.
Blanchard, Pascal, Nicolas Bancel, Sandrine Lemaire: From Scientific Racism to Popular and Colonial Racism in France and the West. In: Human Zoos. Science and Spectacle in the Age of Colonial Empires, ed. by Pascal Blanchard, Nicolas Bancel, Gilles Boëtsch, Eric Deroo, Sandrine Lemaire, Charles Forsdick. Transl. by Teresa Bridgeman. Liverpool: Liverpool University Press 2008, pp. 104-113.
Blom, Philipp: Solimans Körper, Angelos Geist. Anmerkungen zur Erschließung eines Einzelschicksals. In: Angelo Soliman. Ein Afrikaner in Wien, ed. by Philipp Blom, Wolfgang Kos. Wien: Brandstätter 2011, pp. 13-23.
—: Straussenfedern, Muscheln und Glasperlen. Soliman und andere menschliche Präparate in Museen, zwischen Wissenschaft und Ideologie. In: Angelo Soliman. Ein Afrikaner in Wien, ed. by Philipp Blom, Wolfgang Kos. Wien: Brandstätter 2011, pp. 107-119.
Bräunlein, Peter J.: Von Mohren-Apotheken und Mohrenkopf-Wappen. In: Zeitschrift für Kulturaustausch, 41, 1991, 2, pp. 219-238.
Braunstein, Philippe: Wirtschaftliche Beziehungen zwischen Nürnberg und Italien im Spätmittelalter. In: Beiträge zur Wirtschaftsgeschichte Nürnberg, vol. 1, ed. by Stadtarchiv Nürnberg. Nürnberg: 1967, pp. 377-406.
Breitinger, Eckhard: African Presences and Representations in the Principality/Markgrafschaft of Bayreuth. In: Exit. Endings and New Beginnings in Literature and Life, ed. by Stefan Helgesson. Amsterdam [et al.]: Rodopi 2011.
Camara, Babacar: The Falsity of Hegel's Theses on Africa. In: Journal of Black Studies, 36, 2005, 1, pp. 82-96.

Ciarlo, David: Rasse konsumieren. Von der exotischen zur kolonialen Imagination in der Bildreklame des Wilhelminischen Kaiserreichs. In: Phantasiereiche. Zur Kulturgeschichte des deutschen Kolonialismus, ed. by Birthe Kundrus. Frankfurt a. M. [et al.]: Campus 2003, pp. 135-179.
—: Advertising Empire. Race and Visual Culture in Imperial Germany. Cambridge [et al.]: Harvard University Press 2011.
Cohen, Jeremy: Sanctifying the Name of God. Jewish Martyrs and Jewish Memories of the First Crusade. Philadelphia: University of Pennsylvania Press 2004.
Dabydeen, David: Hogarth's Blacks. Images of Blacks in Eighteenth Century English Art. Mundelstrup [et al.]: Dangaroo 1985.
David-Danel, Marie-Louise: Iconographie des Saints médecins Come et Damien. Lille: Morel & Corduant 1958.
Debrunner, Hans W.: Presence and Prestige: Africans in Europe. A History of Africans in Europe before 1918. Basel: Basler Afrika Bibliographien 1979.
Devisse, Jean, Michel Mollat: The Image of the Black in Western Art, Vol. II, 2 Parts. Transl. by William G. Ryan. New York: William Morrow 1979.
Dreesbach, Anne, Helmut Zedelmaier (eds.): ›Gleich hinterm Hofbräuhaus waschechte Amazonen‹. Exotik in München um 1900. München [et al.]: Dölling und Galitz 2003.
Dresser, Madge: Slavery Obscured. The Social History of the Slave Trade in an English Provincial Port. London [et al.]: Continuum 2001.
Eggers, Maureen M., Grada Kilomba, Peggy Piesche, Susan Arndt (eds.): Mythen, Masken und Subjekte. Kritische Weißseinsforschung in Deutschland. Münster: Unrast 2005.
Eliav-Feldon, Miriam, Benjamin Isaac, Joseph Ziegler (eds.): The Origins of Racism in the West. Cambridge [et al.]: Cambridge University Press 2009.
Ellingson, Ter: The Myth of the Noble Savage. Berkeley [et al.]: University of California Press 2001.
Eze, Emmanuel C. (ed.): Race and the Enlightenment. A Reader. Malden [et al.]: Blackwell 1997.
Fichtner, Gerhard: Das verpflanzte Mohrenbein. Zur Interpretation der Kosmas- und-Damian-Legende. In: Medizinhistorisches Journal, 3, 1968, 2, pp. 87-100.
Flaig, Egon: Weltgeschichte der Sklaverei. München: Beck 2009.
Fredrickson, George M.: The Arrogance of Race. Historical Perspectives on Slavery, Racism, and Social Inequality. Middletown: Wesleyan University Press 1988.
Frenzel, Hermann K.: Ludwig Hohlwein. Berlin: Phönix 1926.
Geiss, Imanuel: Geschichte des Rassismus. Frankfurt a. M.: Suhrkamp 1988.
Gilman, Sander L.: On Blackness without Blacks. Essays on the Image of the Black in Germany. Boston: G.K. Hall 1982.
Gissis, Snait B.: Visualizing ›Race‹ in the Eighteenth Century. In: Historical Studies in the Natural Sciences, 41, 2011, 1, pp. 41-103.
Goldberg, David T.: Racist Culture. Philosophy and the Politics of Meaning. Cambridge, Mass. [et al.]: Blackwell 1993.
Grote, Ludwig: Die Tucher. Bildnis einer Patrizierfamilie. München: Prestel 1961.
Gudermann, Rita: Der Sarotti-Mohr. Die bewegte Geschichte einer Werbefigur. Berlin: Links 2004.

Habel, Hubertus: Die Abschaffung des Coburger ›Mohrenkopf‹-Stadtwappens 1934. In: Zwischen Charleston und Stechschritt. Schwarze im Nationalsozialismus, ed. by Peter Martin, Christine Alonzo. Hamburg [et al.]: Dölling und Galitz 2004, pp. 395-407.
Hahn, Sylvia: Das Rätselraten um den Mohren. In: Der Mohr kann gehen. Der Mohr im Wappen des Bischofs von Freising und die Säkularisation 1803, ed. by Sebastian Anneser, Friedrich Fahr, Norbert Jocher, Norbert Knopp, Peter B. Steiner. Lindenberg i. Allgäu: Fink 2002, pp. 17-26.
Hale, Dana S.: Races on Display. French Representations of Colonized Peoples During the Third Republic. Bloomington: Indiana University Press 2008.
Hall, Kim F.: Things of Darkness. Economies of Race and Gender in Early Modern England. Ithaca [et al.]: Cornell University Press 1995.
Hamann, Ulrike: Das M-Wort. In: Rassismus auf gut Deutsch. Ein kritisches Nachschlagewerk zu rassistischen Sprachhandlungen, ed. by Adibeli Nduka-Agwu, Antje Hornscheidt. Frankfurt a. M.: Brandes & Apsel 2010, pp. 146-156.
Hannaford, Ivan: Race. The History of an Idea in the West. Washington: Woodrow Wilson Center Press 1996.
Hegel, Georg W. F.: Vorlesungen über die Aesthetik. Werke, Vol. 10/2, ed. by Heinrich G. Hotho. 2nd ed. Berlin: Duncker und Humblot 1842.
—: Vorlesungen über die Philosophie der Geschichte. Werke, Vol. 9, ed. by Eduard Gans. Berlin: Duncker und Humblot 1837.
Hentges, Gudrun: Schattenseiten der Aufklärung. Die Darstellung von Juden und ›Wilden‹ in philosophischen Schriften des 18. und 19. Jahrhunderts. Schwalbach: Wochenschau 1999.
Herz, Randall (ed.): Die ›Reise ins Gelobte Land‹ Hans Tuchers des Älteren (1479-1480). Untersuchungen zur Überlieferung und kritische Edition eines spätmittelalterlichen Reiseberichts. Wiesbaden: Reichert 2002.
Heyden, Ulrich van der: Gröblicher Rufmord an von der Gröben. Wie eine Straßenumbenennung in Berlin politisch, aber nicht historisch korrekt erfolgte. In: Neues Deutschland, 13.06.2009, http://www.neues-deutschland.de/artikel/150418.groeblicher-rufmord-an-von-der-groeben.html [13.02.2013].
Hinrichsen, Malte: Promoting Racism. Elements of Trademark Stereotyping. In: Racism and Modernity. Festschrift for Wulf D. Hund, ed. by Iris Wigger, Sabine Ritter. Berlin [et al.]: Lit 2011, pp. 257-272.
—: Racist Trademarks. Slavery, Orient, Colonialism and Commodity Culture. Berlin [et al.]: Lit 2012.
Hund, Wulf D.: Die Körper der Bilder der Rassen. Wissenschaftliche Leichenschändung und rassistische Entfremdung. In: Entfremdete Körper. Rassismus als Leichenschändung, ed. by Wulf D. Hund. Bielefeld: Transcript 2009, pp. 13-79.
—: Rassismus. Die soziale Konstruktion natürlicher Ungleichheit. Münster: Westfälisches Dampfboot 1999.
—: Rassismus. Bielefeld: Transcript 2007.
—: Vor, mit, nach und ohne ›Rassen‹. Reichweiten der Rassismusforschung. In: Archiv für Sozialgeschichte, 52, 2012, pp. 723-761.
Isaac, Benjamin: The Invention of Racism in Classical Antiquity. Princeton [et al.]: Princeton University Press 2004.

Jordan, Winthrop D.: White over Black. American Attitudes Toward the Negro, 1550-1812. Chapel Hill: University of North Carolina Press 1968.
Jowitt, Claire: The Culture of Piracy, 1580-1630. English Literature and Seaborne Crime. Farnham [et al.]: Ashgate 2010.
Juterczenka, Sünne: ›Chamber Moors‹ and Court Physicians. On the Convergence of Aesthetic Consumption and Racial Anthropology at Eighteenth-Century Courts in Germany. In: Entangled Knowledge. Scientific Discourse and Cultural Difference, ed. by Klaus Hock, Gesa Mackenthun. Münster: Waxmann 2012, pp. 165-182.
Kahsnitz, Rainer, Achim Bunz (eds.): Die großen Schnitzaltäre. Spätgotik in Süddeutschland, Österreich, Südtirol. München: Hirmer 2005.
Kaplan, Paul H. D.: The Rise of the Black Magus in Western Art. Ann Arbor: UMI Research Press 1985.
—: Black Africans in Hohenstaufen Iconography. In: Gesta, 26, 1987, 1, pp. 29-36.
Kestling, Robert W.: Blacks under the Swastika. A Research Note. In: The Journal of Negro History, 83, 1998, 1, pp. 84-99.
Koerner, Joseph L.: The Epiphany of the Black Magus circa 1500. In: The Image of the Black in Western Art, Vol. III, 1, new ed., ed. by David Bindman, Henry L. Gates, Jr. Cambridge, Mass. [et al.]: Belknap Press of Harvard University Press 2010, pp. 7-92.
Křížová, Markéta: Frontiers of Race, Frontiers of Freedom. The Fabrication of the ›Negro slave‹ in Early Modern European Discourse. In: Imagining Frontiers. Contesting Identities, ed. by Steven G. Ellis, Lud'a Klusáková. Pisa: Pisa University Press 2007, pp. 109-123.
Kuhn, Christian: Generation als Grundbegriff einer historischen Geschichtskultur. Die Nürnberger Tucher im langen 16. Jahrhundert. Göttingen: V&R unipress 2010.
Lusane, Clarence: Hitler's Black Victims. The Historical Experiences of Afro-Germans, European Blacks, Africans, and African Americans in the Nazi Era. New York [et al.]: Routledge 2003.
Macco, Hans: Die Entstehungsgeschichte der Schokoladenfabrik Sarotti. Manuskript im Auftrag von Nestlé verfasst. Berlin: 1931.
—: Rasseprobleme im Dritten Reich. Berlin: P. Schmidt 1933.
Martin, Peter: Schwarze Teufel, Edle Mohren. Afrikaner in Bewußtsein und Geschichte der Deutschen. Hamburg: Junius 1993.
McClintock, Anne: Imperial Leather. Race, Gender and Sexuality in the Colonial Contest. New York [et al.]: Routledge 1995.
Meijer, Miriam C.: Race and Aesthetics in the Anthropology of Petrus Camper (1722-1789). Amsterdam [et al.]: Rodopi 1999.
Meyer, Manuela, Bettina Fleischanderl: Es ist eben mehr als nur ein Logo. Die Bedeutung der Mohrenbrauerei in Bezug auf Rassismus und ihre Repräsentationen und Rezeption in Vorarlberg aus kultur- und sozialanthropologischer Perspektive. Wien: Universität Wien 2009, http://othes.univie.ac.at/7508/ [4.3.2013].
Mielke, Andreas: Nigra sum et formosa. Afrikanerinnen in der deutschen Literatur des Mittelalters, Texte und Kontexte zum Bild des Afrikaners in der literarischen Imagologie. Stuttgart: Helfant Edition 1992.
Miles, Robert: Racism. London [et al.]: Routledge 1989.

Mills, Charles W.: The Racial Contract. Ithaca [et al.]: Cornell University Press 1997.
Möseneder, Michael: Bevorzugung statt Wortstreit. In: Der Standard, 25./26.7.2009, http://derstandard.at/1246542990720/Kontra-Rassismusvorwurf-gegen-Mohren-Bevorzugung-statt-Wortstreit [21.11.2012].
Morrison, Heather: Dressing Angelo Soliman. In: Eighteenth-Century Studies, 44, 2011, 3, pp. 361-382.
Mosse, George L.: Die Geschichte des Rassismus in Europa. Transl. by Elfriede Burau, Hans Günter Holl. 2nd German ed. Frankfurt a. M.: Fischer 1990.
Nederveen Pieterse, Jan: White on Black. Images of Africa and Blacks in Western Popular Culture. New Haven [et al.]: Yale University Press 1992.
Nussbaum, Felicity: The Limits of the Human. Fictions of Anomaly, Race, and Gender in the Long Eighteenth Century. Cambridge [et al.]: Cambridge University Press 2003.
Pirschner, Claus, Claudia Unterweger: Will i mohr? Ein heimischer Eishersteller wirbt mit alten rassistischen Stereotypen für den eisgekühlten ›Mohr im Hemd‹. In: http://fm4.orf.at/stories/1620176/ [21.11.2012].
Polaschegg, Andrea: Der andere Orientalismus. Regeln deutsch-morgenländischer Imagination im 19. Jahrhundert. Berlin [et al.]: De Gruyter 2004.
Ramamurthy, Anandi: Imperial Persuaders. Images of Africa and Asia in British Advertising. Manchester [et al.]: Manchester University Press 2003.
Rodney, Walter: Africa in Europe and the Americas. In: The Cambridge History of Africa, Vol. 4, ed. by Richard Gray. Cambridge [et al.]: Cambridge University Press 1975, pp. 578-622.
Ruepprecht, Hans-Ulrich von: Der Mohr als Wappenfigur. In: 12. Internationaler Kongress für genealogische und heraldische Wissenschaften, München 1974. Kongressbericht, ed. by Hans-Ulrich von Ruepprecht. Stuttgart: Deutsche Arbeitsgemeinschaft genealogischer Verbände 1978.
Schnoor, Mira A.: Der Mohr im Wappen. Wie Afrikaner in bayerische Wappen kamen. In: Geschichte quer, 4, 1995, pp. 5-12.
Schreiber, Georg: Medizin und Charisma. Die hl. Ärzte Kosmas und Damian. In: Münchener theologische Zeitschrift, 9, 1958, 4, pp. 257-266.
Seelig, Lorenz: ›Ein Willkomme in der Form eines Mohrenkopfs von Silber getriebener Arbeit‹. Der wiederentdeckte Mohrenkopfpokal Christoph Jamnitzers aus dem späten 16. Jahrhundert. In: Der Mohrenkopfpokal von Christoph Jamnitzer, ed. by Renate Eikelmann. München: Bayerisches Nationalmuseum 2002, pp. 19-123.
Simon-Aaron, Charles: The Atlantic Slave Trade. Empire, Enlightenment, and the Cult of the Unthinking Negro. Lewiston [et al.]: Edwin Mellen Press 2008.
Smedley, Audrey: Race in North America. Origin and Evolution of a Worldview. Boulder [et al.]: Westview 1993.
Snowden, Frank M., Jr.: Before Color Prejudice. The Ancient View of Blacks. Cambridge, Mass. [et al.]: Harvard University Press 1983.
Soemmerring, Samuel T.: Über die körperliche Verschiedenheit des Mohren vom Europäer. Mainz: n.p. 1784.
—: Über die körperliche Verschiedenheit des Negers vom Europäer. Frankfurt [et al.]: Varrentrapp und Wenner 1785.

Suckale-Redlefsen, Gude: Mauritius. Der heilige Mohr; The Black Saint Maurice. Houston: Menil Foundation 1987.

Taylor, Gary: Buying Whiteness. Race, Culture, and Identity from Columbus to Hip Hop. New York [et al.]: Palgrave 2005.

Tognetti, Sergio: The trade in black African slaves in fifteenth-century Florence. In: Black Africans in Renaissance Europe, ed. by Thomas F. Earle, Kate J. P. Lowe. Cambridge [et al.]: Cambridge University Press 2005, pp. 213-224.

Valls, Andrew (ed.): Race and Racism in Modern Philosophy. Ithaca [et al.]: Cornell University Press 2005.

Walter, Rolf: Oberdeutsche Kaufleute und Genuesen in Sevilla und Cadiz (1525-1560). In: Oberdeutsche Kaufleute und Genuesen in Sevilla und Cadiz (1525-1560). Eine Edition von Notariatsakten aus den dortigen Archiven, ed. by Hermann Kellenbenz, Rolf Walter. Stuttgart: Franz Steiner 2001, pp. 11-64.

Wigger, Iris, Katrin Klein: ›Bruder Mohr‹. Angelo Soliman und der Rassismus der Aufklärung. In: Entfremdete Körper. Rassismus als Leichenschändung, ed. by Wulf D. Hund. Bielefeld: Transcript 2009, pp. 81-115.

Winant, Howard: The World is a Ghetto. Race and Democracy Since World War II. New York: Basic Books 2001.

Wittmann, Anneliese: Kosmas und Damian. Kultausbreitung und Volksdevotion. Berlin: Erich Schmidt 1967.

Wolter, Stefanie: Die Vermarktung des Fremden. Exotismus und die Anfänge des Massenkonsums. Frankfurt a. M. [et al.]: Campus 2005.

Zeller, Joachim, Heiko Wegmann: ›Mohren‹ – ein Stereotyp der Alltagskultur In: Freiburg Postkolonial, 2008, http://www.freiburg-postkolonial.de/Seiten/Mohren-Stereotyp.htm [3.3.2013].

Bittersweet Temptations
Race and the Advertising of Cocoa
Emma Robertson

Abstract: From the mid-nineteenth century, cocoa – once a tropical delicacy available only to wealthy elites – became an increasingly affordable, more palatable drink for an expanding market of British consumers. At the same time, developments in advertising and packaging allowed British confectioners to sell cocoa in new ways as a branded product. This chapter explores cocoa advertising in Britain, from the late nineteenth to the late twentieth century, to reveal the racialised meanings created for, and by, the commodity. In contrast with other colonial products, cocoa in Britain has been typically divorced from its tropical origins, with an emphasis instead on respectable white consumption. Yet images of black people have been employed in cocoa marketing at particular moments. Such raced imaginings of cocoa consumption have both reflected and fed into a broader culture of racism in the west. They have also functioned within the specific dynamics of British imperialism and of the chocolate industry. By taking the analysis into the postwar period, this chapter provides new insights into the operation of commodity racism in chocolate advertising as the British Empire imploded.

In 2011, the Cadbury firm apologised to supermodel Naomi Campbell following an advertising campaign in which she was seemingly associated with a bar of chocolate. The slogan, »Move over, Naomi, there's a new Diva in town«, equated the model with the new brand of Bliss chocolate. Whilst the Advertising Standards Authority (ASA) dismissed the complaints, determining that the advert would be understood to relate to Campbell's behaviour, rather than her skin colour, the company withdrew the advert.[1] Just two years earlier, Cadbury had celebrated their Fair Trade credentials through an advertising film depicting happy, dancing Ghanaian people and a giant god-like cocoa bean bounding through the streets of their village. The campaign received twenty-nine complaints for perpetuating racist stereotypes. The ASA again dismissed the accusations: whilst they accepted that the company had used stereotyping, this was not found

---

[1] Adam Sherwin: ASA says Cadbury was not racist when it compared Campbell to chocolate bar.

to be harmful or offensive.² However muted the response to this campaign, and whatever the positive intentions of the advertisers in terms of portraying active African involvement and ownership of cocoa farming, the stereotyping of black people as happy-go-lucky, as entertainers, and as believers in magic (in the cocoa bean god, which the implicit presence of the western manufacturer serves to discredit) is hard to avoid. Moreover, both campaigns connected with long-standing traditions of equating black people with chocolate. Such representations can never be innocent of the histories of colonialism and racism which enabled the chocolate industry; nor can they be understood outside of wider visual and textual discourses of race.

The history of chocolate in the west is deeply interwoven with the history of imperial exploitation of non-white peoples: from the first contact with the commodity as part of the Spanish conquest of central America, to the slave-grown sugar which would prove key to chocolate's success. Jan Nederveen Pieterse has observed how commodities initially made available through the use of slave labour, such as coffee and cocoa, often used, and many still use, images of black people to enhance their luxury status for potential consumers.³ Elements of this can be seen in early advertising for cocoa in Britain, Europe and America. Yet these representations of black people are neither constant, nor associated solely with luxury. For Anne McClintock, British advertising from the Victorian era entailed »the reinvention of racial difference«. She mentions chocolate directly as one of the commodities responsible for taking »scenes of empire into every corner of the home«, alongside »soap boxes, matchboxes, biscuit tins, whiskey bottles, [and] tea tins«.⁴ This analysis elides some key differences in the version of empire and race produced by different commodities; the »organized system« of imperial imagery was not quite so coherent as McClintock suggests.⁵ How did chocolate, then, (re)invent racial difference?

This chapter examines British cocoa advertising from the late nineteenth to the late twentieth century, in order to make explicit how this commodity has been constructed through, and how it has constructed, understandings of race – of blackness and whiteness. Cocoa as a powder, to be mixed with hot water or milk as a beverage, was one of the earliest branded products to be marketed by the major British confectionery firms of Fry, Cadbury, and Rowntree. It is also one of the more stable brands; solid chocolate for eating has taken so many different forms that the cross-

2   Mark Sweney: Cadbury Dairy Milk Ad Cleared of Racism.
3   Jan Nederveen Pieterse: White on Black, pp. 193 f.
4   Anne McClintock: Imperial Leather, p. 209.
5   See, for example, the work of Anandi Ramamurthy: Imperial Persuaders.

firm comparisons and analysis of long-term marketing trends attempted here would be difficult to achieve. The chapter takes a broadly chronological approach, with select European and American examples helping to determine the extent to which British brands need to be understood within the particular context of British imperialism and its decline.

Domesticating the Exotic for Mass Consumption

Advertising images for branded cocoa, ubiquitous from the late nineteenth century, were connected to an existing iconography of chocolate. Eighteenth-century renderings of cocoa consumption – such as Thomas Rowlandson's watercolour ›The Chocolate House‹ (1787)[6] – had marked its transformation from tropical curiosity into a popular drink for the white elites of Europe. In Harold W. Smith's twentieth-century mural of the famous ›White's Chocolate House, Saint James', London, in the Time of Queen Anne, 1708‹, exotic associations persist through the black boy, in ›Moorish‹ costume, seated on the floor.[7] Other images registered increasingly privatised and feminised practices of consumption, sometimes tinged with the fascination of the exotic and with the associations of sex already incorporated into chocolate mythology. The legend of the Spanish Infanta who bore a black child from drinking so much chocolate at breakfast time was just one story in circulation.[8] However, in the François Boucher painting, ›Le Déjeuner‹ (1739), white women and white children consume cocoa served by a white male in luxurious soundings with no black presence.[9] The exotic product, and the elaborate preparation process signalled by the ornate chocolate pot, are absorbed into the bourgeois domestic scene; in much the same way, an Orientalist ornamental figurine of a Buddha sits neatly visible yet unmarked on a shelf in the background. Even into the twentieth century, British advertisements for ›quality‹ brands of chocolate might evoke similar images of European, and particularly French, high-society consumption.[10]

---

6   For image see Sophie D. Coe, Michael D. Coe: The True History of Chocolate, p. 228.
7   This mural decorated the Terrace Restaurant at the Cadbury factory from 1946 (thanks to Sarah Foden, Archivist, Cadbury Archive – Mondelēz International, for further information). For image, see Anandi Ramamurthy: Imperial Persuaders, p. 65. On the use of ›Moorish‹ costume in representations of black people, see Jan Nederveen Pieterse: White on Black, pp. 124-129; also the chapter of Malte Hinrichsen in this volume.
8   See Emma Robertson: Chocolate, Women and Empire, p. 68.
9   Sophie D. Coe, Michael D. Coe: The True History of Chocolate, p. 237. Although it is difficult to distinguish between coffee and chocolate pots, Roche suggests that the presence of children as consumers in this image marks the commodity as cocoa. Daniel Roche: A History of Everyday Things, p. 191.
10 See Emma Robertson: Chocolate, Women and Empire, p. 26.

Such narratives of feminised luxury in a white world distanced from, yet deeply imbricated with colonial associations, became standard in nineteenth-century British cocoa advertising. Posters and packaging depict white female servants bearing trays of elaborate chocolate pots and crockery. Servants by implication had carried out the labour of preparing the drink, perpetuating a fantasy of leisured consumption. Their employers typically remain out of sight, allowing the viewer of the advert to imagine themselves as the recipient. Tropes of domestic service as a social marker for the Victorian middle classes merged with an earlier iconography of elite chocolate consumption to sell branded cocoa to an expanding market. This was not restricted to Britain: in 1862 the American company Walter Baker & Co. claimed as their trademark the image of ›La Belle Chocolatière‹, made famous in the eighteenth-century painting by Jean-Étienne Liotard (c.1743-1744).[11] In the 1880s, Rowntree adopted a strikingly similar image but re-imagined through a local frame as the ›White Rose of York‹ (in reference to the headquarters of the firm in this northern English city).[12] By the turn of the century, one Rowntree poster offered a more playful, familial version of this visual narrative, as two mischievous white children risk overturning the tray of hot chocolate being carried by their white maid: »Mother's Cocoa in Danger«.[13] In each of these adverts the tropical product appears thoroughly domesticated, part of a private realm of white bourgeois consumption and implicated in the correct performance of class and gender identities. Unlike earlier representations of the seventeenth and eighteenth centuries, in which black figures had appeared, luxury does not figure explicitly as the product of the British Empire. Rather, as Catherine Hall suggests, imperialism has already been absorbed into the domestic sphere and so disappears from the frame.[14]

The figure of the exotic black Moor, especially as a child, lived on in chocolate advertising in mainland Europe. Although David Ciarlo notes the disappearance of the Orientalised black character in Germany at the outbreak of the First World War, these images soon resurfaced, most notably in the form of the Sarotti-Mohr from 1918.[15] The Sarotti-Mohr was dressed in brightly coloured harem pants, a turban and gold earrings. As Nederveen Pieterse suggests, he invoked long-standing narratives of the black eunuch of the harem, enhancing the sensual appeal of the commodity. Yet his diminutive stature and childlike features rendered him safe and

11   For image, see Carole Bloom: All About Chocolate, p. 111.
12   Robert Fitzgerald: Rowntree and the Marketing Revolution, Colour Plate 1.
13   Michael Jubb: Cocoa and Corsets, Figure 13.
14   Catherine Hall: Turning a Blind Eye, p. 41.
15   David Ciarlo: Advertising Empire, p. 319.

endearing to both adults (especially men purchasing chocolate for women) and children.[16] Orientalised black figures (like the white servants already discussed) framed the consumption of cocoa as the luxurious practice of social elites. Moreover, they retained for the commodity an air of the exotic that was being lost in Britain.

Although uncommon in British cocoa advertising, at least by the three major Quaker firms, Orientalised images did appear in British advertising for other commodities such as tea.[17] There was no clear national trend, then, which made such images of blackness unacceptable to white British consumers. The trend away from the exotic in cocoa advertising within Britain may thus be related, at least in part, to the politics of the Quaker confectionery manufacturers, whose brands became associated with wholesome white consumption in the domestic, national context. Their anti-slavery stance (though challenged in the early twentieth century as we shall see), their support for temperance, and their reputation as ›enlightened‹ employers, had implications for how their businesses and products were perceived, and therefore for the kinds of marketing strategies which might make sense to consumers. The emphasis on cocoa as a drink for the respectable white working class in a national frame was also the product of the democratisation of chocolate as an everyday food-beverage. Even where images of elite consumption remained for certain brands, the medium of mass advertising democratised such practices.[18] Overall, the visual iconography of cocoa was shifting towards the white working classes.[19]

Re-visioning the Plantation Commodity

At the same time, in both British and European advertising, new associations of chocolate with black people were emerging. In place of ornamental black figures displayed in the arena of consumption, these black plantation workers visibly toil to produce the tropical product. Two late nineteenth-century adverts, one for Baron Liebig's and one for Cadbury's Cocoa, each displayed male workers carrying a basket laden with pods. Liebig's evoked the elite consumption of earlier cocoa images through the well-dressed white lady in the centre of the advert, who appears at home in a tropical setting. Industrial manufacture is absent from this vision, with tins of prepared cocoa powder inserted into the tropical scene at the feet

---

16 Jan Nederveen Pieterse: White on Black, p. 159; see also Silke Hackenesch: Advertising Chocolate, Consuming Race, p. 8.
17 Joanna de Groot: Metropolitan Desires and Colonial Connections, p. 184.
18 Jan Nederveen Pieterse: White on Black, p. 158.
19 On class, see Emma Robertson: Chocolate, Women and Empire, chapter one.

of the black labourer. In the Cadbury poster, a black female cocoa worker crouches next to two full baskets, looking up at the standing black male worker. They are situated in a fertile scene of tropical plants in the bottom left of the frame. Selected images of the manufacturing process in Britain have been framed and superimposed over the plantation backdrop. These include a seated white female cocoa packer and a standing white male machine tender (closely echoing the positioning of the plantation workers), with the caption, »Cocoa Essence is not touched by human hands during whole process of its preparation«. Once transported to Britain, the raw tropical material became, as the main text proclaimed, »Absolutely Pure« through the intervention of industrial technology.[20]

Other companies also adopted images of plantation agriculture. Lipton's, for example, used a scene purporting to be of their Ceylon cocoa estates, with a white male supervisor in the foreground directing black men carrying the pods. A large storehouse in the background is emblazoned with the company name, emphasising their direct involvement. The Indian Tea Planters Association (established 1880 in London) created ›Coolie Brand Pure Cocoa‹. Invoking indentured labour through its title, the packaging for this brand made images of black workers absolutely central. One tin displayed a typical plantation scene in which male workers (naked from the waist up) harvest cocoa pods, with a ship in harbour in the distance waiting to transport the beans to overseas consumers. The brand was marketed as a comforting supper-time drink: »It helps our rest, it helps our sleep, | New strength it doth endow; | So Coolie Brand Pure Cocoa makes | Us all take suppers now«.[21] Plantation scenes created a visual narrative of the vertical integration of production, in which ultimate ownership of the process rested with the manufacturers whose company name dominated the advert. In the late nineteenth century, the major British confectioners, Cadbury and Rowntree, had indeed established their own cocoa plantations in the West Indies, employing both descendants of African slaves and indentured labourers from South East Asia.[22]

In the wake of scandals over the adulteration of manufactured foods, a re-visioning of cocoa as part of a well-managed commodity chain, in which racial hierarchies were maintained, could have reassured consum-

---

20   Images reproduced in Anandi Ramamurthy: Imperial Persuaders, pp. 66 f.; for the following image (Lipton's) see ibid., p. 78.
21   ›Auckland Star‹, 3.5.1909, p. 6.
22   Although Rowntree were still reticent about marketing at this time, both Cadbury and Rowntree promoted their responsible ownership of plantations in the Caribbean: producing stories and visual displays of ›exotic‹ workers and objects both in the factory and in their inhouse journals for employees in the early twentieth century. Emma Robertson: Chocolate, Women and Empire, pp. 146-149.

ers. Here was a ›natural‹ tropical product which had been appropriately ›purified‹ by British industrial modernity.[23] Both Lipton's and the Indian Tea Planters Association were producers of another colonial commodity – tea. This would continue to be marketed through plantation scenes, remaining distanced from processes of industrial manufacture. For cocoa, however, the positive associations advertisers wanted to create through their depiction of regulated black labourers in a system of plantation agriculture were increasingly being challenged by events in Africa.

»Cocoa, Sah!«: Willing African Labour

Just as the British confectioners became more involved in cocoa growing in the West Indies, the geographical focus for production was shifting. West African farmers in the Gold Coast were taking an increasing share of the market they would come to dominate after the First World War. British firms were already buying West African cocoa on the open market from the Portuguese colonial islands of São Tomé and Príncipe. However, conditions for the ›indentured‹ labourers on plantations there were coming under scrutiny as a form of slavery, with high death tolls recorded. British manufacturers were held accountable in the press for supporting this corrupt industry, delaying a boycott until they had conducted their own investigations. Although Cadbury successfully sued the ›Standard‹ newspaper in 1908 for libel over accusations of buying slave-grown cocoa, the scandal was damaging to the reputation of the British Quaker firms.[24]

Anandi Ramamurthy argues convincingly that the subsequent need of these firms, in the first decade of the twentieth century, to be seen to be sourcing cocoa from willing African farmers, coupled with their support for indirect rule in British West Africa, led to the construction in advertising discourse of an individualised African male and a shift away from images of plantation workers. Although typically young (in line with conventional stereotypes of childlike black people), this character presents the cocoa pod and beans as the product of his (frequently invisible) labours. Women, important workers in the cocoa economy in both the West Indies and West Africa, were typically absent from the frame. An early glass slide from Cadbury, for example, depicts a black boy in a red-and-white striped

---

23   Prior to the adoption in Britain of the Van Houten press (initially by Cadbury) from the late 1860s, British cocoa had generally had starch and other materials added to counteract the fat from the cocoa butter. George Cadbury was consulted over the Adulteration of Food Act in 1872, by which time he could lay claim to ›pure‹ cocoa – see Gillian Wagner: The Chocolate Conscience, p. 34.
24   See Lowell J. Satre: Chocolate on Trial and Catherine Higgs: Chocolate Islands.

shorts suit and straw hat, in bare feet, with his arms so overloaded with cocoa pods that one is falling to the ground. Cocoa trees bearing more fruit are visible in the background.[25] In 1906, in a fantastical advert for Fry's, the abundance of beans was transformed into one enormous cocoa pod, from which a single African man, standing barefoot astride the African continent, fills the white cups of the European nations with Fry's Cocoa. This image is unusual in locating the figure explicitly in Africa. As Ramamurthy suggests, Fry may well have been responding to the scandal over African slave-grown cocoa, given that they were not dealing directly with African farmers at this stage.[26] However, such images were not confined to Britain: Ciarlo observes a similar trend in Germany towards associating Africans with abundant raw materials and with commodities which expand to fill the frame. He links this both to contemporary colonial ideology and a »visuality-driven dynamic of exaggeration« in the early twentieth century.[27] Representations of black cocoa workers were operating on multiple levels.

The association of the African male with the colonial raw material could be still more direct. In one Fry's image from 1907, the same black male character from their 1906 advert is encased in a cocoa pod. Such an image relied partly on long-standing stereotypes of black people ›as‹ chocolate.[28] Here, the African man wears the cocoa pod as protection against the snow – his head and bare feet are all that is visible. The label on the pod of ›Fry's Pure Concentrated Cocoa‹ thus serves a double meaning as the pod contains both the raw cocoa and the cocoa producer, which are effectively merged through the logic of the advert. The main character fits the ›Sambo‹ stereotype of smiling black man but he was at least allowed a distinctly human, young adult face.[29] Images of individualised black characters in cocoa advertising differ markedly from the derogatory and grotesque images of black people being used to market brands such as Pears Soap, which Ramamurthy argues were directly related to the soap industry's commitment to European-owned plantations in Africa.[30]

Some British cocoa adverts placed black and white characters side by side. In one poster for Fry's from 1908, a young black farmer (identical to the figure from earlier Fry's adverts but of a more diminutive stature) pre-

---

25   For image see Angell Antiques.
26   Anandi Ramamurthy: Imperial Persuaders, p. 73.
27   David Ciarlo: Advertising Empire, pp. 149, 204 f.
28   Jan Nederveen Pieterse: White on Black, p. 193.
29   For image see Anandi Ramamurthy: Imperial Persuaders, p. 76. On the ›Sambo‹ stereotype, see Marilyn Kern-Foxworth: Aunt Jemima, Uncle Ben, and Rastus, pp. 79 f.
30   Anandi Ramamurthy: Imperial Persuaders, p. 60; the following quote is from ibid., pp. 83, 84.

sents an oversized cocoa pod to an older white buyer/consumer of the John Bull type, with the words, »Dat's for Massa Fry 'cos it's de best«. The imperial dynamic is visually rendered through differences in age, height and clothing but also through their implied positions as producer and consumer of the raw cocoa. These two figures are directly connected and mutually dependent in a vertically integrated commodity chain.

By imagining chocolate production and consumption through children, a seemingly more equal relationship between black and white could be envisioned.[31] In one Cadbury advert (undated but most likely from the early twentieth century), a black boy and a white girl sit side-by-side on a picnic rug, sharing the frame of the image. However, as Catherine Hall and Anandi Ramamurthy demonstrate, any apparent equality is illusory. The boy is barefooted and dressed as a peasant farmer; the girl is in frills and shoes. The boy offers the girl a cup of cocoa but does not consume anything himself. Cocoa is thus configured as the willing gift of the colonies to the white consumer.[32] An advert for Epp's Cocoa provides another example of a pairing of white girl and black boy but here the boy is westernised in a top hat and suit. Featuring one black and one white character created a visual symmetry that may have been appealing to consumers, especially when featuring charming (safely desexualised) children. They personified the unity of tropical agriculture and western manufacturing, or to take the analogy with natural produce one step further, of brown cocoa powder and white milk. They also embodied gendered, as well as racialised understandings of the commodity chain, with white female consumers distinct from black male producers.

Coterminous with such representations of African males as producers and willing suppliers of the raw material for chocolate were images that evoked and revised earlier stereotypes of black people as servers of prepared cocoa. At the turn of the century, Fry's used a realistic painting of a black boy carrying a breakfast tray with a cup of Fry's Cocoa. The caption read, »Cocoa, Sah!«[33] This image drew on visual and linguistic stereotypes of the subservient and unthreatening ›Sambo‹, originating in the United States. However, it cannot be divorced from the context of European imperial politics. The implication of a male consumer – perhaps a colonial official with a native servant – is interesting in diverging from earlier representations of servants supplying their mistresses with cocoa. It is in keeping with the construction of cocoa as a health- and strength-giving

---

31 See also Nicholas Thomas: Colonial Conversions, pp. 305 ff.
32 Catherine Hall: Turning a Blind Eye, p. 41; Anandi Ramamurthy: Imperial Persuaders, pp. 72 f.; the following image is from ibid., p. 87.
33 Anandi Ramamurthy: Imperial Persuaders, p. 68.

drink for men – a ready prop for the masculine imperial adventure stories popular at the time.³⁴

Black people in British cocoa advertising before the Second World War do not actively consume: they are either the faceless plantation labourers, the obedient individual producer or the ready servant/provider. In contrast, the French chocolate-banana drink, Banania, was marketed explicitly from 1915 through images of an individual black consumer: a realistically rendered painting of a Senegalese soldier in the French colonial army. His gaze was directed outwards to the potential consumer, sharing his pleasure in consumption directly. Whilst this relied to a degree on the symbolic fusion of chocolate with the black soldier, it also allowed for a vision of black people as active consumers and ambassadors for a product, rather than as foils for white consumption. This consumer was contained within the archetype of the ›good savage‹, however, and was disciplined by wearing his service uniform. In a product aimed at children, he was an embodiment of the physical strength the black cocoa claimed to provide (a theme which we shall see reoccurring in postwar advertising for Rowntree's Cocoa).³⁵

The appearance of black Africans in British cocoa advertising from the late nineteenth century into the early twentieth century, though never overriding images of white consumers, aligns with a distinctive British national-imperial history of commodities and manufacturing politics. Yet there are similarities with the marketing approaches for other European brands from this period. In some cases, this is related to the direct influence of both British imperialism and British marketing techniques: Ciarlo presents a convincing case in this vein for German advertising and finds evidence of the direct theft of one soap advertising image by a German company.³⁶ It is not always possible to trace the circulation of images and meanings with such precision: the ›Kleine Coco‹ (Little Coco) trademark of one German brand foreshadows a Rowntree figure by the same name by almost forty years but there is no evidence of a direct connection. Such striking similarities in European racialised imaginings of cocoa are not pure coincidence; they are evidence of a shared history of European colonial exploitation of Africa from the 1880s, and of the complicated intertextuality of white western racist popular culture. While the politics of British colonial cocoa production, of business and of individual business owners,

---

34 The popular novel, King Solomon's Mines by Henry Rider Haggard, had been a best-seller from its release in 1885. On the playing out of a crisis of late-Victorian masculinity in the empire, see Anne McClintock: Imperial Leather, p. 233.
35 For more on this figure, see Malte Hinrichsen: Racist Trademarks, and Susan Terrio: Crafting the Culture and History of French Chocolate, p. 249.
36 David Ciarlo: Advertising Empire, pp. 114, 261; for the following see ibid., p. 308.

influenced marketing strategies, we should be wary of underestimating the role of advertising agents in constructing campaigns that drew from wider racist understandings of the world. For whatever the politics of the manufacturers, the aim of the adverts was to sell cocoa. Whilst assessing the impact of advertising remains an imprecise science, advertisers have to at least try to create an image that appeals to their market. This, rather than the political leanings of their clients, is their primary concern.

The Marginalising of the Colonial Producer

Reticent about entering the tawdry world of advertising, the York-based Rowntree firm also appears to have been slow to adopt any images of black people in their marketing. In 1919, in an effort to gain ground on their Cadbury rivals, they embarked on a new marketing strategy through the characters of a white girl and white boy (and occasionally their pet dog). Whilst cocoa and chocolate have often been used as euphemisms for people of colour,[37] in the Rowntree case it was these white children who became known as the ›Cocoa Nibs‹ – a term meaning crushed cocoa beans and also adopted to refer to young white workers at the York factory. These popular child characters seemingly align with Ramamurthy's analysis that, after 1910, the images that came to dominate cocoa advertising were »those of sugary-sweet white boys and girls«.[38] Yet there was another, less well remembered, Cocoa Nib, promoted both in the ›Cocoa Works Magazine‹ and in shop window displays.[39] This Nib was a smiling, wide-eyed black boy, barefooted, wearing dungarees. He carried an over-sized cocoa pod and tin of Rowntree's Elect Cocoa. He was firmly located ›out‹ in the rural empire and no images survive of any contact between him and white children – in contrast to the adverts mentioned above.

This ›other‹ Nib was not alone in British interwar cocoa advertising. Fry also adopted a single young black male character during the 1920s, in a reprise of the »Cocoa, Sah!« slogan. This figure was more stylised than his earlier incarnation: with a wide grin and a yellow shirt with red polka dots, he offers a large cocoa pod to the viewer/consumer.[40] In contrast to the earlier campaign, this boy was unambiguously located outside of west-

---

37   Susan Terrio: Crafting the Culture and History of French Chocolate, p. 248.
38   Anandi Ramamurthy: Imperial Persuaders, p. 91.
39   ›Cocoa Works Magazine‹, March 1922; the magazine was the inhouse journal for Rowntree.
40   Image reproduced on Lambeth Landmark. This website makes a fascinating juxtaposition between this image and photos of a young boy in Lambeth whose father was a West African cocoa farmer in Ghana. The poster is used solely as an illustration of the boy's connection to the cocoa industry, with no discussion of the nature of the image

ern society: rather than a tray bearing the prepared drink, he is the bearer of the raw material before it has been packaged for shipment to Britain. The existence of such figures problematise Ramamurthy's chronology of the ›receding‹ black boy in British cocoa advertising, although they fit her thesis that interwar representations of black figures avoided the domestic frame given the racial tensions which emerged in the economic downturn after the First World War.[41]

Cadbury continued to present plantation labour into the 1930s, even as they now purchased the majority of their cocoa from farming families in West Africa. Black producers were represented as being under the supervision, if indirectly, of Cadbury buyers. One advert explained, »How to make chocolates as good as Cadbury's«: »Take the pick of the world's cocoa plantations. [...] Send your own buyers abroad and instruct them to follow the methods of Cadbury's experts who buy on the spot, rigorously rejecting all beans that fall below the high Cadbury standard«. This point was illustrated by an image of four faceless African women, carrying baskets of cocoa pods on their heads.[42] Now that Cadbury had effectively lost direct control of cocoa production, except through their buying strategies, the cocoa labourer was no longer male but an unthreatening, faceless, exotic female.

By the 1930s and 40s, however, cocoa was rapidly losing any lingering association with its colonial, or even tropical origins. Consumption was the preserve – and the preserver – of white men, women and children within a British domestic, often domesticated, context. Photo stories for Rowntree from the mid-1930s focused on white children, engaged in appropriately gendered tasks, growing stronger through drinking cocoa. These healthy white children were the new generation of Britons being brought up on Rowntree products. Interwar cocoa advertising in Europe followed a somewhat different path, whereby key brands retained non-white figures as their signature trademarks: the Sarotti-Mohr and the Banania soldier are perhaps the most famous. Nonetheless, as Ciarlo suggests for Germany, saccharine images of white children were the dominant trope.[43]

In wartime advertising, cocoa consumption was credited with the production of healthy white British subjects capable of beating the enemy and forging a new postwar society. A Rowntree's Cocoa advert from 1941, headlined, »And that's what Amazons are made of«, features a group of

itself, or of the social context in which the child consumed free mugs of cocoa at the local Mission club for children in the 1920s.

41 Anandi Ramamurthy: Imperial Persuaders, pp. 91, 151.
42 Cadbury Archive – Mondelēz International, 196/520/003552, Cadbury's Special Ads: May 1930 to December 1932.
43 David Ciarlo: Advertising Empire, p. 303.

white women workers on a construction site. Instead of sugar and spice and all things nice, these women workers are made of »10 stone of cheerfulness, grit and hard work« – all »the ingredients for a British demolition worker, 1941 model«.⁴⁴ In the postwar period, the dominant model purchaser/consumer reverted to the white British housewife dealing with the stresses of shopping and feeding her family. It was to this housewife, and her children, that two new fictional consumers of Rowntree's Cocoa were designed to appeal. Unusually, given the context just discussed, both these characters were black.

The Return of the Native?

In 1946, cinema audiences in Britain were introduced to »Little Coco«, the »charming new salesman for Rowntrees«.⁴⁵ This cartoon caricature of a black Boy Scout appeared nationally in cinema advertising, with each short film seen by 11,000,000 people.⁴⁶ In keeping white audiences amused while they waited for the main film to begin, Coco aligns with the black stereotype of the entertainer.⁴⁷ His features conformed to existing cartoon stereotypes of black people: an oversized head, large eyes, and the large lips associated with minstrels. He was clearly intended to have positive associations for audiences through his child-like appearance.

As a happy-go-lucky male figure, Coco fits the long-standing stereotype of ›Sambo‹ that had been drawn upon in earlier cocoa advertising. Yet he embodies an element of the stereotype not seen in previous campaigns: the potential for savage strength. Though westernised and ›civilised‹ by virtue of his Boy Scout uniform, Coco battles with dangerous wildlife, fortified by Rowntree's.⁴⁸ In one early film, he deliberately tackles a wild bear. A later piece played on the comic aspect of his being blissfully unaware of the danger from wild animals – busy instead with more conventional Boy Scout activities such as cooking, climbing and fishing. His seriousness in undertaking these tasks, and his innocence of the dangers, are a source of amusing dramatic irony. But like Popeye with his spinach, Coco can rely on Rowntree's for the temporary strength to tackle any situation. Safely contained within a distant foreign landscape, he inhabits the

---

44 Borthwick Institute, York (BI), Rowntree Archive (RA), N41, Cocoa 1941-2.
45 BI, RA, N44, Cocoa 1946-50.
46 BI, RA, N44, Cocoa 1946-50.
47 Jan Nederveen Pieterse: White on Black, p. 136.
48 As a Scout, like the Senegalese soldier of the French Banania campaign, Coco may be ›contained‹ within a Western imperialist mission – see also Susan Terrio: Crafting the Culture and History of French Chocolate, p. 250. For an analysis of the connections between empire and the Scout movement, see Allen Warren: Citizens of the Empire.

comic margins of masculine adventure stories.[49] Where the white Cocoa Nibs of the 1920s had appeared largely in urban settings, Coco (like his forerunner, ›The Other Cocoa Nib‹), was clearly felt to be more at home in the stereotypical setting of the wilderness.[50] While this exotic, dangerous location might appeal to white British children, they were presumably not meant to identify too closely with Coco and his violent tendencies.

In 1947, another black character was created for the marketing of Rowntree's Cocoa: a girl named »Honeybunch« who happily recommended the Rowntree brand to animals, people and nursery rhyme characters alike.[51] Susan Terrio notes that images of black women tended to displace those of black men in lending an ›exotic‹ element to chocolate advertising in postwar France.[52] Honeybunch was employed rather differently: she clearly belongs to the »pickanniny« stereotype, with her »braids and spindly legs«.[53] Like Little Coco, she had the large ›lap-dog‹ eyes and childish oversized head typical of black stereotypes, though her features were not of the grotesque proportions of many nineteenth- and early twentieth-century images.[54]

In contrast to Coco, Honeybunch was both westernised and feminised through her light skin, blue eyes (in colour images), and hair ribbons, making her more acceptable in the company of white characters. She exhibits many of the characteristics Kern-Foxworth identifies as typical of representations of black women: a happy-go-lucky nature, a desire to please, and a folksy wisdom about food.[55] Her name, meanwhile, is a sugary term of endearment, encouraging the audience to assume a position of powerful familiarity over the character.

Whilst her youth and femininity made her a safe figure, Honeybunch, too, had adventures. She travelled far and wide, meeting a variety of hungry wild animals and ravenous ›natives‹ who were usually in the midst of eating something comically inappropriate. The ads made use of grotesque racial stereotypes: an ›Eskimo‹, for example, whose in-turned feet suggest stupidity, attempts to eat a candle; in another image a ›cannibal‹, complete

49 The extraordinary alter-egos of Popeye (created in 1929) and Little Coco do not occupy a place in ›normal‹ society; the ›ordinary‹ characters are themselves marginal figures. As a sailor, Popeye exists in the liminal spaces between land and sea. Coco, meanwhile, is positioned between western civilisation and the wilderness.
50 On stereotyped settings, see Marilyn Kern-Foxworth: Aunt Jemima, Uncle Ben, and Rastus, p. 95. David Hand's involvement may be the key to the American tone of the films in terms of both setting and language.
51 BI, RA, N44, Cocoa 1946-50.
52 Susan Terrio: Crafting the Culture and History of French Chocolate, p. 251.
53 Marilyn Kern-Foxworth: Aunt Jemima, Uncle Ben, and Rastus, p. 41.
54 Jan Nederveen Pieterse: White on Black, p. 193, discusses large eyes in terms of rendering black people as »lap dogs«.
55 Marilyn Kern-Foxworth: Aunt Jemima, Uncle Ben, and Rastus, pp. 79 f.

with a spear and a top hat, is about to cook a white explorer.⁵⁶ Perhaps the Cocoa Nibs would have been worryingly (for white consumers) out of place confronting a hungry ›Eskimo‹ or wild animals. Nederveen Pieterse argues that, »Africans and crocodiles together within a single frame appear to be the European counterpart to the morbid American myth that crocodiles are particularly fond of black flesh«.⁵⁷ Although Honeybunch is not in immediate danger of being eaten (the characters she confronts are all engrossed in eating something else), the adverts may have been understood in this framework by consumers. Instead of eating the ›chocolate‹ girl, the animals and savage humans are calmly advised by Honeybunch to consume real cocoa. The caption, »So grateful, so genial, so good«, by association applies to Honeybunch herself. These adjectives have connotations of supposedly safe female African American characters such as Aunt Jemima.⁵⁸ Where Coco was active and occasionally aggressive, Honeybunch took on a more persuasive feminine role.

In later adverts, Honeybunch steps out of her cartoon world into photographs of ›real‹ white families, advising them to »have a cuppa Rowntree's«. She becomes a more modern incarnation of black child figures from the early twentieth century, serving the best cocoa to white consumers as a member of the »imperial family«.⁵⁹ Although now part of a domestic scene within Britain, Honeybunch remains safely distanced by appearing in a different medium – that of animation. As in the earlier adverts, her bare feet are a marker of her inferior status in comparison to the well-dressed white families with whom she is juxtaposed. She is also smaller than the white characters, never positioned centre stage, and takes on a service role rather than actively participating in family life. As a black woman, she has some authority as regards what is good to eat and drink. Although not the ›mammy‹ stereotype of the US context, she does take on a knowledgeable role about food, which connects her to such American representations.⁶⁰ She is certainly unusual as a black female character in British cocoa advertising.

Whilst much of the appeal of Little Coco and Honeybunch relied on visual and situation comedy, racial ›difference‹ was also created through

---

56 BI, RA, N44, Cocoa 1946-50. This ad is dated 1948. It should be compared with the 1957 TV advert discussed in the following section.
57 Jan Nederveen Pieterse: White on Black, p. 44.
58 On Aunt Jemima, the mammy character used to market a brand of pancake mix in the US from the late nineteenth century, see Maurice M. Manring: Slave in a Box, and Marilyn Kern-Foxworth: Aunt Jemima, Uncle Ben, and Rastus, pp. 101-104.
59 Anandi Ramamurthy: Imperial Persuaders, pp. 84 f.
60 Whilst it is important to keep in mind the different political and cultural contexts of the US and Britain, certain stereotypes had resonance in both countries thanks to their close relationship.

language. The dialect of both characters drew on stereotypes of black speech: influenced by imperialism, minstrel shows and other African and African American stereotypes. Coco's ›Yessah!‹ is reminiscent of Fry's ›Cocoa, Sah!‹ campaign, evoking once again the stereotype of obedient black men, which allowed these characters to be construed as unthreatening by white audiences. Honeybunch's advice, meanwhile, was given in a folksy dialect: »Feelin' kinda hungry? Me, I'd have a cuppa Rowntree's«.[61] There is an (African) American ›Southern hospitality‹ discourse at work here.[62] The use of non-standard English by infantilised black characters was deliberately employed for comic effect: for instance, the pun on running ›roun' trees‹ and drinking ›Rowntree's‹ in one Little Coco ad. Both characters were positioned through language as ›different‹ to white British consumers – as black, and as American. Nevertheless, Little Coco and Honeybunch each spoke from a position of active, independent consumption.

So why did Rowntree and their advertising agents choose to adopt black characters in their cocoa advertising at this particular moment? Although products of the postwar era, these figures belong to, and modify, long-standing traditions of associating black people and chocolate. As Terrio notes, chocolate has been used as a »euphemism for people of color« in many western cultures.[63] In the context of the Rowntree ads featuring Honeybunch, and particularly those featuring Coco, this symbolic logic was reversed. The signifier and signified switched places as the black characters were made to serve as visual and – for Little Coco – linguistic metonyms.[64] Coco's bald head visually connected him to a cocoa bean (though this also distanced him from the ›Gollywog‹ character which was at that time being employed by the Robertson jam firm).[65]

---

61 BI, RA, N44, Cocoa 1946-50.
62 Marilyn Kern-Foxworth: Aunt Jemima, Uncle Ben, and Rastus, p. 95, has identified the connections between African American speech and the speech patterns of the white American South, suggesting that the presence of slaves (particularly as nannies within the white household) would have had an impact on white children. The ›hospitality‹ of the American South, meanwhile – the genteel practices of a white elite – was built upon the labour of slaves.
63 See Susan Terrio: Crafting the Culture and History of French Chocolate, p. 248; Anandi Ramamurthy: Imperial Persuaders, pp. 64 f. ›Chocolate‹ has sometimes been used by black people themselves to differentiate based on skin tone.
64 Jan Nederveen Pieterse: White on Black, p. 193, similarly notes that, »In Germany a chocolate cake [...] is referred to as the ›edible negro‹«. The racist histories behind the association of black people and chocolate in advertising raise questions about the analysis of colour in advertising as »simply a *technique* [...] to make correlations between a product and other things« as formulated by Judith Williamson: Decoding Advertisements, p. 24.
65 See Jan Nederveen Pieterse: White on Black, pp. 156 ff. for a more detailed discussion of the ›Gollywog‹ character; also Michael Pickering's chapter in this volume.

Unlike earlier campaigns, such symbolic links were employed without any recognition of the actual connections between cocoa and the labour of black people in the colonies. In an advert from 1950, Honeybunch's body is replaced by a spring as she is shown bouncing, like a jack-in-the-box, out of a tin of cocoa.[66] She is being consumed by the product and losing her individual, physical identity. In one sense, this is typical of the »equation of Africans with natural produce«.[67] Honeybunch's name, suggesting the naturally sweet product of honey, is another way this association is achieved. Yet Honeybunch becomes the ›manufactured‹ cocoa tin – rather than the cocoa pod as was the case in the earlier Fry's advert mentioned above. The image has been revised for a postwar world in which the modern convenience of tinned cocoa held more meaning for consumers than any representation of the cocoa in its natural state. Still, of all the Rowntree products, cocoa powder was closest to the ›raw‹, colonial, material. In the British adverts studied, it is significant that black figures were used to advertise cocoa powder rather than chocolate. Like Aunt Jemima and her pancake mix, as a black woman in the ›mammy‹ tradition Honeybunch lent cocoa powder authenticity as a natural food.

The postwar social, economic and cultural context in which Coco and Honeybunch appeared is certainly significant. They embodied in turn the strength-giving, soothing and nutritious properties of cocoa that Rowntree aimed to promote at a time when food was still subject to rationing. Each character offered an American folksy wisdom about chocolate consumption, which may have been appealing in the context of Americanisation – especially to those consumers who remembered the American GIs (white and black) bringing chocolate and other luxuries with them when stationed in Britain. However, unlike black GIs, black British soldiers, and black (post)colonial migrants, Coco represented a safe version of black masculinity. As a child he was desexualised; he was never put into contact with white people; and he was contained within a distant location. As Terrio comments in relation to postwar France, »[t]he presence of large numbers of Africans tended to blur the line between the metropolis and the colonies, the dominant and the dominated, creating profound anxiety«. This led to a shift in the image of the black soldier used to advertise Banania chocolate; the figure »became progressively stylized, abstract, and incidental to the marketing of the product«.[68] Where Little Coco was, briefly, central to the marketing of the Rowntree brand, he was similarly stylised and abstracted from the national, postcolonial context. As non-threatening

66 BI, RA, N44, Cocoa 1946-1950.
67 Anandi Ramamurthy: Imperial Persuaders, p. 75.
68 Susan Terrio: Crafting the Culture and History of French Chocolate, pp. 250 f.

images of blackness, Little Coco and Honeybunch may thus have soothed white consumer anxieties, just as the product promised to do.

For the advertising agents, however, because such strategic concerns as brand differentiation would dominate the rationale for these characters, race was never explicitly discussed.[69] In the mid 1940s, Rowntree and their agents, J. Walter Thompson (JWT) were searching for a campaign with the potential to create long-lasting brand loyalty. JWT noted that a »merchandising idea« was needed which could attract children through stories involving lovable characters, with associated merchandise to collect. They decided on the ›Adventure-Continuity Campaign‹. There is nothing to suggest that they had envisaged a black character. This may have been the idea of Coco's creator, David Hand (an American who had been a Disney animator for many years). Yet even in 1945 the agents already had high hopes for the Little Coco films: »it is feasible to think that we have got on to so outstanding a technique as to raise to some extent the basic value of cinema as a medium«.[70] Documents and correspondence from 1947 reveal Little Coco was indeed intended to have a life outside the films: »a Press campaign using the ›Coco‹ character is far in production, and supporting display material using the character is also contemplated«. Unfortunately for Rowntree and JWT, they had not considered fully the copyright claims of the artist David Hand and the production company GB Animation, and this appears to have hampered any meaningful extension of Little Coco merchandising.[71]

JWT saw the late 1940s as a crucial period in preparing consumers for the lifting of wartime measures and ensuring that Rowntree would be in a strong competitive position. As the continuation of wartime restrictions forced advertisers to rely on small-scale newspaper ads to keep the brand name in view, Honeybunch provided a simple but striking image. Little Coco, meanwhile, was developed as a character suited to animated films, allowing JWT to overcome some of the immediate postwar restrictions on other forms of advertising. From a competitive viewpoint, Honeybunch and Coco were visually ›different‹ to the images of sturdy white youths being employed by Cadbury and were therefore potentially more memorable. In a survey of 400 housewives in 1948, 200 were shown an edited version of ›Honeybunch and the Swordfish‹ and asked to identify the product and the firm; the remaining 200 women were shown a Cadbury advert

---

69 History of Advertising Trust, UK (HAT), JWT, Box 294, A710, Study of the Long-Term Prospects for the Cocoa Powder Market, 28.8.1945, p. 6.
70 HAT, JWT, Box 294, A710, Study of the Long-Term Prospects for the Cocoa Powder Market, 28.8.1945, pp. 4, 6.
71 HAT, JWT, Box 297, A61, Summary of ›Little Coco‹ copyright negotiations; letter from G. J. Harris to J. D. Watson, re. ›Coco‹ Copyright, 10.3.1947.

with 3 white children of different ages all growing stronger from drinking cocoa. Whilst 78 per cent of each sample were able to identify that it was cocoa being advertised, only 29 per cent correctly identified the Cadbury firm, compared to 42 per cent who associated Honeybunch with the name of Rowntree.[72] Ramamurthy has highlighted the »racialisation« of brands in the late nineteenth and early twentieth centuries; clearly, distinguishing otherwise similar products by associating them with a distinct racial caricature remained a useful marketing tactic.[73]

Although copyright negotiations may have limited the range of the Little Coco campaign, it is telling that both Coco and Honeybunch were short lived. I have found no references to Coco after his first series of films in the late 1940s; only Honeybunch seems to have been acceptable in the context of the 1950s and even she did not survive the decade. In view of violent colonial uprisings, increasing racial tensions in Britain and the development of legislation against public expressions of racism in the 1960s, as well as the influence of the Civil Rights movement, Rowntree may have decided these characters were no longer so appealing. Ramamurthy observes that »[i]n the postwar period, as decolonisation became a reality, and immigration from the colonies began to change the face of Britain, consumer advertising stopped using the image of black people to sell products«.[74] Yet some black mascots survived for British commodities: most famously the ›Gollywog‹ of Robertson's jams. This figure remained until the early 2000s, although the firm felt the need to repeatedly distance him from associations with ›real‹ black people. The popularity of the BBC's ›Black and White Minstrel Show‹ into the late 1970s also suggests that we should not underestimate the continued attractions of the black entertainer stereotype.[75] Perhaps Rowntree and their agents had simply overestimated the appeal of overtly American characters in the late 1940s and 50s.

Cocoa on a Civilising Mission

One advert for Rowntree from the late 1950s tellingly shifted the action back to a comic anachronism of the British Empire in Africa, just as the cocoa-producing Gold Coast was about to become independent. This tel-

---

72 BI, RA, R/DD/MT/OMR/28f, Cocoa Advertisement Recognition Test Report. November 1948.
73 Anandi Ramamurthy: Imperial Persuaders, p. 15.
74 Ibid., p. 215.
75 The show reached audiences of almost 17 million. BBC4: Black and White Minstrel Show – Revisited. Television Documentary. Originally broadcast 6.6.2004; see also Michael Pickering: Blackface Minstrelsy in Britain.

evision animation from 1957 featured a group of ›cannibals‹, with bodies resembling cocoa beans, dancing around a cauldron.[76] Again, this visual conflation of black people and cocoa erased the material relations of production. A worried-looking white ›explorer‹ (dressed in safari clothing, with a large white moustache) stands by the pot, flanked by two »dusky guards«. He clearly fears he is about to be eaten. The advert begins with a witch doctor character, wearing a chef's hat, dancing around the steaming pot whilst waving a large bone. This is accompanied by a »[b]ackground of beating drums« and a »[c]hant sung by various natives«. The Chief, sitting on a throne next to the cauldron, begins: »What is it soothes the savage beast?«. His words are accompanied by him »smacking his lips« and »rolling his eyes«. Preying on the racist fears of white audiences, these words and actions suggest that the explorer is about to be cooked. Then, by magic, the pot turns into a cup of Rowntree's Cocoa. The white explorer looks relieved and joins in the chanting: »What is it all housewives request? [...] Rowntree's, Rowntree's, Rowntree's«. White housewives are still the dominant consumers, despite their exclusion from the jungle setting. It is white domesticity that prevails, neutralising the threat of black savagery.

Cannibal jokes, according to Nederveen Pieterse, have been a clichéd staple of western humour. He suggests a slight change in emphasis between the nineteenth and the twentieth century, with »the ironization of the cannibalism motif« through the figure of the »cannibal gourmand«. He sees this figure as the »icon of the colonized savage and of a pacified Africa«: a »cannibal with refined manners, with the attributes (chef's hat, implements) and attitudes of European cuisine«.[77] The witch doctor character conforms to this trope, complete with chef's hat. However, the advert goes further than Nederveen Pieterse suggests, by dispensing with cannibalism altogether. By converting the ›cannibals‹, the power of Rowntree's Cocoa as a civilising force, and indeed as a food not just a drink, is stressed.

This postwar advert entirely erased the labour of African farmers and rendered women invisible. Cups of cocoa appear by magic, rather than as a result of the labour of farmers and factory workers, obscuring the inequalities of consumption and production faced by those in British colonies and former colonies. Africans are depicted first and foremost as savages and cannibals. Even when they turn away from cannibalism, they remain contained within the stereotype of ›the native‹ through their clothes and actions. Ironically, although these cartoon characters literally *are* cocoa

---

76 BI, RA, W24, Rowntree Cocoa – Television.
77 Jan Nederveen Pieterse: White on Black, pp. 114, 119.

beans, they consume processed cocoa owned by Rowntree. The product and the relations of production and consumption are exoticised, even as the civilising powers of cocoa are revealed. The histories of African cocoa farming, the cocoa trade, and the exploitations of British colonialism are forgotten.

By the latter half of the twentieth century, imperial conquest was treated almost as a joke. It is the white explorer who is made to look a fool, but only because of the success of Rowntree in penetrating even the depths of the African jungle.[78] Whilst there is an initial suggestion of resistance to white exploration, this is overturned by the friendly sharing of cocoa. The advert relies on collective white perceptions about savagery and cannibalism, even as these are comically undermined (though not entirely discredited). Mirroring but distorting the economic reality of colonial and postcolonial relations between Britain and Africa, British companies magically send manufactured cocoa back to producers in the final irony of the cocoa chain.[79] With the empire collapsing, the former imperial rulers looked to ›civilised‹ black people to run the former colonies and continue the civilising mission. Across the Little Coco, Honeybunch and Cannibals campaigns, a Rowntree brand, the product of invisible African labour, was shown to be a reassuringly civilising force.

Conclusion

In contrast to other colonial drinks – particularly tea – cocoa became divorced from its tropical origins in British advertising discourse during the twentieth century. Visual reminders of ›raw‹ cocoa, and of cocoa farming, became rare in advertising after the First World War (they have recently returned in relation to fair trade and ›high quality‹ cocoa). White consumers became the dominant trope. This may in part be related to the extent of industrial processing of the beans, which distanced chocolate as a drink and a food from its ›exotic‹ roots. Yet associations of cocoa with black people have remained elsewhere in Europe, despite industrial processing. It may then, as Ramamurthy argues, be connected to the politics of the British Quaker manufacturers themselves, who dominated the

---

[78] On the treatment of imperial masculinity as a joke in the postwar period, see Wendy Webster: Englishness and Empire, pp. 184, 186; also Stuart Ward: ›No Nation Could be Broker‹.

[79] As I observed during a research trip to Nigeria in 2002, cocoa farmers have indeed been consumers of Cadbury's Bournvita chocolate and other western imports. However, such items are expensive.

chocolate market.[80] There can be no conclusive explanation for this but it is important to note the extent to which cocoa adverts depicted white working-class consumers. The food values which came to be associated with cocoa made it suitable for hard-working white men, as well as for the more susceptible white women, children and invalids suggested by some advertising. British cocoa adverts over the course of the twentieth century created a bittersweet world of respectable white consumers in which the black producers of cocoa beans and the black consumers of chocolate within Britain were marginalised.

The use of black characters to market branded cocoa can be seen as part of strategic decisions by advertising agents to visually differentiate their product. Yet the use of such characters was never neutral, and has been encoded with particular racist ideologies. The forms and meanings of black characters have been unstable: shifting, as Ciarlo suggests for German advertising, from an exotic to a colonial trope.[81] The figure of the black male producer/server of cocoa was aligned in British cocoa advertising, particularly before the First World War, with contemporary imperial and industrial politics which placed black cocoa producers, white British confectionery workers, and white British consumers into dependent yet unequal interrelationships through the economics of commodity manufacture. Black characters after the Second World War were not employed in recognition of African labour or as a reflection of the increasing presence of black people within the metropole; such figures worked within contemporary white western (and Americanised) cultural understandings of ›blackness‹, part of cultural traditions such as minstrelsy which were still popular in Britain.

The decision by Rowntree and their agents to use black cartoon characters to sell cocoa in the late 1940s and into the 1950s runs against the dominant trends in British chocolate advertising. Although short-lived, Little Coco and Honeybunch deserve analysis for their place in postwar advertising history as departures from what had become the standard trope of white cocoa consumers. The characters of Honeybunch and Little Coco were intended as amusing novelties contained within a cartoon world. They were part of a postwar society in which American culture had taken hold, but they were also part of a decolonising British Empire, where former racial hierarchies were on increasingly shaky ground. Despite the racism inherent in the stereotyped representations of Coco and Honeybunch, these characters were essentially cast in the role of civilising imperialists.

80 Anandi Ramamurthy: Imperial Persuaders, p. 70.
81 David Ciarlo: Advertising Empire, p. 211.

They each used cocoa, the product of African labour, to tame wild animals or to show uncivilised humans how to consume correctly. With the British Empire imploding, other postwar campaigns for cocoa drew satirically on this civilising motif. As the bitter cocoa beans had found success in western Europe through the sweetening addition of slave-grown sugar, so in these adverts the bitter pill of racism was sugar-coated.

References

Archival Sources

Angell Antiques (http://www.angellantiques.com/content/cadburys-cocoa-advertising-lantern-slide, accessed March 2013).
›Auckland Star‹, Vol. XL, Issue 104, 3.5.1909, p. 6.
Borthwick Institute, York (BI), Rowntree Archive (RA), N41, Cocoa 1941-2.
BI, RA, N44, Cocoa 1946-1950.
BI, RA, W24, Rowntree Cocoa – Television.
BI, RA, TV1, Television Guard Book 1955-1960.
BI, RA, R/DD/MT/OMR/28f, Cocoa Advertisement Recognition Test Report. November 1948.
Cadbury Archive – Mondelēz International, 196/520/003552, Cadbury's Special Ads: May 1930 to December 1932.
›Cocoa Works Magazine‹, March 1922.
History of Advertising Trust, UK (HAT), JWT, Box 294, A710, Study of the Long-Term Prospects for the Cocoa Powder Market, 28.8.1945.
HAT, JWT, Box 297, A61, Summary of ›Little Coco‹ copyright negotiations; letter from G. J. Harris to J. D. Watson, re. ›Coco‹ Copyright, 10.3.1947.
Lambeth Landmark (http://landmark.lambeth.gov.uk/siteimages/landmark_learning/1920/large/frys.jpg – accessed March 2013).

Literature

BBC4: Black and White Minstrel Show – Revisited. Television Documentary. Originally broadcast 6.6.2004.
Bloom, Carole: All About Chocolate. The Ultimate Resource for the World's Favourite Food. New York: Macmillan 1998.
Ciarlo, David: Advertising Empire. Race and Visual Culture in Imperial Germany. Cambridge, Mass.: Harvard University Press 2011.
Clarence-Smith, William Gervase: Cocoa and Chocolate, 1765-1914. London: Routledge 2000.
Coe, Sophie D., Michael D. Coe: The True History of Chocolate. London: Thames and Hudson 1996.
De Groot, Joanna: Metropolitan Desires and Colonial Connections. Reflections on Consumption and Empire. In: At Home with the Empire, ed. by Catherine Hall, Sonya O. Rose. Cambridge: Cambridge University Press 2006.

Fitzgerald, Robert: Rowntree and the Marketing Revolution, 1862-1969. Cambridge: Cambridge University Press 1995.

Hackenesche, Silke: Advertising Chocolate, Consuming Race? On the Peculiar Relationship of Chocolate and Blackness. Unpublished Conference Paper. Between Local and Global. The History of Cocoa and Chocolate. Cologne: October 2010.

Hall, Catherine: Turning a Blind Eye. Memories of Empire. In: Memory, ed. by Patricia Fara, Karalyn Patterson. Cambridge: Cambridge University Press 1998.

Higgs, Catherine: Chocolate Islands. Cocoa, Slavery and Colonial Africa. Athens: Ohio University Press 2012.

Hinrichsen, Malte: Racist Trademarks. Slavery, Orient, Colonialism & Commodity Culture. Berlin [et al.]: Lit 2012.

Jubb, Michael: Cocoa & Corsets. London: HMSO 1984.

Kern-Foxworth, Marilyn: Aunt Jemima, Uncle Ben, and Rastus. Blacks in Advertising, Yesterday, Today, and Tomorrow. Westport: Greenwood Press 1994.

Manring, Maurice M.: Slave in a Box. The Strange Career of Aunt Jemima. Charlottesville [et al.]: Indiana University Press 2009.

McClintock, Anne: Imperial Leather. Race, Gender and Sexuality in the Colonial Contest. London: Routledge 1995.

Nederveen Pieterse, Jan: White on Black. Images of Africa and Blacks in Western Popular Culture. New Haven: Yale University Press 1992.

Pickering, Michael: Blackface Minstrelsy in Britain. Aldershot: Ashgate 2008.

Ramamurthy, Anandi: Imperial Persuaders. Images of Africa and Asia in British Advertising. Manchester: Manchester University Press 2003.

Robertson, Emma: Chocolate, Women and Empire. A Social and Cultural History. Manchester: Manchester University Press 2009.

Roche, Daniel: A History of Everyday Things. The Birth of Consumption in France, 1600-1800. Cambridge [et al.]: Cambridge University Press 2000.

Satre, Lowell J.: Chocolate on Trial. Slavery, Politics and the Ethics of Business. Athens: Ohio University Press 2005.

Sherwin, Adam: ASA says Cadbury was not racist when it compared Campbell to chocolate bar. In: Independent, 21.6.2011 (http://www.independent.co.uk/news/media/advertising/asa-says-cadbury-was-not-racist-when-it-compared-campbell-to-chocolate-bar-2300278.html – accessed April 2013).

Sweney, Mark: Cadbury Dairy Milk Ad Cleared of Racism. In: Guardian, 11.11.2009 (http://www.guardian.co.uk/media/2009/nov/11/cadbury-dairy-milk-cleared-racism – accessed April 2013).

Terrio, Susan: Crafting the Culture and History of French Chocolate. Berkeley: University of California Press 2000.

Thomas, Nicholas: Colonial Conversions. Difference, Hierarchy, and History in Early Twentieth-Century Evangelical Propaganda. In: Cultures of Empire. A Reader, ed. by Catherine Hall. Manchester: Manchester University Press 2000, pp. 298-328.

Wagner, Gillian: The Chocolate Conscience. London: Chatto and Windus 1987.

Ward, Stuart: ›No Nation Could be Broker‹. The Satire Boom and the Demise of Britain's World Role. In: British Culture and the End of Empire, ed. by id. Manchester: Manchester University Press 2001, pp. 91-110.

Warren, Allen: Citizens of the Empire. Baden-Powell, Scouts and Guides, and an Imperial Ideal, 1900-40. In: Imperialism and Popular Culture, ed. by John M. MacKenzie. Manchester: Manchester University Press 1986, pp. 232-256.

Webster, Wendy: Englishness and Empire, 1939-1965. Oxford: Oxford University Press 2005.

Williamson, Judith A.: Decoding Advertisements. Ideology and Meaning in Advertising. London: Marion Boyars 1978.

›The German Alternative‹
Nationalism and Racism in ›Afri-Cola‹
Katharina Eggers, Robert Fechner

Abstract: Commodity racism was historically coined through colonial and imperial motifs. However, it was and is not limited to those. The aim of this study is to examine the different stages of post-colonial commodity racism in Germany. The study will discuss the advertisements of Afri-Cola and the visualisation of colonial revisionism, racism, National Socialism and anti-Americanism since the 1930s. Hereby continuities and disruptions will become apparent. The brand was presented as a colonial drink, a defence drink, a whiteness drink, an ecstasy drink and a German drink. Despite all the flexibility Afri-Cola showed by adapting to the circumstances at the time, the racist tradition prevailed.

At the beginning of the 20th century, several Cola-drinks developed independently from each other. However, it was the success of Coca-Cola and a trip to America in 1931 which gave a German entrepreneur the idea to launch a rival drink. It was not a coincidence that he named the drink Afri-Cola. The name did not only signal the relation between the drink and the cola nut native to Africa, but it also had an exotic-racist and colonial-revisionist dimension.

At the beginning of the 1930s in Germany a new product with the label ›Africa‹ conjured up a whole realm of connotations. One of them was, without a doubt, the racist propaganda surrounding the so-called ›Black Shame‹ which was a reaction by all political camps in response to the occupation of the Rhineland by the French after the First World War. Yet the blatant racism of the campaign against the ›Black Shame‹ was embedded in a complex ideological network. It was possible that the propaganda directed against ›coloured‹ soldiers at the feet of the Lorelei could have been expressed in the sort of bourgeois establishment which Wulf D. Hund portrayed in a constructed genre scene. Such establishments came complete with an African sculpture at the fireside and a gramophone playing Jazz while ladies and gentlemen consumed chocolate, cigars and coffee, all advertised with a ›Moor‹ on the packaging, before leaving to see the latest

›Negro-revue‹. It must be added that several of those present could well have been members of the German Colonial Society. Under the pretext of German involvement being necessary, this organisation was arguing for an imperialist mission to ›civilise‹ so-called primitive people while urging for the re-occupation of resource-rich colonies.[1] Other than the exotic and colonialist dimension of the name Afri-Cola, there is also an implicit anti-American dimension to it, resulting from the rivalry with Coca-Cola which had been producing for the German market since 1929.

All these dimensions influenced the advertisements for Afri-Cola in different ways. However, at every phase of development, specific elements were highlighted. Naturally, the commercialisation of Afri-Cola as a ›colonial drink‹ played a special role, as it indicated an affiliation with the colonial revisionism which was spreading throughout the German Colonial Society and the Reich Colonial League. Just as important was the ›defence drink‹ which was reinforced by antisemitic discrimination against the ›American‹ enemy. After 1945 both these advertising strategies became intolerable and had to be abandoned. However, one could rely on general racism to advertise the brand as a ›whiteness drink‹, which symbolised the connection to the white race after the military and moral surrender of fascism. After a phase in which the aesthetics of commodities stagnated during the politically conservative Adenauer era, Afri-Cola tried to take advantage of the dynamic of the global youth movement by advertising the drink as an ›ecstasy drink‹. In doing so, the promotion was reconnected with the racist dimensions of exoticism. Towards the end of the 1980s, the brand harnessed the general sentiment in the country to launch the ›German drink‹ which meant a return to its early roots of advertising.

›Colonial Drink‹

In an interview, the son of the ›inventor‹ of the drink responded to a question on how the company came up with the name and the logo by saying that the food regulations at the time required »the usage of the cola nut« in cola drinks. Since those came from Africa, and »of course the palm tree belongs to Africa« and back then the palm also represented »a very special kind of exoticism«, the naming of the brand was self-evident.[2]

---

1 Cf. Wulf D. Hund: Negative Vergesellschaftung, p. 36; for the propaganda against the occupation of the Rhineland see Iris Wigger: Die ›Schwarze Schmach am Rhein‹; for colonial revisionism see Michael Schubert: Der schwarze Fremde, pp. 307 ff.; for the different contemporary ideological connotations of blackness see the articles in Peter Martin, Christine Alonso: Zwischen Charleston und Stechschritt.
2 Mineralbrunnen Überkingen-Teinach AG: ›80 Jahre anders‹.

That »palm trees [...] express exoticism«, which »was not synonymous with ›jungle‹« is an opinion which continues to be voiced often until this very day.³ One has to add that this is a profitable form of exoticism. Seen through this lens, palm trees have played a huge role in Germany, and not only in the promotion of Afri-Cola. Since the German Empire the palm has served in advertisements for all sorts of goods – from coffee, tea, alcohol,

Fig. 1: ... ›Germany needs her colonies back‹ ...

tobacco, cigarettes, cigars to starch, baking soda, adhesive right through to accordions. But it also played a part in the advertising of margarine and soap.⁴ That is why every consumer at the beginning of the 1930s would have known that ›Africa‹ and ›palm trees‹ were not only ›exotic‹ but were also an important economic factor.⁵

Since cola nuts do not grow on palm trees, the symbol on the logo of Afri-Cola can only indicate a combination of calculated exoticism and commercial acumen. In the early years of the 1930s, the colonial aspect was also present. Germany had lost all its colonies in the wake of the treaty of Versailles and the German Colonial Society started a strong movement for the re-instatement of the colonial territories. After the society merged with the Reich Colonial League in 1933, the united revisionism was able

---

3   Pierre Bourdieu: The Social Definition of Photography, p. 76 (›exotism‹); Michel Racine: The Gardens of Provence and the French Riviera, p. 96 (›jungle‹).
4   Cf. several figures in David Ciarlo: Advertising Empire.
5   This applied especially to the fat processing industry, which produced the cooking oil ›Palmin‹ from the coconut and the cleansing agent ›Palmöl-Borax-Seife‹ from the oil of the oil palms.

to demand this with the backing of the state.⁶ However, this claim was not only politically supported. This becomes obvious in the advertising of Afri-Cola.

Afri-Cola produced advertisements »in association with the Reich Colonial League for the German colonies in Africa«. With its permission the company published the »Colonial-Prospect« which included sketches of »our colonies«.⁷ The intended message was also shown on beer caps (see fig. 1). It shows the outline of Africa including former German colonies. Around the edge of the cap there are three advertising messages written in different fonts. The slogan ›the stimulating refreshment drink‹ is written in pseudo-personalised handwriting. The political advertisement is a central heading, demanding in capital letters ›Germany needs her colonies back‹. In addition, both messages are combined in a political-economic doctrine, with arrows pointing towards the colonies explaining that it is there we find ›the home country of the valuable ingredients of Afri-Cola‹.

Due to colonial revisionism, it is no wonder that the trade mark symbol – the palm tree – is not standing on the former colonies but rather right in the middle of the continent, signalling even greater territorial claims.⁸ This is a combination of private indulgence with national greatness and capitalist profit. Analogous with this are the company's thoughts on the colonial question: »If the colonial problem is not solved quite soon, Afri-Cola's worries about resources will cease to exist«.⁹ Similar to the beer cap, an advertisement (see fig. 2a) shows that this was not only about colonial revisionism but also about Germany as a whole. On one side the aim is the return of the colonies. On the other hand, the advertisement places the product centrally and oversized on the continent of Africa and shows the connection between exploitation and underdevelopment.

This symbolises the coming together of advertisements not only for the success of the brand but also for the good of the fatherland. This is not only about the consumption of lemonade but also about ›German consumerism‹ playing its part in regaining national greatness.¹⁰ The request for national consumption combines enjoyment and aggression by asking the individual to say: »I support the German economy, because Afri-Cola is the German

6   Cf. Karsten Linne: Deutschland jenseits des Äquators, pp. 26-30.
7   Afri-Post, 2, 1937. The Afri-Post was an in-house publication without page numbers. The editions were kindly provided as copies by Jeff Schutts.
8   Cf. Afri-Post, 1, 1937.
9   Afri-Post, 19, 1939; for the following cf. ibid. The brand logo was registered on the 3th of March 1938 and was removed on the 3th of February 2000 – cf. German Patent and Trademark Office: register number 500456, old reference number B76431.
10 With regard to the advertising industry under National Socialism cf. Uwe Westphal: Werbung im Dritten Reich; Dirk Reinhardt: Von der Reklame zum Marketing, pp. 423-428.

Fig. 2 a & b: ... ›drinking in favour of Germany's (and Afri-Cola's) greatness‹ ...

Cola-drink whose resources are partly being imported from German colonies«.[11] Consumption is presented to the *Volksgemeinschaft* as a service and the well-being of the consumer is equated with the profit of the entrepreneur as well as with the claim to national greatness. Whoever drinks Afri-Cola is protecting the importance of ›Germanness‹ in the world.

Another advertisement clearly shows that this is about supremacy and symbolically combines the brand Afri-Cola with the first verse of the national anthem (›Deutschland über alles‹) and with the image of colonial revisionism showing the ›Kaiser-Wilhelm-peak‹ of Mount Kilimanjaro (see fig. 2b).[12] The contemporary viewer can clearly identify the clouded scene. However, ›Germany's (former) highest mountain‹ is not topped with a national flag, but rather serves as a bottle holder for Afri-Cola. The success of the company is put on the same level as the greatness of the nation.

In fact, the restitution of the African colonies would remain wishful thinking. All the more fatal was the Nazi policy of expansion in Eastern Europe. The producer of the ›colonial drink‹ had no problem profiting from the war and the internal colonisation of Europe. The company obtained three production facilities through the conquest: in Kiew, Kamjan-

11 Afri-Post, 19, 1939.
12 The advertisement was published in ›Deutsche Mineralwasser-Zeitung‹, 25, 24.7.1938; concerning the motif of the picture cf. Christof Hamann, Alexander Honold: Kilimandscharo, pp. 121-148; see also the essay by Wulf D. Hund in this volume.

ez-Podilskyi and Skoczów. The companies that were taken over solely produced for army supplies and the *Wehrmacht* had the exclusive right to disposal of the commodities. The production also used forced labourers, which can be seen from a report which speaks of »›workers being transferred from the Ukraine‹«.[13]

›Defence Drink‹

While Afri-Cola presented itself as a ›colonial drink‹, the company also attempted to construct an internal enemy – the rival Coca-Cola was attacked with anti-American and antisemitic sentiments in order to establish the label Afri-Cola as a ›defence drink‹.

The boss of the company is thought to have found a link between ›American‹, ›Coca-Cola‹ and ›Jewish‹ during his trip to the USA with the German Labour Front in 1936. He came upon a Coca-Cola bottle top with Hebrew writing on it. This was because a Rabbi certified the brand as kosher and the company then produced a bottle cap with that certification in Hebrew.[14] For the German antisemite, this was sufficient to identify the competing lemonade as ›Jewish‹.

He strengthened the discriminatory tradition of »anti-Jewish messages« by emphasising the »lettering that was reminiscent of Hebrew writing«. This behaviour was not different from those of a designer who utilised pseudo-Hebrew letters to form the text ›The eternal Jew‹ on a placard a few years later.[15] In order to show the ›Jewish character‹ of Coca-Cola, the Afri-Cola company supplied photographs of the bottle top with the Hebrew letters to its customers, to workers in the industry for alcohol-free drinks and to members of the NSDAP.[16] From a marketing point of view, trying to discredit a rival through its supposed connections to Jewry was

---

13   Note by Dr. Wicharz dated 22.4.1944; concerning the manufacturing facilities cf. the letter from Karl Flach to the fruit, vegetable and potato headquarters Ukraine GmbH, dated 29.3.1944; for the right of disposal see the certification from the Heeresverpflegungsmagazin Kiew, Abt. II, dated 1.9.1943.
14   Cf. Marcie Cohen Ferris: Matzoh Ball Gumbo, p. 319.
15   Wolfgang Benz: Was ist Antisemitismus, p. 235 (›messages‹); Hans-Christoph Goßmann: ›...denn das Heil kommt von den Juden‹, pp. 99 f.(›eternal Jew‹); for an image of the poster by Horst Schlüter see http://www.deutsches-museum.de/fileadmin/Content/010_DM/060_Verlag/030_Forschung/BN_46802_PlakatJude.jpg.
16   Concerning the antisemitic discrimination of Coca-Cola cf. Jeff Schutts: ›Die erfrischende Pause‹, p. 166; id.: Coca-Colonization, ›Refreshing‹ Americanization, or Nazi Volksgetränk, p. 276; Mark Pendergast: For God, Country and Coca-Cola, pp. 224 f.; Uwe Westphal: Werbung im Dritten Reich, pp. 53 f.; Silke Horstkotte, Olaf Jürgen Schmidt: Heil Coca-Cola, p. 81; the trip to the USA is mentioned in Frederick Allen: Coca-Cola Story, p. 328; on the certification see Tom Segev: How Coca-Cola became kosher for Passover.

still a risky move even though this was consistent with the antisemitic tradition in Germany in general and the racial antisemitism of the Nazis in particular. However, at least in the first years of fascism even the latter had to consider its repellent effect, especially during the Olympics in Berlin. Admittedly, there were attempts to use anti-Semitism as advertising at North Sea spas during the German Empire by pointing out that they were ›free of Jews‹. During the Weimar Republic there were so many spas advertising with this slogan that the Central Association of German Citizens of Jewish Faith (CV) felt compelled to establish its own ›travel service‹ giving advice on which spas Jews could still visit without being in danger.[17] And the infamous boycott slogan of the Nazis demanded ›Germans, do not buy from Jews‹.[18]

Against this background the antisemitic agitation of Afri-Cola produced short-term success. The NSDAP headquarters cancelled their Coca-Cola orders. But Coca-Cola fought against the ›allegations‹ and enforced a cease and desist order against Afri-Cola, although they avoided further legal action, expecting it may lead to negative publicity.[19] In fact, Coca-Cola published three advertisements in the antisemitic Nazi-propaganda journal ›Der Stürmer‹ to placate the Nazis. Incidentally, the concessionaires of Coca-Cola were quite well integrated in German society. One of the concessionaires, Leopold Kretschmann, was an early NSDAP member councilman in his home town of Hof and director of the Imperial Federation of the German Mineral Water Manufacturers.[20]

Despite the failed antisemitic campaign, Coca-Cola remained a negative point of reference. Afri-Cola complained that »the spread of the American Cola drink in the German beverage market [...] could not be prevented by the indigenous trade« and presented itself as the advocate of productive German labour in opposition to the »foreign-based capital power«. Antisemitic resentment merged with the Anti-American stance and Coca-Cola was branded as a destructive and un-German element against which Afri-Cola was organising resistance. They promoted »healthy and active defence forces« – declaring that »a successful defence can only be imagined to be successful through a great German united front«. This political slogan was directly connected to their own marketing: »According

---

17 Cf. Frank Bajohr: ›Unser Hotel ist judenfrei‹; Cornelia Hecht: Deutsche Juden und Antisemitismus in der Weimarer Republik, p. 304.
18 Cf. Hannah Ahlheim: ›Deutsche, kauft nicht bei Juden!‹.
19 Cf. Mark Pendergast: For God, Country and Coca-Cola, p. 225; Jeff Schutts: Coca-Colonization, ›Refreshing‹ Americanization, or Nazi Volksgetränk, p. 276.
20 Cf. Jeff Schutts: ›Die erfrischende Pause‹, p. 167; Deutsche Mineralwasser-Zeitung, 25, p. 357 and 39, p. 736.

to the judgement of the greatest specialists in the field, this defence front is called: Afri-Cola, the German quality drink«.[21]

The brand's economic rivalry was stylised as representing the destiny of the whole industry while it was declared the will of the people through militaristic eugenic and racist rhetoric. The demand for a »defence-organisation against the foreign intruder« was supposed to stop the »foreign infiltration of the German mineral water trade«.[22] The economic rival, Coca-Cola, was declared a destructive enemy which Afri-Cola opposed, labelling itself the ›defence drink‹. In military language, the »German corporate-conscious colleague« was ordered to the »front defence line« »not only to overrule this alien intruder, but also to destroy his desire to expand«. In this important battle nobody was allowed to »stand back«: »There is only one option: everybody to the defence front! German mineral water manufacturer wake up before it's too late«.[23]

The implementation of the *lingua tertii imperii* interconnected several connotations: a warning about the ›health of the people‹ endangered by ›foreign intruders‹ and the aggressive call to protect linked to the appeal to finally ›wake up‹. These elements had a strong antisemitic dimension which must have been obvious to the audience of the contemporary discourse. Jews were being labelled as internal enemies whose influence had to be curbed by banning them from their professions and by the introduction of laws for the ›protection of German blood‹ right at the beginning of the National Socialist rule. They were also seen as external enemies who controlled international financial capital in an attempt to damage Germany. Dietrich Eckart, the first editor of the ›Völkisch Observer‹ began early on in his ›Storm song‹ to complain about ›Judas‹ who was trying to annex the ›Empire‹. He coined the common Nazi slogan which later decorated their flags: ›Germany awake‹.[24]

The identification of the internal and external enemy implied fighting all supposedly un-German elements and thereby implied the *völkisch* consolidation of institutional powers and discipline. The warning that nobody should ›stand back‹ is easily identifiable as an appeal to integrate oneself into the collective of the *Volksgemeinschaft* as well as into the collective of the company. For the beverage industry this meant that everybody »who had not yet fallen under the influence of the American dollar-company«

---

21 Afri-Post, 1, 1937; concerning the affinity of antisemitism and anti-Americanism cf. Heiko Beyer, Ulf Liebe: Antiamerikanismus und Antisemitismus.
22 Afri-Post, 13, 1939 (›intruder‹); Afri-Post: 1, 1937 (›foreign infiltration‹).
23 Afri-Post, 3, 1937 (›defence drink‹); Afri-Post: 1, 1937 (›defence line‹).
24 Cf. Victor Klemperer: The Language of the Third Reich; Cornelia Esser: Die ›Nürnberger Gesetze‹ (›protection of German blood‹); Günter Hartung: Deutschfaschistische Literatur und Ästhetik, pp. 165 ff. (›Germany awake‹).

›The German Alternative‹ 205

had to collect »German strength for defence« and to focus »on one single defence-speciality« – Afri-Cola of course.²⁵

This demand was obviously not only related to the beverage market but also to the employees of this industry. The slogan »the individual is nothing« was aimed at them, calling them to integrate into »the Afri-loyalty front« so that »the common interest comes before the individual«.²⁶ In fact, this was also the message to the consumers: they were supposed to choose the ›German‹ Cola and by doing so they were drinking the enemy of the German people under the table. Drinking what was both a ›defence drink‹ and a ›colonial drink‹ at the same time, converted the enjoyment of Afri-Cola into a national act which was aggressive towards others. The commodity racism of the Afri-Cola advertisement was not satisfied with the defamation of others. It openly aimed at their submission or elimination.

›Whiteness drink‹

In spring 1945 not only was German fascism defeated, but Afri-Cola had also lost their fight against their American rival to become the ›German refreshment beverage‹. Coca-Cola was present on both sides of the front, it invaded the European neighbours with the German army and subsequently marched through to Berlin with the allied troops.²⁷ It was no wonder that Afri-Cola saw itself as a victim of the »favoured rival«²⁸ which they could no longer even attack on an ideological level. Coca-Cola presented itself as the drink of the »consumer-democrats« and hovered successfully between old anti-Americanism and the new Americanism in Germany. This became apparent when the parliament of the new Federal Republic tried »to ban the soft drink« while at the same time »members of the newly established [...] Bundestag in Bonn were downing some fifteen thousand bottles of Coca-Cola a month«.²⁹

Once Afri-Cola could not hang on to their colonial revisionist propaganda, they fell back on the usual racism which was not likely to be resisted by the Western occupying powers. This is indicated by the continuing advertisement of a chocolate brand with its ›Sarotti-Mohr‹ in Germany as

25   Afri-Post, 1, 1937.
26   Afri-Post, 3, 1937.
27   Cf. Mark Pandergrast: For God, Country, and Coca-Cola, pp. 195-226.
28   Afri-Post, 6, 1951, p. 1.
29   Jeff R. Schutts: Born Again in the Gospel of Refreshment?, pp. 142 f. (›consumer-democrats‹), 125 (›ban‹, ›downing‹); concerning the ambivalent relation of Americanisation and anti-Americanism cf. Bernd Greiner: ›Test the West‹; Axel Schildt: Zur so genannten Amerikanisierung in der frühen Bundesrepublik – einige Differenzierungen.

well as the French ›bonhomme Banania‹ and the US advertising characters ›Aunt Jemima‹ and ›Uncle Ben‹.[30]

The same also became apparent through a film produced during the Nazi era but not shown before the end of the war. At first it was censored by the allied forces but after much back and forth concerning the political past of the main actor, ›Quax in Africa‹ was allowed to premier in 1953.[31] One episode of this sexist and racist film production was set in an imaginary ›Africa‹ populated by half naked ›savages‹, drumming away in grass skirts and suspected of cannibalism. In addition to the infamy of the presentation there was the iniquity of the production – next to actors in ›blackface‹ there were also black actors and extras forced to participate, who were not only exposed to daily racism due to the National Socialist race ideology but had also to be in fear of their lives. They were portrayed as ›natives‹ who praised the hero, stranded in ›Africa‹, as a ›white God‹. The latter declared: »I think I know these brothers. I have seen them before in the Berlin Zoo«. Logically, due to the stereotypical nature of the portrayed native combined with the projection of uncivilised and rampant libidinal urges, he is offered a topless young woman.

Afri-Cola had no problem latching on to such discriminatory supremacist images. It presented its drink as a ›whiteness drink‹. A cinema advertisement from 1955 by Hans Fischerkoesen[32] with the obvious title ›Bimbus‹ clearly shows the shift from colonial to exotic-patriarchal racism. The image of the deserted and resource-rich Africa found in the National-socialist advertising was now being transformed into a desert populated by underdeveloped ›tribes‹. First, a nearly naked, dark black caricature of an African is shown in cartoon style with a grass skirt, earrings and oversized lips. He walks through the desert, visibly exhausted, looking for something to drink until he finds the white Afri-Cola palm tree on which grow the black Afri-Cola bottles that rescue him. He climbs up the tree to get the bottles (see fig. 3a) and quickly carries them back to his fellow ›tribe members‹. Thanks to Afri-Cola, the African village, consisting of mud huts, survives and celebrates by dancing to the beat of drums. At this point the film switches from a cartoon to a realist style focusing on a street in a city in the Occident. A well-dressed white man steps into a bar decorated with

---

30 Cf. Malte Hinrichsen: Racist Trademarks; see also his essay in this volume.
31 Cf. Rita Morrien: ›Africa mon amour‹? p. 262; Manuel Köppen: Mit dem ›Dritten Reich‹ um die Welt, p. 270 – the complete movie on youtube: http://www.youtube.com/watch?v=CQikGbYhLV8.
32 Hans Fischerkoesen was one of the most distinguished animators in Nazi-Germany and in the Adenauer era. He also produced other commercials in the 1950s, which included racist iconography – cf. the commercials »The flotsam and jetsam« (1951) and »The alluring target« (1957) in Joachim Kellner, Deutsches Werbemuseum e.V. (ed.): Die besten Kinospots der 50er Jahre.

the Afri-Cola logo and enjoys an Afri-Cola. This is not very reminiscent of the African scene except perhaps for the carefree zest for life.

The commercial (which was still shown in a corporate video for the 80th anniversary of Afri-Cola in 2011) shows the contrast between barbarism and civilisation. The Africans are caricatured as hunter gatherers on the lowest level of the human scale of development propagated since the Enlightenment.[33] The European belongs to a highly developed goods producing society, where one can buy pleasure or indulgence any time. The two-sided point of view can also be applied to the environment (desert and city), and to the architecture of the huts (mud huts and houses).

Fig. 3 a & b: ... ›revelling racism‹ ...

›Africa‹ seems to be a continent that is populated by ›primitive tribes‹. Its infantile ›natives‹ would not survive without the Europeans and their ›white‹ products.

Through the rescue of the ›blacks‹, the underdeveloped Africa in the cartoon signals a shift from colonial to postcolonial civilising missions. The subsequent exuberance of the survivors demonstrates the exoticism of the drink as well as the bottles hanging from a palm tree. Yet this was not a native but a commercial logo of the ›civilised world‹ and hereby emphasised the necessity of ›development aid‹. A contemporary commercial for ›Dallmayr coffee‹ directly vocalises this message. The coffee might be from ›Africa‹ but before the refinement of it by the Europeans it was being consumed in such a primitive manner that it would have horrified you. ›Development aid‹ was needed right from the start.[34]

33 Cf. Wulf D. Hund: Rassismus, pp. 61 ff.
34 The advertising film ›Men talk about Dallmayr-Kaffee‹ (about 1958) also used the opposition of animation and real movie footage, but the relationship to patriarchal development aid was explicit: »They could have used development aid back then« – see

The calamity of losing the war and the final end of the colonial dream is compensated by the affiliation to the ›white race‹. The ›Germanness‹ of Afri-Cola has to momentarily take a back seat because the ›whiteness‹ of the Afri-Cola palm tree is the only opportunity to latch on to the supremacist advertising agenda of National Socialism and while doing so, also allows Germany's integration into the Western Bloc. The portrayed superiority can be seen in a coin tray (see fig. 3b), an article of company merchandise, decorated with caricatures of infantile ›blacks‹.[35] One of the concessionaires of Afri-Cola understood the message literally and took »a small Negro boy with him on his delivery runs as a living promotional character for Afri-Cola« where he served as a »living ›mascot‹«.[36]

›Ecstasy Drink‹

The 1960s were shaped by dramatic economic, political and social changes. The economy slipped into a financial crisis and strikes increasingly occurred. The German Emergency Acts prompted huge protests and anti-authoritarian resistance was building in the universities. Combined with this were new forms of protest and the search for alternative life styles. Rock'n'Roll, Blues and Beat music were imported from America, flower power served as an esoteric surrogate religion and sexual morals began to crumble.[37]

The advertising campaign initiated by Afri-Cola between 1968 and 1972 seized upon these developments and used them to promote their product. The placards and films produced by Charles Wilp would not miss their target. Sales rose about 34 percent in Germany and by about 40 percent in Austria.[38] This was due not least to the calculated breaking of taboos. The advertisements were aimed foremost at young buyers who were trying to free themselves from bourgeois-authoritarian structures. Displays of nakedness and a thrill of ecstasy, with psychedelic music and hints of esotericism in the background, served to distinguish them from the older generation.

Joachim Kellner, Deutsches Werbemuseum e.V. (ed.): 50 Jahre Werbung in Deutschland.
35 A picture of the coin tray is published in GoodTimes. Kult!, 1, 2010, p. 41.
36 Afri-Post, 1, 1952, p. 2 f.
37 Cf. Wolfgang Kraushaar: 1968 als Mythos, Chiffre und Zäsur; Stephan Malinowski, Alexander Sedlmaier: ›1968‹ als Katalysator der Konsumgesellschaft.
38 The turnover of Afri-Cola was 200 million Deutsche Mark (DM), clearly behind Coca-Cola with a turnover of 600 million DM. The market share of Afri-Cola amounted to 15 percent and Coca-Cola's to 55 percent – cf. Karl Günter Simon: Der Werbe-Hippie; N.N.: Seit 20 Jahren im Expansionsrausch.

The main subject of the ›sexy-mini-super-flower-pop-op-cola‹-campaign was the portrayal of sex, where women were presented topless or in tight clothing and illustrated the incarnated fantasy of men: stewardesses bending down in miniskirts, sexy nurses and hippy women under the influence of drugs. During the Afri-Cola-thrill they allowed their supposed nature to run free and consumed the beverage, promoted as an ›ecstasy drink‹. The sexism in the campaign was supplemented by racism. Charles Wilp thought of black women as ›close to nature‹ and ›animalistic‹. He explained in an interview that the »real strong woman« »is the sexual black«, who »has her roots in Africa«: she »exudes sexuality«. And he explains what is to be understood when he speaks of ›strength‹: sex includes the »lowest instincts to appeal to humans«.[39]

The sexist-racist ideology on which the Afri-Cola campaign was founded, is encapsulated in a commercial called ›Bushbaby‹. In it a black woman with an afro hairstyle dances, expressing her apparent »unlimited zest for life«.[40] Donna Summers went through a similar transformation when she was engaged to take part in the campaign. She was well-known by German consumers through the German version of the musical ›Hair‹ and the popular crime thriller ›11 Uhr 20‹. The musical, which, considering the fact that it was staged for easy viewing, was surprisingly time-critical, had its premiere in Munich in 1968. Donna Summers played a pagan esoteric and attractive black virgin. In the feature film ›11 Uhr 20‹, shown at the beginning of the 1970s, she played the part of a black slave in an oriental harem. Writhing half-naked on the floor she sang about ›black power‹, understood here as sexual adventure, while completely depriving the word of its political meaning: »Black power | that's the glamour of the night | when you're holding me so tight«.[41]

In this case, the discrepancy between protest and commerce was comparably small so that Wilp was able to easily stage his sexist-racist view of women. One of the posters shows Donna Summers behind a window, an image which was also used in other advertisements. However, the window, usually displayed iced-over, in this case Wilp's ideology of the black women exuding sex has made the commercial ice melt. The supposed hot atmosphere seemed to come from this woman, sitting naked with nearly closed eyelids behind Afri-Cola bottles to which her mouth is connected by a straw. The accompanying text strongly suggest that the drink is a

39 Cit. by Moritz Ege: Schwarz werden, p. 32; regarding the relations of racism and sexism see Ina Kerner: Differenzen und Macht.
40 Cf. »Es ist eine Lust zu Leben. ›Buschbaby‹« (advertising spot from the personal inventory of Alexander Flach).
41 Donna Summer: Black Power (http://www.golyr.de/donna-summer/songtext-black-power-13951.html); cf. Gerome Ragni, James Rado: Haare.

»stimulant« and »atmosphere elixir« promising »social games with the Afri-Cola straw«. The phallic association is supported through the positioning of the bottles (see fig. 4). At the same time, the caption of the

Fig. 4: ... »exuding sexuality« ...

advertisement is ambivalent: »the source of God with the Afri-Cola straw« could either mean the bottle or the black woman.

If the message of an advertisement like this is supposed to show the »heady rush of blackness«,[42] it does not do that from an emancipatory per-

42   Moritz Ege: Schwarz werden, p. 38; the author certainly remains ambivalent regarding Wilps alleged innovations in the representation of blacks and writes that the representations are »a new (perhaps an old) ›myth‹« (p. 40). Wholly one-sided is the judgement of Alexander Grönert: Politik, Pop und Afri-Cola, p. 165, when he claims, that the »self-confident view« of the blacks in the advertisements of Wilp are a »provocative to all those who had racist and colonial attitudes«. Even then contemporaries were already criticising, although cut and dried, the racism contained in the advertisement – cf. Peter

spective. Rather it has a pornographic dimension which started even before the presentation of »black women on the auction block« in the southern states of the USA.[43] Wilp's commodity racism had a »porno-tropic tradition« including the description of black women as »hot constitution'd ladies« who have »no scruple to prostitute themselves to the Europeans«.[44] And in 1893 at the Chicago World's Columbian Exposition, not only was ›Aunt Jemima‹ created a ›black mammy‹, but there was also a ›Dahomey Village‹ whose black women were photographed for different purposes with different degrees of nakedness.[45]

Also speaking in Chicago was the black feminist Anna Julia Cooper in front of the Women's Congress, while at the same time the black civil rights activist Ida B. Wells was strongly criticising the World Exposition. Both women, who were born as slaves, were part of the emancipation movement which would fight for the civil rights of black Americans. One of their successors was Angela Davis who studied in Germany and joined the Socialist German Student Union (SDS) in the middle of the 1960s. The kind of ›black power‹ which she represented was attacked by Wilp's campaign. The resistant elements in the biographies of his models were undermined and ridiculed. In spite of the new trendy exterior of Afri-Cola, the advertisements remained true to racist tradition.

›German Drink‹

In 1981, fifteen German professors published the ›Heidelberger Manifest‹ in which they declared: »It is with great concern that we observe the infiltration of the German people by the immigration of millions of foreigners and their families, the foreign infiltration of our language, our culture and our folklore«. The language uses blatant biological racism and supports the slogan ›foreigners out‹, which was circulating in the political sphere, with pseudo-scientific rhetoric. It went on along the lines that »it would be impossible to integrate great masses of non-German foreigners [...] while

---

Böhmer, Thomas Leber, Jürgen Martini, Hans Seidemann, Reinhard Wagner: Der Rassenkonflikt in den USA, p. 136; N.N.: Schwarze Haut für weiße Kassen. The copyright of figure 4 lies with Stiftung Preußischer Kulturbesitz.
43 Cf. Patricia Hill Collins: Pornography and Black Women's Bodies, p. 39.
44 Anne McClintock: Imperial Leather, pp. 31 ff. (›commodity racism‹), 22 (›porno-tropic tradition‹); Winthrop D. Jordan: White Over Black, p. 35 (quoting ›hot ladies‹, ›no scruple‹).
45 Cf. Kimberly Wallace-Sanders: Mammy, p. 60 (Aunt Jemima); Christopher Robert Reed: ›All the World is Here!‹ (Dahomey Village, images p. 162 f.); concerning the following see ibid, pp. 102 (Anna Julia Cooper), 30 ff. and passim (Ida B. Wells); Bruce Levine: ›Black Prussians‹, pp. 76 ff. (Angela Davis).

at the same time conserving the German people« because this will lead »to the well-known ethnic catastrophes of multicultural societies«.[46]

The racism of the professors became apparent at a time when newly found self-confidence was intermingling with old xenophobic attitudes. This also became obvious in the statements and actions of high ranking government officials. For example chancellor Helmut Kohl made *Ausländerpolitik* an element of exceptional urgency in his government dec-

Fig. 5: ... ›Afri Cola – the German alternative‹ ...

laration of 1982 and, somewhat later, managed to compel Ronald Reagan to visit a military cemetery near Bitburg in 1985, where members of the SS were also buried (even though the overwhelming majority of the US House of Representatives asked the president not to attend).[47]

This aggressive saturation, which at the same time insisted on appreciation (of its own importance) and exclusion (of unwanted others) also became apparent in the commercial campaign of ›Afri Cola – the German alternative‹ in 1983. The campaign was aimed at young adults who, according to the marketing boss of Afri-Cola, »were able to use the word

---

46 ›Heidelberger Manifest‹, pp. 29 f.; cf. Andreas Wagner: Das ›Heidelberger Manifest‹ von 1981.
47 Cf. Ulrich Herbert: Geschichte der Ausländerpolitik in Deutschland, pp. 249 ff. (›policy towards foreigners‹), Maren Röger: Bitburg-Affäre.

›German‹ again without having a complex«.⁴⁸ The advertisements introduced young Germans by name, seen dressed in contemporary clothes and showed them justifying why they preferred the ›German‹ brand. National resentment was being spread, disguised as individual opinion. A ›Steffi Böhm‹ (see fig. 5) declares that if »they« do not like it »here« they should »get lost«. This recommendation correlates with the tougher handling of procedures for asylum seekers and with the prevalent opinion that claimed that the problem of unemployment was due to »too many guest workers«.⁴⁹ ›Hatred of foreigners‹ became the catch phrase of political discourse and the topic of scientific analysis.

While the message against the ›foreigners‹ was directed inwards, the focus of a ›Susanne Sommer‹ was on the anti-Americanism ticket. She confronts American modernism, which she perceives to be alienated from Germany's down-to-earth approach. America, represented through an abstract New York, is being confronted with homey Germany.⁵⁰ The press of the right-wing ›Homeland Association of East Prussia‹ was full of praise for these statements, since it saw »obvious reactivation of German self-confidence« through Afri-Cola and its advertisement as »a cause for further hope« in »conservative circles«.⁵¹

On an ideological level, the campaign linked to already field-tested concepts and thereby closed a circle that started with the anti-Americanism of the Nazi era. In the meantime, racism had been modernised many times and appeared again in the robe of a new nationalism which was copied from the French *nouvelle droite*. The lessons taken from there included discrimination in the form of asking the ›others‹ to go back to their ›ancestral‹ countries or even better, to stay there in the first place in order not to lead to disputes about our ›own‹ ›German homeland‹.⁵²

Afri-Cola adjusted the commodity racism of its advertisements according to varying historical circumstances. During National Socialism, the brand presented itself as a ›colonial drink‹ and a ›defence drink‹. The ›colonial drink‹ sold the German consumer racist exoticism and revisionist colonial politics. It combined the brand logo of the palm tree with a claim to reoccupy the German colonial Empire. In its fight against rivals, Afri-Cola established itself as a ›defence drink‹. Coca-Cola was defamed

---

48 AP: Africola sieht sich als ›deutsche Alternative‹.
49 Emnid-Informationen: 1/2, 1982; cf. Georgios Tsiakolos: Ausländerfeindlichkeit. The advertisement is printed in ›Stern‹, 22, 1983, p. 129.
50 ›Spiegel‹, 20, 16.5.1983, p. 43.
51 A.G.: Nach den Cowboys kommt jetzt Bismarck, p. 10.
52 Cf. Wieland Eschenhagen (ed.): Die neue deutsche Ideologie; Margret Feit: Die ›Neue Rechte‹ in der Bundesrepublik.

as a company ruled by Jews and was used again and again as a point of negative identification by the German *Volksgemeinschaft*.

After the defeat of German fascism, the Afri-Cola palm tree developed as a symbol for white supremacy and Afri-Cola was defined to be the ›whiteness drink‹. Afri-Cola saw itself as presenting ›white‹ civilisation in contrast to a ›primitive‹ Africa. Through this, they gained ground again in the 1960s, and as a brand felt strong enough to return to patterns of aggressive discrimination. By declaring the drink an ›ecstasy drink‹ they disguised old racist stereotypes about gender and race with a trendy advertising campaign. Finally, the brand went back to its roots with the campaign for a ›German drink‹, which, in a period of increasing racism, promised to be on the ›right‹ side. Without directly naming the main rival, Afri-Cola appealed once again for people to consume only ›German‹.

References

Archival Sources

Certification from the Heeresverpflegungsmagazin Kiew, Abt. II, dated 1.9.1943. In: BArch R 33-I / 54.
Letter from Karl Flach dated 29.03.1944 to the fruit-, vegetable and potato headquarters Ukraine GmbH. In: BArch R 33-I / 54.
Note of Dr. Wicharz dated 22.4.1944. Production facilities in poor condition. In: BArch R 33-I / 54.

Literature

Afri-Post. Vertrauliches Informations- und Mitteilungs-Blatt für unsere Afri-Freunde. Köln: Hausverlag bei F. Blumhoffer Nachfolger.
Afri-Post. Hausmitteilungen der Afri-Cola-Organisation. Köln: Hausverlag bei F. Blumhoffer Nachfolger GmbH.
A.G.: Nach den Cowboys kommt jetzt Bismarck. ›Die deutsche Alternative‹ – Langsam paßt sich die Werbung neuem Trend an. In: Das Ostpreußenblatt, 3.12.1983.
Ahlheim, Hannah: ›Deutsche, kauft nicht bei Juden!‹. Antisemitismus und politischer Boykott in Deutschland 1924 bis 1935. Göttingen: Wallstein 2011.
Allen, Frederick: Coca-Cola Story. Die wahre Geschichte. 2nd ed. Köln: vgs 1995.
AP: Africola sieht sich als ›deutsche Alternative‹. Trotz zahlreicher Proteste hält die Firma an ihrer aggressiven Werbung fest. In: Frankfurter Rundschau, 19.7.1983.
Bajohr, Frank: ›Unser Hotel ist judenfrei‹. Bäder-Antisemitismus im 19. und 20. Jahrhundert. Frankfurt: Fischer Taschenbuch Verlag 2003.
Benz, Wolfgang: Was ist Antisemitismus. München: Beck 2004.

Beyer, Heiko, Ulf Liebe: Antiamerikanismus und Antisemitismus. Zum Verhältnis zweier Ressentiments. In: Zeitschrift für Soziologie, 39, 2010, 3, pp. 215-232.

Böhmer, Peter, Thomas Leber, Jürgen Martini, Hans Seidemann, Reinhard Wagner: Der Rassenkonflikt in den USA. Sozialisation und Probleme der Emanzipation am Beispiel der Afroamerikaner. Band I. Frankfurt: Europäische Verlagsanstalt 1972.

Bourdieu, Pierre: The Social Definition of Photography. In: id. [et al.], Photography. A Middle-brow Art. Stanford: Stanford University Press 1990, pp. 73-98.

Ciarlo, David: Advertising Empire. Race and Visual Culture in Imperial Germany. Cambridge [et al.]: Cambridge University Press 2011.

Cohen Ferris, Marcie: Matzoh Ball Gumbo. Culinary Tales of the Jewish South. Chapel Hill: University of Carolina Press 2005.

Ege, Moritz: Schwarz werden. ›Afroamerikanophilie‹ in den 1960er und 1970er Jahren. Bielefeld: transcript 2007.

EMNID-Informationen: 1/2, 1982. Bielefeld : EMNID-Institut 1982.

Eschenhagen, Wieland (ed.): Die neue deutsche Ideologie. Darmstadt: Luchterhand 1988.

Esser, Cornelia: Die ›Nürnberger Gesetze‹ oder Die Verwaltung des Rassenwahns 1933-1945. Paderborn [et. al.]: Schöningh 2002.

Feit, Margret: Die ›Neue Rechte‹ in der Bundesrepublik. Organisation – Ideologie – Strategie. Frankfurt [et al.]: Campus 1987.

Goßmann, Hans-Christoph: ›...denn das Heil kommt von den Juden‹. Christliche Zugänge zum Judentum und zum christlich-jüdischen Dialog. Münster: Waxmann 2005.

Greiner, Bernd: ›Test the West‹. Über die ›Amerikanisierung‹ der Bundesrepublik Deutschland. In: Westbindungen. Amerika in der Bundesrepublik, ed. by Heinz Bude, Bernd Greiner. Hamburg: Hamburger Edition 1999, pp. 16-54.

Grönert, Alexander (ed.): Politik, Pop und Afri-Cola. 68er Plakate. Bottrop: Pomp 2008.

Hamann, Christof, Alexander Honold: Kilimandscharo. Die deutsche Geschichte eines afrikanischen Berges. Berlin: Wagenbach 2011.

Hartung, Günter: Deutschfaschistische Literatur und Ästhetik. Gesammelte Studien. Leipzig: Leipziger Universitätsverlag 2001.

Hecht, Cornelia: Deutsche Juden und Antisemitismus in der Weimarer Republik. Bonn: Dietz Nachf. 2003.

›Heidelberger Manifest‹. In: Nation Europa, 12, 1981, p. 29 f.

Herbert, Ulrich: Geschichte der Ausländerpolitik in Deutschland. Saisonarbeiter, Zwangsarbeiter, Gastarbeiter, Flüchtlinge. München: Beck 2001.

Hill Collins, Patricia: Pornography and Black Women's Bodies. In: Gender Violence. Interdisciplinary Perspectives, ed. by Laura L. O'Toole, Jessica R. Schiffman, Margie L. Kiter Edwards. New York [et al.]: New York University Press 1997, pp. 395-399.

Hinrichsen, Malte: Racist Trademarks. Slavery, Orient, Colonialism & Commodity Culture. Berlin [et al.]: Lit 2012.

Horstkotte, Silke, Olaf Jürgen Schmidt: Heil Coca-Cola! Zwischen Germanisierung und Re-Amerikanisierung. Coke im Dritten Reich. In: Amerikanische Populärkultur in Deutschland, ed. by Heike Paul, Katja Kanzler. Leipzig: Leipziger Universitätsverlag 2002, pp. 73-86.

Hund, Wulf D.: Negative Vergesellschaftung. Dimensionen der Rassismusanalyse. Münster: Westfälisches Dampfboot 2006.
—: Rassismus. Bielefeld: transcript 2007.
Jordan, Winthrop D.: White Over Black. American Attitudes Toward the Negro, 1150-1812. Chapel Hill: University of North Carolina Press 1968.
Kellner, Joachim (ed.): Die besten Kinospots der 50er Jahre. Werbewelten im Zeichentrick. Hans Fischerkoesen zum 100. Geburtstag. Ingelheim: Westermann Kommunikation 1996.
— (ed.): 50 Jahre Werbung in Deutschland. 1945 bis 1995. Ingelheim: Westermann Kommunikation 1995.
Kerner, Ina: Differenzen und Macht. Zur Anatomie von Rassismus und Sexismus. Frankfurt [et al.]: Campus 2009.
Klemperer, Victor: The Language of the Third Reich. LTI, Lingua Tertii Imperii. A Philologist's Notebook. London [et al.]: Athlone Press 2000.
Köppen, Manuel: Mit dem ›Dritten Reich‹ um die Welt. Kodierungen der Fremde im fiktionalen Film. In: Kunst der Propaganda. Der Film im Dritten Reich, ed. by id., Erhard Schütz. 2nd ed. Bern: Peter Lang 2008, pp. 247-282.
Kraushaar, Wolfgang: 1968 als Mythos, Chiffre und Zäsur. Hamburg: Hamburger Edition 2000.
Levine, Bruce: ›Black Prussians‹. Germany and African American Education from James W. C. Pennington to Angela Davis. In: Crosscurrents. African Americans, Africa, and Germany in the Modern World, ed. by. David McBride, Leroy Hopkins, C. Aisha Blackshire-Belay. Drawer: Camden House 1998, pp. 65-81.
Linne, Karsten: Deutschland jenseits des Äquators. Die NS-Kolonialplanungen für Afrika. Berlin: Links 2008.
MacDermot, Galt, Gerome Ragni: Haare. München: Die Fünf 1969.
Malinowski, Stephan, Alexander Sedlmaier: ›1968‹ als Katalysator der Konsumgesellschaft. Performative Regelverstöße, kommerzielle Adaptionen und ihre gegenseitige Durchdringung. In: Geschichte und Gesellschaft, 32, 2006, 2, pp. 238-267.
Martin, Peter, Christine Alonso (ed.): Zwischen Charleston und Stechschritt. Schwarze im Nationalsozialismus. Hamburg [et al.]: Dölling und Galitz 2004.
McClintock, Anne: Imperial Leather. Race, Gender and Sexuality in the Colonial Contest. New York [et al.]: Routledge 1995.
Mineralbrunnen Überkingen-Teinach AG: ›80 Jahre anders. Interview mit Alexander Flach, Sohn des afri Erfinders Karl Flach‹ (http://www.afri.de/upload/files/9895336784d500b48819fe.pdf).
Morrien, Rita: ›Africa mon amour‹? Der Afrika-Diskurs im populären deutschen Spielfilm. In: Deutsch-afrikanische Diskurse in Geschichte und Gegenwart. Literatur- und kulturwissenschaftliche Perspektiven, ed. by Michael Hofmann, Rita Morrien. Amsterdam: Rodopi 2012, pp. 253-284.
N.N.: Seit 20 Jahren im Expansionsrausch. In: Industriekurier, 23.12.1969.
N.N.: Schwarze Haut für weiße Kassen. In: konkret, 16, 1972, pp. 22-24.
Pendergast, Mark: For God, Country and Coca-Cola. The Unauthorized History of the Great American Soft Drink and the Company that Makes it. 5th ed. London: Orion Books 1995.
Racine, Michel: The Gardens of Provence and the French Riviera. Cambridge [et al.]: MIT Press 1987.

Reed, Christopher Robert: ›All the World is Here!‹ The Black Presence at White City. Bloomington [et al.]: Indiana University Press 2000.

Reinhardt, Dirk: Von der Reklame zum Marketing. Geschichte der Wirtschaftswerbung in Deutschland. Berlin: Akademie Verlag 1993.

Röger, Maren: Bitburg-Affäre. In: Lexikon der ›Vergangenheitsbewältigung‹ in Deutschland. Debatten- und Diskursgeschichte des Nationalsozialismus nach 1945, ed. by Torben Fischer, Matthias N. Lorenz. Bielefeld: transcript 2007, pp. 227-229.

Schildt, Axel: Zur so genannten Amerikanisierung in der frühen Bundesrepublik – einige Differenzierungen. In: Modernisierung als Amerikanisierung? Entwicklungslinien der westdeutschen Kultur 1945-1960, ed. by. Lars Koch. Bielefeld: transcript 2007, pp. 23-44.

Schubert, Michael: Der schwarze Fremde. Das Bild des Schwarzafrikaners in der parlamentarischen und publizistischen Kolonialdiskussion in Deutschland von den 1870er bis in die 1930er Jahre. Stuttgart: Steiner 2003.

Segev, Tom: How Coca-Cola became kosher for Passover. In: Haaretz, 30.3.2012 (http://www.haaretz.com/weekend/the-makings-of-history/how-coca-cola-became-kosher-for-passover-1.421675).

Schutts, Jeff: Born Again in the Gospel of Refreshment? Coca-Colonization and the Making of Postwar German Identity. In: Consuming Germany in the Cold War, ed. by David Crew. Oxford [et al.]: Berg 2003.

—: Coca-Colonization, ›Refreshing‹ Americanization, or Nazi Volksgetränk? The history of Coca-Cola in Germany, 1929-1961. Ann Arbor, Mich.: UMI Diss. Services 2004.

—: ›Die erfrischende Pause‹. Marketing Coca-Cola in Hitler's Germany. In: Selling Modernity. Advertising in Twentieth-Century Germany, ed. by Pamala E. Sweet, Jonathan S. Wiesen, Jonathan R. Zatlin. Durham [et al.]: Duke University Press 2007, pp. 151-181.

Simon, Karl Günter: Der Werbe-Hippie. In: Die Zeit, 11.4.1969.

Tsiakalos, Georgios: Ausländerfeindlichkeit. Tatsachen und Erklärungsversuche. München: Beck 1983.

Wagner, Andreas: Das ›Heidelberger Manifest‹ von 1981. Deutsche Professoren warnen vor ›Überfremdung des deutschen Volkes‹. In: Manifeste. Geschichte und Gegenwart des politischen Appells, ed. by Johanna Klatt, Robert Lorenz. Bielefeld: transcript 2011, pp. 285-313.

Wallace-Sanders, Kimberly: Mammy. A Century of Race, Gender, and Southern Memory. Ann Arbor: University of Michigan Press 2008.

Westphal, Uwe: Werbung im Dritten Reich. Berlin: Transit 1989.

Wigger, Iris: Die ›Schwarze Schmach am Rhein‹. Rassistische Diskriminierung zwischen Geschlecht, Klasse, Nation und Rasse. Münster: Westfälisches Dampfboot 2007.

Racism Analysis – Series B: Yearbooks
edited by Wulf D. Hund (Hamburg University)

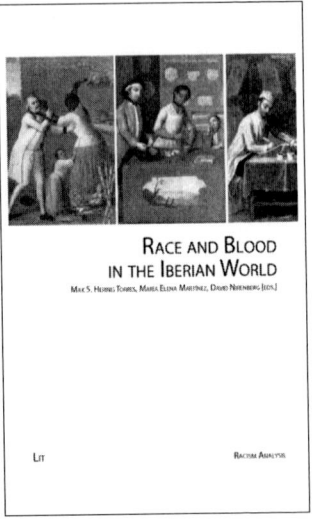

Wulf D. Hund; Christian Koller; Moshe Zimmermann (Eds.)
Racisms Made in Germany
Contents | Christian Koller: Racisms Made in Germany. Without ›Sonderweg‹ to a ›Rupture in Civilisation‹ | Moshe Zimmermann: Between Jew-Hatred and Racism. The German Invention of Antisemitism | Wulf D. Hund: ›It Must Come From Europe‹. The Racisms of Immanuel Kant | Claudia Bruns: Antisemitism and Colonial Racism. Transnational and Interdiscursive Intersectionality | Arno Sonderegger: Racist Fantasies. ›Africa‹ in Austrian and German African Studies | Ulrike Hamann, Stefanie Michels: From Disagreement to Dissension. African Perspectives on Germany | Wolfgang Wippermann: Purification of the National Body. Racial Policy and Racial Murder in the ›Third Reich‹ | Gudrun Hentges: Between ›Race‹ and ›Class‹. Elite Racism in Contemporary Germany | Boris Barth: Racism Analysis in Germany. The Development in the Federal Republic
Bd. 2, 2011, 240 S., 24,90€; im Abo: 19,90 €, br., ISBN 978-3-643-90125-5

Max S. Hering Torres; María Elena Martínez; David Nirenberg (Eds.)
Race and Blood in the Iberian World
›Racism Analysis‹ is a research series that explores racial discrimination in all its varying historical, ideological and cultural patterns. It examines the inven-tion of race, the dimensions of modern racism and inquires into racism avant la lettre. The series brings together scholars from various disciplines and schools of thought. A key aim is to contribute to the conceptualisation of racism and to identify the practices of dehumanisation intrinsic to it.
Bd. 3, 2012, 216 S., 24,90 €, br., ISBN 978-3-643-90259-7

LIT Verlag Berlin – Münster – Wien – Zürich – London
Auslieferung Deutschland / Österreich / Schweiz: siehe Impressumsseite